NEW UNDERSTANDING SCIENCE 2

REVISED NATIONAL CURRICULUM EDITION

JOE BOYD
St Augustine's High School, Edinburgh

WALTER WHITELAW
Science and Technology Adviser, City of Edinburgh Council

JOHN MURRAY

© Joe Boyd and Walter Whitelaw 1990, 1996

First published 1990
by John Murray (Publishers) Ltd
50 Albemarle Street
London W1X 4BD

Reprinted 1990, 1991 with revisions, 1992, 1995
Second edition 1996

All rights reserved. No part of this publication may be reproduced in any material form (including photocopying or storing in any medium by electronic means and whether or not transiently or incidentally to some other use of this publication) without the written permission of the publisher, except in accordance with the provisions of the Copyright, Designs and Patents Act 1988 or under the terms of a licence issued by the Copyright Licensing Agency.

Layouts by Fiona Webb
Cartoons by Ainslie McLeod and Richard Duszczak
Line drawings by Jeff Edwards and Philip Ford
Natural history drawings by Nancy Sutcliffe and Peter Bull Art Studio

Typeset in $11\frac{1}{2}/13$pt Futura Book by Wearset, Boldon, Tyne and Wear
Printed and bound in Great Britain by Cambus Litho Ltd, East Kilbride
Colour separations by Dot Gradations Limited, Wickford, Essex

A CIP catalogue record for this book is available from the British Library

ISBN 0-7195-7288-6

Contents

Acknowledgements vi

Unit 1 Lively places

Exploring environments

1.1	Measuring the environment	2
1.2	Life on Earth	4
1.3	Adaptations	6
1.4	Counting living things	8
1.5	Helping or harming the environment	10
1.6	Problem – Winning an award	12
1.7	Talkabout – Making an impact	14
1.8	Readabout – Life on the edge	15

Unit 2 Tiny ideas

Thinking about particles

2.1	Scientific thinking	18
2.2	Finding patterns	20
2.3	Bits and pieces	22
2.4	Likely explanations	24
2.5	Moving particles	26
2.6	Spaced out particles	28
2.7	Making a hypothesis	30
2.8	Making predictions	32
2.9	Model predictions	34
2.10	Problem – Build a fire alarm	36
2.11	Talkabout – Good questions	37
2.12	Readabout – Forbidden ideas	38

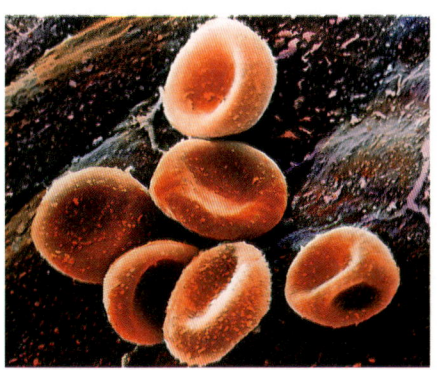

Unit 3 Good health

Finding out about the body

3.1	Body systems	40
3.2	Food for health	42
3.3	The fate of food	44
3.4	Food for thought	46
3.5	Heart and circulation	48
3.6	Lungs and breathing	50
3.7	Fit for nothing	52
3.8	Problem – Design a game	55
3.9	Talkabout – Smoking and health	56
3.10	Readabout – Body defences	57

Unit 4 Everyday forces
Thinking about movement and design

4.1	Describing forces	60
4.2	Forces at a distance	62
4.3	Action and reaction	64
4.4	Balancing act	66
4.5	Turning forces	68
4.6	On the move	70
4.7	Watch your speed	72
4.8	Feel the pressure	74
4.9	Problem – Consumer report	76
4.10	Talkabout – Good and bad design	77
4.11	Readabout – New joints	78

Unit 5 Interacting substances
Describing chemical reactions

5.1	Chemical reactions	80
5.2	Chemical accounts	82
5.3	Slow oxidation	86
5.4	Acids and alkalis	88
5.5	Neutralisation	90
5.6	Word equations	92
5.7	Problem – Kitchen chemistry	94
5.8	Talkabout – Wishing for a new material	96
5.9	Readabout – Time travellers	97

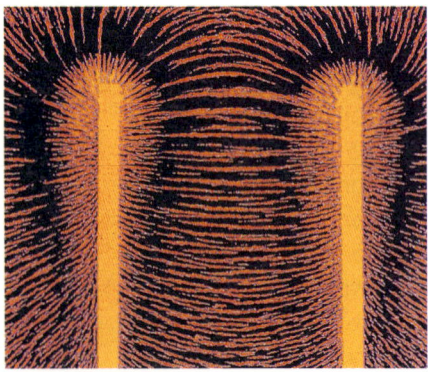

Unit 6 Science in use
Finding out about technology

6.1	The physics of magnetism	100
	Problem – Electromagnets	102
6.2	Microbe biology	104
	Problem – Biological washing powder	107
6.3	Fuel chemistry	108
	Problem – Fire and smoke	111
6.4	Talkabout – Technology	112
6.5	Thinkabout – Your future	113
6.6	Readabout – Electronic processing	114

Extensions

1.1	Map measurements	118	4.1 Force distorts	141
1.2	Key questions	119	4.2 Ring the changes	142
1.3	Growth pattern	121	4.3 What a reaction!	143
1.4	Animal numbers	122	4.4 Floating along	144
1.5	Thermal pollution	123	4.5 Nothing for nothing	145
2.1	Use the clues	124	4.6 Air resistance	146
2.2	Coloured compounds	125	4.7 Speed reading	147
2.3	Asking questions	126	4.8 Pressure puzzles	148
2.4	Joining atoms	127	5.1 More active reactions	149
2.5	Ammonia on the move	128	5.2 Redox reactions	150
2.6	Bumped!	129	5.3 Investigating rust protection	151
2.7	The Solar System	130	5.4 Activity plan	152
2.8	Fortune teller	131	5.5 Sour water	153
2.9	Expansion	132	5.6 Speeding up reactions	154
3.1	Cells and tissues	133	6.1 Electric motors	155
3.2	Investigating vitamin C	134	6.2 Biotechnology with yeast	156
3.3	Digesting fat	135	6.3 New fuels	158
3.4	Cramping your style	136		
3.5	Fit for life	137	**Index**	159
3.6	CPR – Lifesaver technique	138		
3.7	Drug abuse	140		

Acknowledgements

Cover photo: ZEFA

The following have provided photographs or given permission for photographs to be reproduced:

- **p.iii** *top* Henry Ausloos/NHPA; *middle* George Holton/Science Photo Library; *bottom* Prof. P Motta/Dept of Anatomy/University of 'La Sapienza', Rome/Science Photo Library
- **p.iv** *top* Action Images; *middle* Jerry Mason/Science Photo Library; *bottom* Alfred Pasieka/Science Photo Library
- **p.v** Bill Bachmann/Topham Picture Point
- **p.1** Henry Ausloos/NHPA
- **p.2** Simon Fraser/Science Photo Library
- **p.3** *top left* W Schmidt/ZEFA; *top right* W Broadhurst/FLPA; *middle left*; Planet Earth Pictures; *middle right* Planet Earth Pictures; *bottom left* John Heseltine/Science Photo Library; *bottom right* Martin B Withers/FLPA
- **p.6** *from top to bottom* Simon Fraser/Science Photo Library; Planet Earth Pictures; ZEFA; E & D Hosking/FLPA
- **p.7** H Eisenbeiss/FLPA
- **p.8** *top left* Planet Earth Pictures; *top middle* Dr Morley Read/Science Photo Library; *top right* John Shaw/NHPA; *bottom left* Kim Taylor/Bruce Coleman Ltd; *bottom middle* Ecoscene/Beatty; *bottom right* Topham Picture Point
- **p.10** *top left* Terry Whittaker/FLPA; *top middle* Simon Fraser/Science Photo Library; *top right* Ecoscene/Alexandra Jones; *bottom left* D Coutts/FLPA; *bottom middle* Robert Harding Picture Library; *bottom right* J M Martos/FLPA
- **p.11** *top left* Planet Earth Pictures; *top right* Ancient Art & Architecture Collection; *bottom left* Nigel Blake/Bruce Coleman Ltd; *bottom right* Adrian Davies/Bruce Coleman Ltd
- **p.14** *top* Chris Newton/FLPA; *bottom left* Martin Bond/Science Photo Library; *bottom middle* Sue Cunningham; *bottom right* ZEFA
- **p.15** *top left* Planet Earth Pictures; *top right* Neil P Lucas/BBC Natural History Unit; *bottom left* E A Janes/NHPA; *bottom right* Rex Features
- **p.16** *left* Planet Earth Pictures; *right* Jane Burton/Bruce Coleman Ltd
- **p.17** George Holton/Science Photo Library
- **p.18** David Scharf/Science Photo Library
- **p.26** *top left* Henningsen/ZEFA; *bottom left* K Benser/ZEFA; *top middle* David Nunuk/Science Photo Library; *bottom middle* Adrienne Hart-Davis/Science Photo Library; *left* Klaus Hackenberg/ZEFA
- **p.27** National Portrait Gallery
- **p.29** Luke Dodd/Science Photo Library
- **p.31** Andrew Lambert
- **p.37** *top right* Norman Tomalin/Bruce Coleman Ltd; *bottom left* Andrew Syred/Science Photo Library
- **p.38** *top* and *middle* Mary Evans Picture Library; *bottom* NASA/Science Photo Library
- **p.39** Prof. P Motta/Dept of Anatomy/University of 'La Sapienza', Rome/Science Photo Library
- **p.48** David Bassett/Science Photo Library
- **p.50** Alfred Pasieka/Science Photo Library
- **p.52** St. Bartholomew's Hospital/Science Photo Library
- **p.57** *top left* A B Dowsett/Science Photo Library; *top middle* and *bottom left* Dr Jeremy Burgess/Science Photo Library; *top right* CNRI/Science Photo Library; *bottom right* National Institute of Health/Science Photo Library
- **p.58** Simon Fraser/Science Photo Library
- **p.59** Action Images
- **p.60** *top left* Jean F Hosking/FLPA; *top middle* Barnaby's Picture Library; *top right* Robert Harding Picture Library
- **p.65** *top left, top right* and *bottom left* ZEFA; *bottom right* Bruce Coleman Ltd
- **p.72** John Townson/Creation
- **p.76** John Townson/Creation
- **p.78** *top* CNRI/Science Photo Library; *bottom* James Stevenson/Science Photo Library
- **p.79** Jerry Mason/Science Photo Library
- **p.80** *left* and *right* ZEFA; *middle* Planet Earth Pictures
- **p.83** *left* ZEFA, *middle* Robert Harding Picture Library; *right* Jane Burton/Bruce Coleman Ltd
- **p.88** *left* Scotsman Publications Ltd.; *middle* Martin Bond/Science Photo Library; *right* ZEFA
- **p.90** *from left to right* Kodak Ltd; Nigel Cattlin/Holt Studios International; John Townson/Creation; Rex Features
- **p.93** Jerry Mason/Science Photo Library
- **p.95** *top left* Robert Harding Picture Library; *top right* ZEFA; *bottom* John Townson/Creation
- **p.96** *top left* Gore-tex®; *top right* Ronald Sheridan/Ancient Art & Architecture Collection; *bottom left* © Walt Disney Pictures; *bottom right* Philippe/Science Photo Library
- **p.97** *top* D W Haigh/FLPA
- **p.98** Topham Picture Point
- **p.99** Alfred Pasieka/Science Photo Library
- **p.104** *left* Moredun Animal Health Ltd/Science Photo Library; *right* David Scharf/Science Photo Library
- **p.109** Rex Features
- **p.111** Building Research Establishment
- **p.112** *top left* David Parker, 600 Group Fanuc/Science Photo Library; *top middle* Alexander Tsiaras/Science Photo Library; *top right* Barnaby's Picture Library; *middle right* Tony Craddock/Science Photo Library; *bottom left* Dale Boyer/NASA/Science Photo Library; *bottom right* Colorsport
- **p.114** *top left* London Regional Transport; *top right* Dick Luria/Science Photo Library; *bottom left* AGA Infrared Systems/Science Photo Library; *bottom right* Hank Morgan/Science Photo Library
- **p.115** Alfred Pasieka/Science Photo Library
- **p.117** Bill Bachmann/Topham Picture Point
- **p.118** *from left to right* J Hutchings/FLPA; Hugh Clark/FLPA; Dr Jeremy Burgess/Science Photo Library; Life Science Images
- **p.119** *left* Hans Reinhard/Bruce Coleman Ltd; *right* Kim Taylor/Bruce Coleman Ltd
- **p.120** *left* R Wilmshurst/FLPA; *right* M B Withers/FLPA
- **p.121** Stephen Dalton/NHPA
- **p.123** David Woodfall/NHPA
- **p.124** Sinclair Stammers/Science Photo Library
- **p.125** Dr B Booth/GSF Picture Library
- **p.127** Life Science Images
- **p.129** ZEFA
- **p.130** *left* Rex Features; *right* NASA/Science Photo Library
- **p.132** *left* Ray Bird/FLPA; *right* Heini Schneebeli/Science Photo Library
- **p.133** *left* Francis Leroy, Biocosmos/Science Photo Library; *middle* Prof. P Motta, Correr & Nottola/University 'La Sapienza', Rome/Science Photo Library; *right* Secchi-Lecaque/Roussel-Uclaf/CNRI/Science Photo Library
- **p.138** Will & Deni McIntyre/Science Photo Library
- **p.144** *left* David Nunuk/Science Photo Library; *right* Mary Evans Picture Library
- **p.146** *top left* NASA/Science Photo Library; *top right* ZEFA; *bottom* Claude Nuridsany & Marie Perennou/Science Photo Library
- **p.147** *top left* Planet Earth Pictures; *top right* Colorsport; *middle left* and *right* ZEFA; *bottom left* Alan Williams/NHPA; *bottom right* ZEFA
- **p.149** Kim Taylor/Bruce Coleman Ltd
- **p.151** GSF Picture Library
- **p.152** Andrew Lambert
- **p.156** Barnaby's Picture Library
- **p.158** Prof. David Hall/Science Photo Library

1
Lively places

BIG IDEAS IN THIS UNIT

1 There are different habitats. Each habitat has a different set of animals and plants.
2 Living things can be classified into major groups. Living things in the same group have features in common.
3 Living things are adapted to live in a particular habitat.
4 The size of a population depends on factors such as available resources, number of predators and human activity.
5 It is important to conserve our environment and reduce pollution.

1.1 Measuring the environment

A Environmental conditions

The different places in and around a school's grounds are examples of different **habitats**. The conditions in the habitat and the living things present make up the **environment**. A photograph is a good way to show the appearance of a habitat. Measurements of environmental conditions improve the description.

Collect

- Measuring instruments
- Poster paper
- Coloured pencils

1 You are going to study and describe one small habitat in your school's grounds.
   Discuss what environmental conditions you could measure.
   Think about conditions that stay the same and conditions that change.
2 Talk about how to use the available measuring instruments.
   Think about how many measurements to take and how to record them.
3 Go to one of the habitats suggested by your teacher. Make and record your measurements. Make a list of the plants and animals you see.

1 Produce a group poster to describe your habitat. Include drawings or photographs if possible. Include your measurements. Make a list of the plants and animals present and *either* draw some of them, *or* prepare and give (or record) a short talk to describe your habitat to the rest of the class.
2 Help produce a class poster on 'Environmental conditions'. There should be three headings:
   - measurements that stay the same
   - measurements that change throughout the day
   - measurements that change with the seasons.
3 Discuss the class poster. Make a copy of it in your book.

2

MEASURING THE ENVIRONMENT

B Around and about

The photographs below show several different habitats.

Town street and gardens

Parkland

Rocky seashore

Forest

Arable farmland

River bank

 Choose one habitat that you know a lot about. It might be a favourite place nearby, somewhere you visited on holiday or somewhere one of the photographs reminds you of. Describe the place and the living things in it
  a during the summer
  b during the winter.

1.2 Life on Earth

A Animal and plant kingdoms

The animal kingdom

If you want to study an environment you have to describe the environmental conditions. You also have to be able to name the animals and plants present.

Scientists classify living things by grouping them into sets. This makes them easier to name. The three main sets, called **kingdoms**, are animals, plants and bacteria. Each kingdom is divided into smaller groups of living things that have features in common. For example the vertebrates are one of the main groups of the animal kingdom. All of the vertebrates have backbones.

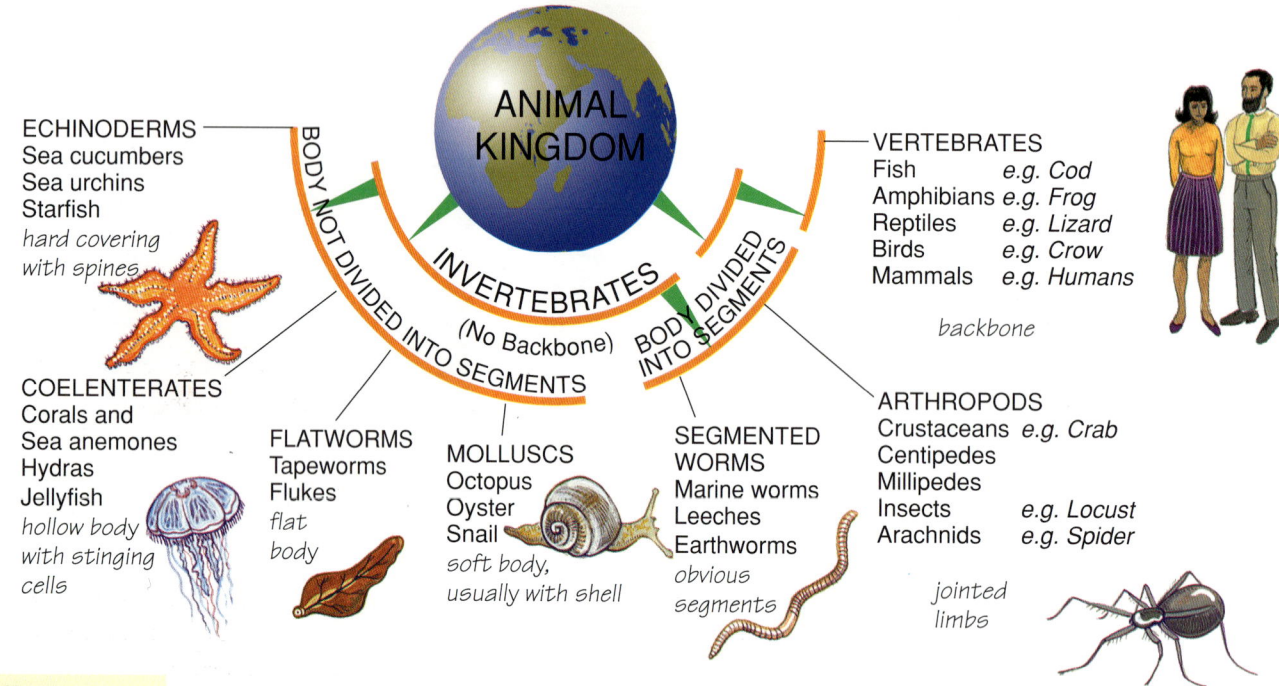

Collect
- Hand lens
- Living invertebrate
- Animal table
- Set of invertebrate animal cards

1 Observe the living creature with a hand lens.
2 Look for details of its structure that will help you to classify it.
3 Use the diagram above to identify which group it belongs to.
4 Repeat this with a second animal.
5 Shuffle the cards. Group them into six invertebrate sets.

Treat all living things with respect.

1 Make a short report about each invertebrate animal. Include
  - a labelled drawing or description
  - the name of the group the animal belongs to
  - your reasons for classifying it in this group.

2 **Collect** and complete the animal table.

LIFE ON EARTH

The plant kingdom
Plants are also classified into several major groups. For example, flowering plants are one of the major groups shown in the table.

Name of major group	Example	Important group features
Mosses and Liverworts		No true roots Simple stems and tiny leaves lacking transport system for food and water Reproduce by spores produced in capsules
Club mosses		True roots and stems bearing true leaves arranged in spirals Transport system for food and water Spores produced in tiny cones
Horsetails		True roots and stems bearing scale-like true leaves in whorls Spores produced in cones
Ferns		True roots and stems, and true leaves divided into tiny leaflets Spores produced in clusters on leaf undersides
Conifers		True roots, stems and needle-like leaves Reproduce by seeds produced in cones
Flowering plants		True roots, stems and leaves Produce flowers and seeds

Until recently **botanists** (plant scientists) also classified fungi – such as mushrooms – and algae – such as seaweed – as plants. These are now put into two different kingdoms altogether.

1 **Collect** a blank plant key. Fill in the missing clues and group names. Stick the completed key in your book.
2 Look at the plants in the classroom. Use your key to identify which group each plant belongs to.

B Sort it out

1 **Collect** the 'Life on Earth' sheet.
2 Work in a group of three or four. Discuss each of the short passages. Decide on how to complete the gaps. Stick the sheet in your book.

1.3 Adaptations

A A place for everything

Each living thing is most often found in the habitat where it has the best chance of survival.

Living thing	Habitat		Useful characteristics for survival
Cactus	Dry desert		Swollen stem that stores water Spiny leaves to reduce water loss Huge root system to catch any rain
Mayfly larva	Fast-flowing stream		Flattened body to cling to rocks Streamlined shape to resist water flow Strong legs for gripping rocks
Mole	Underground		Paddle-shaped front feet for digging Short hair that sticks out in all directions to allow easy movement through tunnels Tiny eyes that do not easily get clogged-up with dirt Bristles on nose and tail to sense surroundings

These living things are **adapted** to their environment. Living things that cannot adapt reasonably well to their surroundings become extinct. This may happen when important features of the environment change, when there is competition from other living things for food or space or when new predators arrive. Dinosaurs became extinct 65 million years ago because of changes in their environment. Nowadays many species are becoming extinct due to human activity. For example, the Great Auk became extinct in 1844 because it couldn't escape from human predators.

Great Auk

1 **Collect** a set of dominoes. Each domino has a picture of an animal in its habitat and a description of a useful characteristic for survival. Play dominoes in the usual way, matching a picture with a correct description.

ADAPTATIONS

Collect
- *Daphnia* in a U-tube (corked at both ends)
- Dropper bottles of: vinegar, sodium bicarbonate solution
- Bench lamp
- Black paper
- Plasticine
- Light filters
- Safety glasses

Daphnia factfile
- Live in fresh water
- Breathe oxygen; most oxygen is near surface of water
- Eat microscopic green algae
- Eaten by small fish

2 The behaviour of an animal often helps it to survive. You can see this in action.

Take care of living things.
Change the following parts of the U-tube environment and watch which way the *Daphnia* move. For each change decide why this movement would help the *Daphnia* to survive.

- Dark/light
- Colour of light
- Acid/alkali
- Up/down

1 Make a table of two columns (*Animal* and *Survival characteristics*) to show how you matched three dominoes.
2 Describe your experiments on the behaviour of *Daphnia*. Include a diagram of what you did, a note of the results and your opinion of how this behaviour helps *Daphnia* survive.

B Design a survivor

1 Design and draw an animal that could survive in this habitat. Label its major structural features.

Habitat factfile
- Weather: cold, wet and windy
- Ground conditions: steep, rocky and slippery
- Food supply: leaves and bark of tall trees
- Atmosphere: oxygen, carbon dioxide, nitrogen

2 Describe the behaviour patterns that would help your animal to survive in this habitat.

1.4 Counting living things

A Populations

Some schools are bigger than others. They have more pupils. Another way of saying this is that big schools have a big pupil **population**. In the same way a woodland habitat has a certain number of foxes called the fox population, a certain number of mice called the mouse population and so on. The size of any population depends on several factors.

Environmental change
Changes in climate over a long time or short-term spells of severe weather can reduce populations.

Human activity
Clearing forests for farming reduces the size of habitat for all the animals and plants.

Number of predators
The more predators there are, the greater the chance of being eaten.

Competition for scarce resources
Animals of the same kind or **species** compete for food, water, space and mates. Animals of different species also compete for the same resources.

Plants compete for water, sunlight and space.

Pests and disease
Populations can be reduced by the spread of disease or by pests. This crop of wheat is being eaten by locusts.

It is important to know the population size of the plants and animals in a habitat. This allows us to decide if there are too many of one species or if that species is in need of protection. It is very difficult to count all the individuals in a population. You have to estimate the population size by counting a sample.

COUNTING LIVING THINGS

Collect

- Tray of sawdust
- Magnetic rod
- Quadrat

There are iron 'fish' hidden in the sawdust 'pond'. You are going to sample the population using a quadrat. Then you can estimate the population size.

1 Work in groups. Put the quadrat anywhere on the tray.
2 Use the magnet to catch **all** the fish **inside** the quadrat. Count the fish.
3 Do this **two** more times. Each time, sample in a **different** place.

1 What factors affect the size of a population?
2 Make a table of your results from the quadrat. The two columns should have the headings

- sample
- number of fish caught.

3 Did you catch the same number of fish each time? Explain this.
4 Work out your **average** number in a sample.
(*Hint:* add up the numbers and divide by three.)
5 It would take ten quadrats to cover the whole pond. Use your average number in a sample to estimate how many fish are in the whole pond.
6 Produce a class bar chart to compare the estimates from each group. Discuss the results.

B Sampling plants

Collect

- Quadrat

1 Find a piece of grassy land.
2 Choose one species of plant that seems to be fairly common in the place. (A daisy, for example, but not grass.)
3 Use the quadrat to take three samples from different places.

Write a report of your survey. Include

- method
- results and average number of plants in a sample
- your estimate of the population size in 100 m² of land.

9

1.5 Helping or harming the environment

A Conservation and pollution

People can affect the environment in good and bad ways. **Conservation** is helping the environment. **Pollution** is harming the environment. The photographs below show examples of conservation and pollution.

a

b

c

d

e

f

Discuss the pictures. Which show conservation? Which show pollution?

1. Pick two pictures showing conservation. Describe what is happening in each.
2. Pick two pictures showing pollution.
   a What is causing the pollution?
   b What effect is the pollution having?
   c How do you think the pollution could be prevented?
3. Write about a local conservation activity **or** a local pollution problem.
   (Your teacher will give you a local newspaper to help you.)

10

HELPING OR HARMING THE ENVIRONMENT

B Pollution detective

You can be a pollution detective. There are clues in the environment that indicate the amount of air pollution. Some plants and animals are good indicators of pollution.

Look for as many of these clues as you can around the school **or** on your way home **or** at home.

1 Lichens

2 Black spot

4 Buildings and statues in clean air (above) and in polluted air (right)

3 Two-spotted ladybirds in clean air (top) and in polluted air (bottom)

1 Write a short report about your detective work.
2 Where do you think air pollution comes from? Make a list of sources.

11

1.6 Problem

Winning an award

You can help to protect the balance of nature in your environment. Take part in the **Conservation Award Scheme**. Everyone's a winner

- you will win a certificate
- the animals and plants in your area will win your care and attention.

1 Complete as many of the tasks as you can on your own or as part of a class group. You can take as long as you want. For each task

- find out **how** to do it
- make a **plan**
- pick the best time and **act** on your plan.

2 Collect and complete an application form for an award. You need to earn

- 600 points for the **gold** award
- 350 points for the **silver** award
- 100 points for the **bronze** award.

Fact-finding tasks

1 Find the addresses of four local conservation groups.
10 points

2 Write to a local conservation group asking for information.
10 points

3 Join a conservation group. **50 points**

4 Go round a nature trail. **50 points**

5 Watch a TV programme on nature **or** read a book about nature. **10 points** per programme or book (up to **100 points**)

6 Collect articles from the local newspaper about local conservation issues. **10 points** per article (up to **50 points**)

PROBLEM – WINNING AN AWARD

Fact-giving tasks

1 Set up a conservation display for the school library.
   100 points

2 Organise a talk from a local conservation group at your school.
   100 points

3 Organise a visit to a local nature reserve.   **150 points**

4 Write an article for the school newspaper or for the local newspaper about nature conservation.
   50 points for school newspaper
   150 points for local newspaper

Action tasks

1 Collect litter from around the school.   **50 points**

2 Take part in a clean-up campaign in your area.
   100 points

3 Make a bird table.   **50 points** for each bird table
   (up to **200 points**)

4 Make a wild garden. You can buy seeds to help you.
   150 points

5 Plant a tree with your classmates. Look after it.
   100 points per tree
   (up to **300 points**)

6 Set up a tree nursery. (You can do this in a window box.)
   300 points

7 Make a nest for insects that live in holes. Use drinking straws or hollow plant stems, or make holes in dead wood.   **50 points**

8 Plant a plot of small shrubs like hawthorn and holly.
   50 points per type of shrub
   (up to **200 points**)

9 Raise some money for a local or national conservation group.   **5 points** per pound

10 Plan and carry out a survey of wild birds in your area.
   10 points per bird species spotted
   (up to **500 points**)

13

1.7 Talkabout

Making an impact

The photograph shows a typical rural environment in Britain.

What effects would each of the following changes have on the local populations of plants and animals?

Nuclear power station

Theme park

Motorway

1.8 Readabout

Life on the edge

Animals and plants that live in extreme habitats have remarkable adaptations that allow them to survive. The animals and plants that are best adapted produce the most offspring.

At a depth of 3000 metres there is no light and the water pressure is 300 times greater than at the surface. Many of the fish produce light themselves – perhaps to attract a mate or prey.

Giant lobelia plants grow in high valleys of Mount Kenya, in Africa. The hairs on their leaves trap air which insulates the plant against the frost at night. The extreme cold would kill them otherwise.

The plants and animals in more familiar habitats are also adapted to live there. In some habitats there are big environmental changes every day.

On the sea shore there are daily changes in temperature, water level and saltiness. Animals that live here have body systems that can cope with the changes.

In deserts the nights can be cool but the days are very hot. Animals cannot afford to lose too much water or to overheat. Body systems are adapted to prevent water loss. Many desert animals also show behavioural adaptations. They rest in a shady spot during the day.

READABOUT – LIFE ON THE EDGE

In other habitats there are big environmental changes with the changing seasons.

Plants lose water through their leaves and replace this with water from the soil. In winter water may not be available because it is trapped in the form of snow and ice.
Some trees have an important adaptation to prevent water loss – they drop their leaves in the autumn.

Some animals would have trouble surviving the extremes of winter. They overcome problems of cold and low food supply with an unusual behaviour – they hibernate and sleep the winter away.

Plant
- How is a Venus flytrap adapted to obtain energy?
- How is marram grass adapted to grow on sand-dunes?
- Why do spider orchid flowers look like spiders?

Animal
- How is a camel adapted to survive life in the desert?
- How is the osprey adapted to be a fish-eating predator?
- Why do some butterflies have large spots on their wings?

Human
- How are humans adapted to keep a constant body temperature?
- How are humans adapted to live on dry land?
- Why do some athletes train at high altitude?

1. You have to carry out some research to find out about adaptations in plants and animals, including humans. You can research some of the questions in the boxes on the left, but you can also research ideas of your own.
   Work in groups of three. Use available books, multimedia CD-ROMs or the library to find answers to *three questions* (from the boxes or from your own ideas) – one about plants, one about humans and one about another animal. Find out

   - where the animal or plant lives
   - what the environmental conditions are like or what the problems for survival are
   - how the animal or plant is adapted to survive.

2. Agree with your teacher on the best way to make a report. You may be able to

   - jointly write a report
   - present a results table
   - record your report
   - make a poster
   - speak about your work
   - make use of a database.

16

2 Tiny ideas

BIG IDEAS IN THIS UNIT

1. Think about how to explain what you observe.
2. Matter is made up of tiny particles called atoms and molecules.
3. These particles are always moving and there is empty space between them. The movement and spacing can be changed.
4. The properties of solids, liquids and gases can be explained using our ideas about particles.

2.1 Scientific thinking

A Begin with ideas

People are very good at thinking – much better at it than animals like cats and dogs. Chimpanzees have been into space but they didn't design and build their own rockets.

Try out this thinking experiment: What would it be like to gradually become tiny? Imagine being small enough to stand on the hair in the photograph. Now imagine that you keep on shrinking. What do you see and hear and feel as you become smaller and smaller?

Science helps people to think. Thinking will help you to explain things.

You **observe** something → You think of **ideas** → You work out an **explanation** → Now you can make **predictions**

Collect
- Activity sheet
- What you need for one activity

Do some (or all) of these activities. The instructions are on the report sheet for each activity.

For each activity you will have to describe what you see. Then you will have to think of an explanation for it.

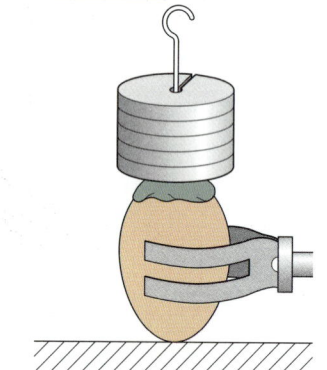

1 Crack an egg

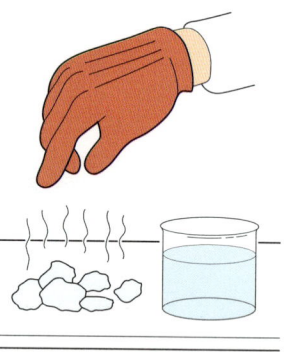

2 Dry ice

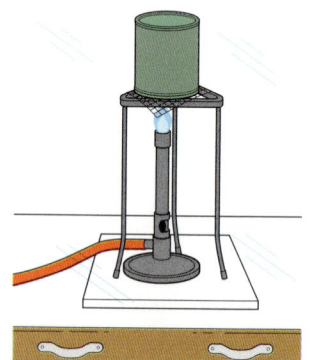

3 Can opener

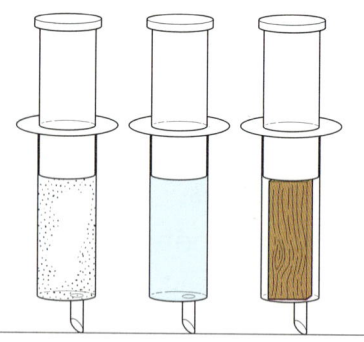

4 Squash it

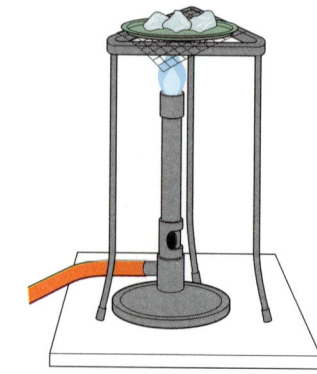

5 Hot stuff

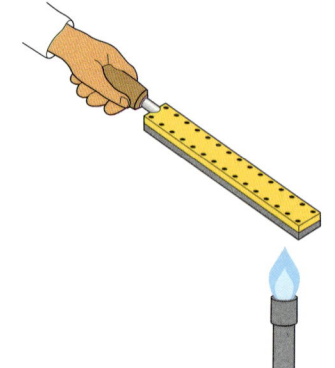

6 Toasted sandwich

SCIENTIFIC THINKING

 For each activity complete the report by

- describing what you saw (your **observations**)
- writing down what you think about it (your **ideas**)
- trying to explain what you saw (your **explanation**).

Here is an example.

Report on Activity 9
Name of activity: *Air freshener*

Method

Place the air freshener on a table and open it.

Observations

A smell of Norwegian wood filled the air in the classroom.

Ideas

There is a small forest growing inside the plastic container.

B Share your ideas

Collect
- Poster paper
- Coloured pencils

Your group has to make a poster to explain one of the activities. You have 30 minutes to make the poster.

What to do

- Each person in the group will read their **observations** aloud. There should be no comment from the other members of the group while this is being done. Everyone in the group then agrees which observations to show on the poster. Write these observations on the poster.
- Each person then reads aloud their **ideas** for explaining the observation.
- The group now has 10 minutes to talk about and then to agree on the best **explanations**. Write these explanations on the poster.

19

2.2 Finding patterns

A Practical clues

There are short cuts that can help you to understand things. For example, it is sometimes useful if you can find a pattern when thinking about things that are new to you.

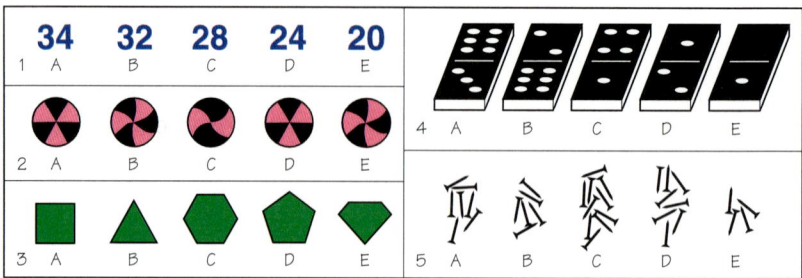

Which is the odd one out in each set? (Answers at the bottom of the page.)

A pattern will help you to

- sort out your observations
- find explanations more quickly
- predict what might happen in a new situation.

Collect
- Set of fingerprints

Fingerprints
The police look for patterns in a fingerprint, for example

Arch   Whorl   Loop

Collect and examine the suspects' fingerprints – which person has left this small print?

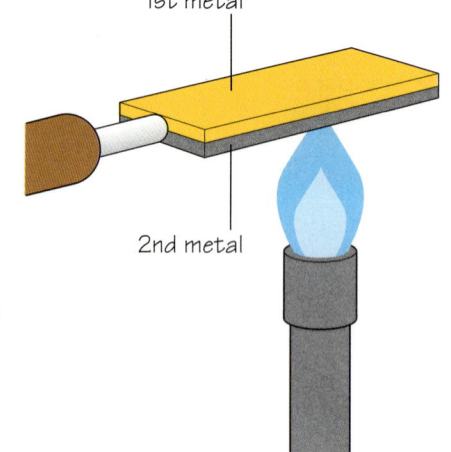

1st metal

2nd metal

Collect
- Thin bimetallic strip
- Bunsen burner and mat
- Safety glasses

The magic strip
1. Look at the bimetallic strip. It is made of two different metals.
2. Heat then cool each of the metal sides of the strip in turn. Observe.
3. Look for a pattern in how the strip changes.

20

Puzzle answers: 1 A, 2 C, 3 E, 4 B, 5 A

FINDING PATTERNS

 1 The police often store information in a computer database. Explain how such a database helps the police to find patterns in their information.
2 What happens to the bimetallic strip when
   a the first metal side is heated? Draw the shape.
   b the other metal side is heated? Draw the shape.
   (Colour the two sides of the strip differently.)
3 What does the strip do when it begins to cool?
4 From the pattern of results predict what might happen if the strip is cooled with ice. (Test the strip to see if you were right.)

B Flame colours

A pattern is clearer from the results of a number of experiments. A pattern can help you to work out what will happen in a future experiment.

Collect
- Set of solids
- Test rod
- Bunsen burner and mat
- Safety glasses

1 Light the bunsen burner. Use a blue flame.
2 Dip the rod into one of the solids. Hold it in the flame.
3 Note the name of the chemical and the colour of the flame.
4 Clean the cooled rod in water. Repeat for all the solids. Look for a pattern in the results.

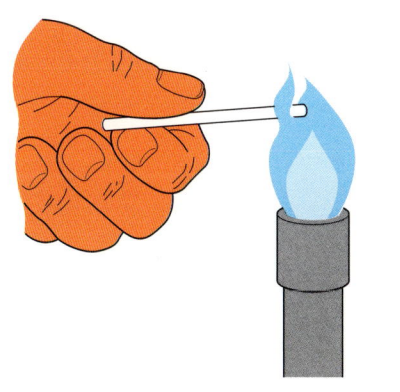

 1 What do these solids do to a blue bunsen flame?
2 What colour would you expect if the following solids were put in a flame?

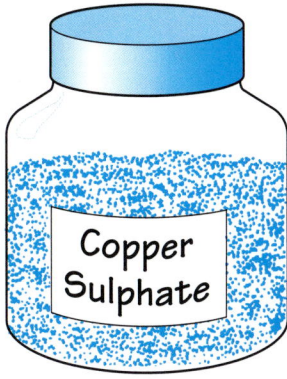

Try them and see if you were right.

2.3 Bits and pieces

A Break up

Everything that you can touch is made up of stuff called **matter**. Even substances like air have 'stuff' in them. You can feel this matter pushing you in a high wind.

In the following experiments you are going to

- make observations about solid matter
- find a pattern to these observations
- using the pattern, try to explain your observations.

Collect
- Purple crystal
- 5 test tubes
- Beaker of water
- Purple pencil
- Test-tube rack

Experiment 1

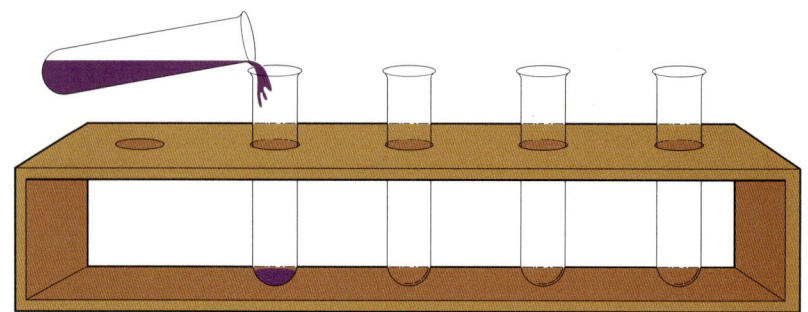

1. Add **one** purple crystal to a test tube of water. Mix until the crystal dissolves.
2. Pour one-fifth of the coloured liquid into a second test tube. Fill with water and mix.
3. Pour one-fifth of the contents of this tube into a third tube filled with water.
4. Continue until there seems to be no colour left in the liquid.

Collect
- Petri dish
- White crystal
- Blue crystal
- Spatula

Experiment 2

1. Fill a petri dish with water.
   Put it on the table. It must remain steady.
2. Gently put a white crystal into the water at one end of the dish.
3. Gently put a blue crystal into the water at the other end of the dish.
4. Wait for a few minutes.

BITS AND PIECES

1 **Make observations about matter**
   a How many purple crystals did you put into the first tube?
   b Was there any purple substance in the second tube?
   c Draw a diagram of your results in experiment 1 to show how many tubes contained the purple substance at the end.
   d Draw a diagram to show what happens after a few minutes in experiment 2.

2 **Find a pattern**
Discuss the two experiments with your partner and try to find similarities in the results. Describe what crystals do in water. Use words like *crystal*, *spread*, *colour*, *cannot be seen* and *still there*.

3 **Likely explanations**
Discuss the similarities that you found in the two experiments. What do you think has happened in the experiments?
Use words like *matter*, *pieces*, *tiny*, *spread* and *break up*.

B Tiny pieces

Collect

- 5 test tubes
- Test-tube rack
- Mustard powder
- Wooden splint

This experiment will help to explain how a substance can spread if it is made of tiny pieces.

1 Add a tiny amount of mustard powder to a test tube of water. (Use just enough to cover the end of a wooden splint.)
2 Follow the instructions for experiment 1 on page 22.

1 Write a title for your experiment. Describe what you did.
2 Copy the diagram below.

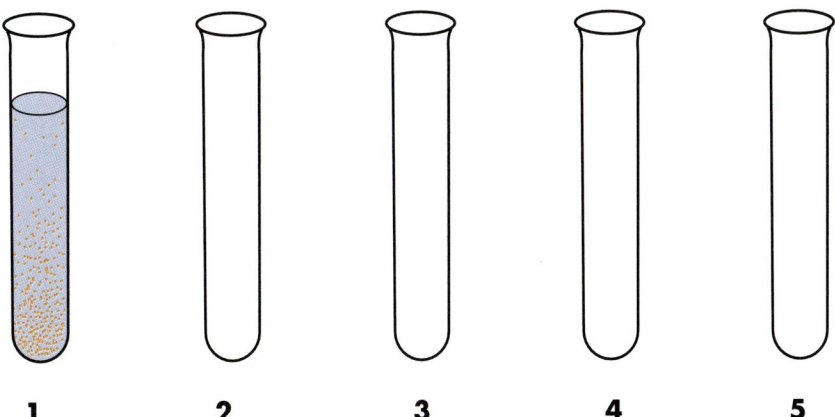

Add dots to your diagram to represent the number of mustard grains that you can see in each test tube.
3 Write down a likely explanation of why mustard can spread so far.

23

2.4 Likely explanations

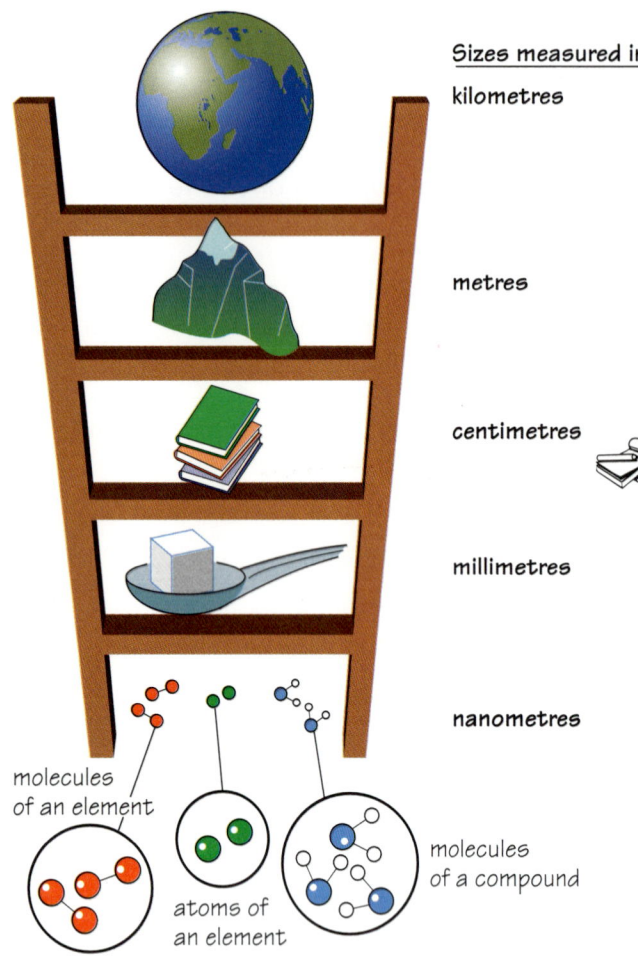

A Particles

When you dissolve sugar in tea the sugar seems to disappear. However, it must still be there as the tea tastes sweet. You tried to explain this kind of observation in Topic 2.3. One likely explanation is that the sugar breaks up into tiny bits called **particles**.

The smallest particles are called **atoms**. Several atoms can join together to make a **molecule**. Your little fingernail contains millions and millions of molecules!

1 What happens to the size of an object as you climb up the ladder?
2 Copy the ladder into your book. Discuss which rung your fingernail should be shown on.
3 **Explain** why you cannot see one molecule of sugar.
4 **Explain** the difference between
   a atoms of an element and molecules of an element
   b molecules of an element and molecules of a compound.

Collect

- Clean container
- Bunsen burner and mat
- Tripod stand
- Bottled liquid
- Safety glasses

1 Inspect the container. Make sure that it is clean.
2 Pour some bottled liquid into the container and heat it as shown in the diagram.
3 The water in the liquid will eventually disappear. Look at the container when it is cool.
   Explain what you see. Use the words *tiny particles*, *molecules* and *atoms* in your explanation.

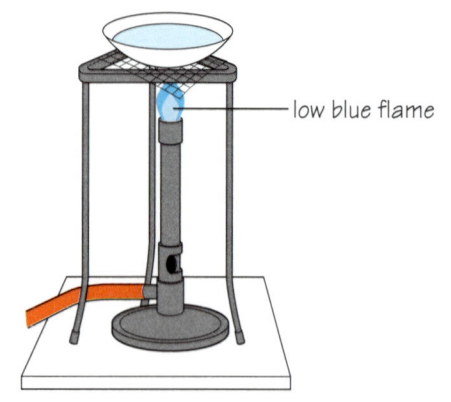

24

LIKELY EXPLANATIONS

B Words represent ideas

It is important to understand new ideas and how they fit in with ideas that you already use.

The diagram below has new ideas in red, quite new ones in green and familiar ones in blue.

Matter is like a story

Collect
- Idea cards

Sort the cards as shown below.

1 Copy one card from each separate pile (or group) of cards.
2 Describe what Topic 2.4A is about using all the words in the diagram above.

2.5 Moving particles

A Smells

Smells get around. A male emperor moth can smell a female at a distance of 11 km. Your nose is also an excellent smell detector. It can detect over 3000 smelly substances. You detect a smell when particles of a substance get up your nose.

1 Your teacher will place a dish of ammonia solution in the room.
2 Move slowly towards the dish. Find out where you can detect the smell.

 1 Copy the plan below.

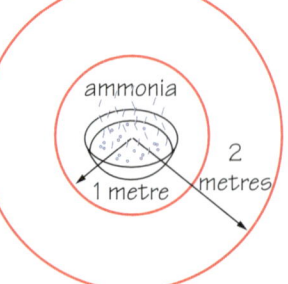

2 Add dots to your plan to show how many ammonia molecules were present at different distances.
   Hint: Use a lot of dots for a strong smell.
3 What must ammonia molecules be able to do to spread through a room?
4 Describe the nicest smell that you know.
   Draw a picture to show how this smell can spread around a room. Use dots to represent molecules.

MOVING PARTICLES

Portrait of Robert Brown taken in 1855

B Brownian motion

In 1827, a Scottish scientist called Robert Brown discovered something that amazed him. When he looked at pollen grains under a microscope they looked as if they were dancing!

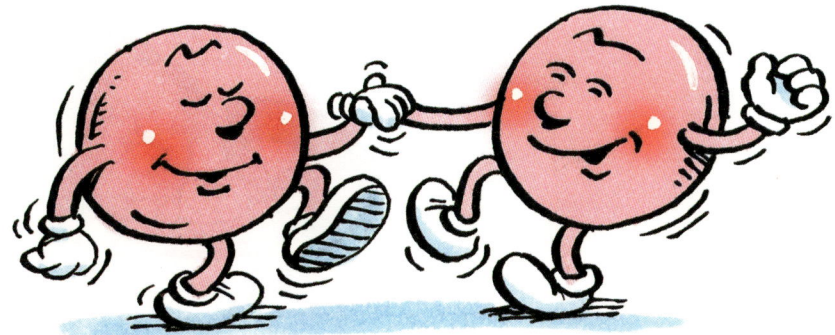

This kind of movement is now called **Brownian motion**. You can also observe Brownian motion.

Collect
- Microscope
- Bench lamp
- Slide
- Cover slip

1 Use a high-power magnification.
2 Take the slide to the hot milk in the room.
3 Put one drop of hot milk on the slide and cover it with a cover slip.
4 **Quickly** return to the microscope. Focus the microscope on the slide.

1 Describe what you did.
2 Describe what you saw. Use words like *droplets*, *shaped like*, *moving*, *quick/slow*, *direction* and *jiggle*. Draw a diagram if it will help your description.
3 Your teacher may show you how smoke looks under a microscope.

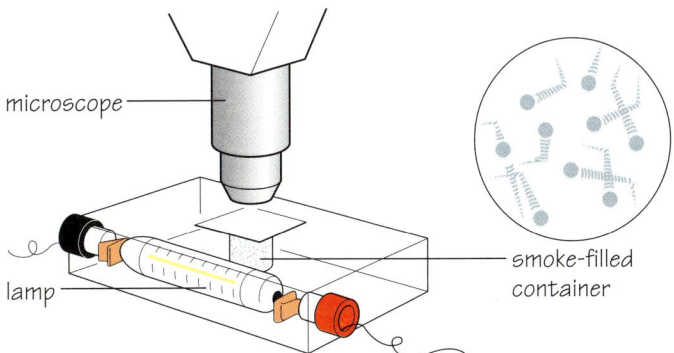

Draw and describe what you see.
4 What explanations can you think of for Brownian motion? Make a list of your ideas.
Then discuss these in class with your teacher.

27

2.6 Spaced out particles

A Diffusion

You can add sugar to a cup which is already full of tea. The tea will not slop over the side of the cup. Why is this? Where do the sugar molecules go?

Particles are held together by forces between them. However, there are spaces between the molecules. The sugar moves into the spaces between the water molecules.

Collect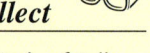

- Dish of jelly
- Tweezers
- Borer
- Dropper
- Bottle of acid
- Bottle of alkali
- Safety glasses

1 The jelly has universal indicator in it. Use the borer to cut two small holes in the jelly. Pull the bits out with tweezers.
2 Fill one hole with acid and the other with alkali, as shown in the diagram.

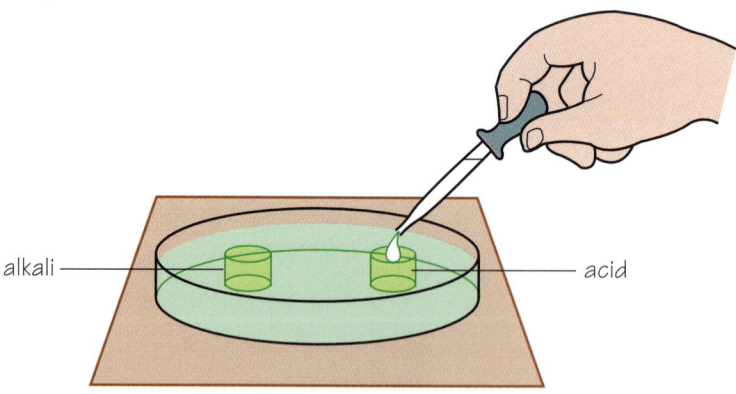

3 Leave the dish **without touching it** for about 10 minutes.

1 **Explain** why a full cup of tea does not slop over when sugar is added carefully to it.
2 Draw and describe the result of your experiment with the jelly.
3 Why was universal indicator added to the jelly?
4 Write down a likely explanation for the result of your experiment. Use words like *molecules*, *move* and *spaces between*.
5 Find out the meaning of the word **diffusion** and write it down.

28

SPACED OUT PARTICLES

B Empty space

Look at the photograph of stars in part of our galaxy. There is space between the stars. Scientists think that there is also space between particles. The space is empty.

Collect
- Two 100 cm³ measuring cylinders
- 250 cm³ measuring cylinder
- Bottle of peas
- Bottle of rice

1 Your teacher is going to add exactly 100 cm³ of water to exactly 100 cm³ of alcohol.
   Write down the result that you **expect** when the two are added together.
2 Write down the **measured** amount when the two are added together.
3 Repeat instructions 1 and 2, but add 100 cm³ of rice to 100 cm³ of peas, instead of water to alcohol.

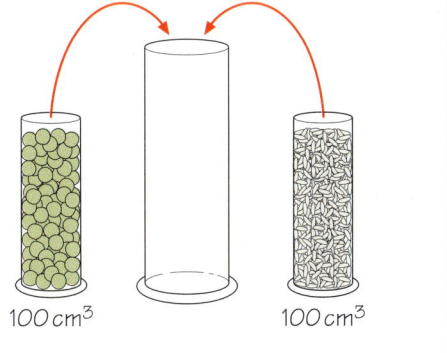

1 Put your results in a table with the headings Mixture, Expected result and Actual result.
2 Draw a diagram to show what happened to the rice when it was added to the peas.
3 **Explain** the results of both experiments. Use words like *particles* and *spaces*.
4 Copy the drawing of the molecules in a test tube full of air. Add something to your drawing to show what is between these molecules.

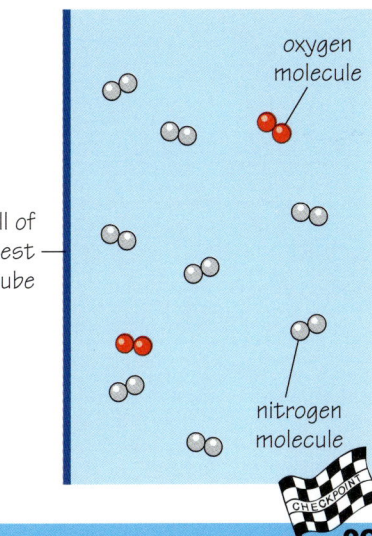

29

2.7 Making a hypothesis

A About particles

When you think of a likely explanation for an observation then you are making a **hypothesis**. You can test out your ideas by doing experiments and examining your results.

We now have several hypotheses about particles.

- Everything is made of particles (molecules and atoms).

- Particles are tiny.

- Particles are always moving.

- Particles can be spaced out.

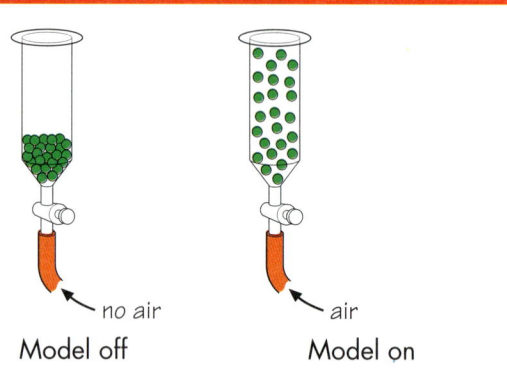

Look at the model. It shows how particles probably behave. Each ball represents a tiny particle.

1 When the model is switched on, what do the 'particles' do?
2 When the model is switched on, what happens to the distance between the 'particles'?
3 If the particles were given more movement energy what would happen to
   a the spaces between them
   b their shape
   c their mass?
4 **Collect** and complete the summary diagram. Stick it into your book.
5 Look again at your work from Topic 2.1 (page 18). Rewrite two or three of your explanations using the hypotheses about particles.

MAKING A HYPOTHESIS

B Smoke without fire

The molecules of a substance can sometimes be changed when they bump into molecules of a different substance. This is what happens when ammonia molecules meet hydrogen chloride molecules.

The substances **react**. The atoms that make up their molecules are rearranged to make a new substance.

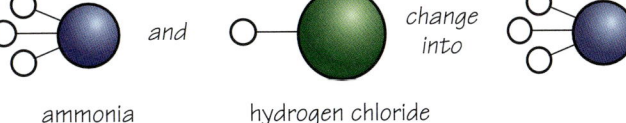

ammonia molecule   and   hydrogen chloride molecule   change into   ammonium chloride molecule

1. Using the hypotheses about particles write down what you predict will happen in the experiment below. Be exact about what you expect.
2. Observe the experiment. Was the result as you predicted?

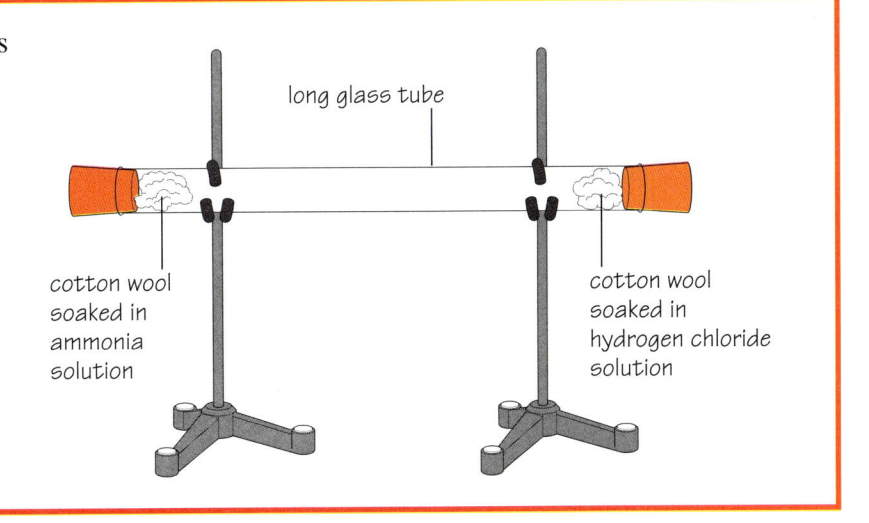

long glass tube

cotton wool soaked in ammonia solution

cotton wool soaked in hydrogen chloride solution

Draw a diagram of the result. **Explain** the result using labels such as *molecules, reaction, meet, atoms are rearranged* and *diffusion*.

31

2.8 Making predictions

A Scientific forecasting

The following drawings represent the spacing of particles in three different substances. Remember that the spaces are big when the particles move a lot. They are small when the particles move a little.

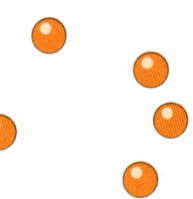

Substance A   Substance B   Substance C

Copy the diagrams above and predict which substance will
a contain particles that move around most
b be easiest to push (compress) into a different shape
c will contain particles that stay in place on a flat surface and do not flow
d will be most dense.

Collect

- Plastic stoppered bottles of substances A, B and C
- Empty plastic box
- Evacuated bottle (presealed)
- Balance

1 Your teacher will measure the mass of an empty bottle for you. Measure the mass of a bottle full of substance. You can now estimate the density of the substance:

$$\left(\frac{\text{mass}}{\text{volume}}\right)$$

2 Open each of the bottles in turn. Stand the open container on the bench. Decide which substance moves out of the container most easily.
3 Try to pour each substance into an empty box. Decide which substance takes up the shape of the box most easily.
4 Put the box on its side each time. Decide which substance stays in place most easily.

A   B   C

1 Write a short description of each experiment.
2 You made four predictions about substances A, B and C. How many of your predictions were correct?
3 Look at the ten kitchen substances in the collection. Decide if each substance is like A, B or C. Write these sets into your book.

MAKING PREDICTIONS

B Property patterns

Substances come in all shapes and colours. However, they all belong to one of the three sets of substances called **solids**, **liquids** and **gases**.

Solid

Liquid

Gas

1 There are lots of substances laid out around the room. Each of them has a number. Go to each one in turn. Write down the number of the substance and its name (if you know it). Also write down which set of substances you think it belongs to.
2 When you have finished, join a discussion group of three or four people.
   The group has to discuss the answers to three questions.

   - What is similar about the properties of all solids?
   - What is similar about the properties of all liquids?
   - What is similar about the properties of all gases?

Write your ideas about the discussion questions under these headings.

- I know a substance is a solid because . . .
- I know a substance is a liquid because . . .
- I know a substance is a gas because . . .

2.9 Model predictions

A Solid, liquid, gas

Particles move. The more they move, the more space there is between them. If the particles are heated then they gain energy and move faster. The particles can therefore change their arrangement but they do not change their shape or mass (they are still the same little particles!). This hypothesis can be shown in a model.

Particles in a solid vibrate

Particles in a liquid roll over one another

Particles in a gas zoom around

> Your teacher may allow the class to act out the water cycle.
> When you hear the word *ice*, you should all act as particles in a **solid**. When you hear the word *water* you should all act as particles in a **liquid**. When you hear the words *water vapour*, you should all act as particles in a **gas**.

Predict which arrangement of particles should be easiest to press together (compress).

Collect
- Plastic syringe
- Rubber stopper
- Wood

1 Fill the syringe with the **gas** air.
2 Hold the end against a rubber stopper and press the plunger hard.
3 Fill the syringe with the **liquid** water.
  Carefully repeat step 2.
4 Fill the syringe with **solid** wood.
  Carefully repeat step 2.

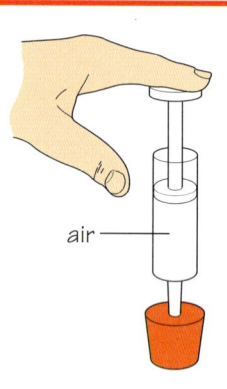

1 Write a short description of your experiment.
2 Was your prediction correct?
  Explain why particles with this arrangement can be pressed together more easily.
3 Draw your own labelled diagrams to show the arrangement of particles in a solid, a liquid and a gas.
4 *When ice changes into water and then water changes into water vapour, the mass of substance is conserved.*
  Explain this sentence, using your class model of the water cycle to help you.

MODEL PREDICTIONS

B Hot stuff

The diagram shows a model of the spacing of particles in a solid at different temperatures.

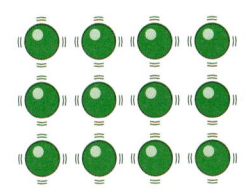

Cold solid   Hot solid

Predict what will happen to
a the length of a solid when it is heated
b the volume of a solid when it is heated
c the length and volume of a solid when it is cooled.

Collect

- Bunsen burner
- Heatproof mat
- Safety glasses
- Tongs
- Telephone wire
- Ball and ring

1 Set up the model telephone wire. Heat it as shown. Find out what happens to the length of the wire.

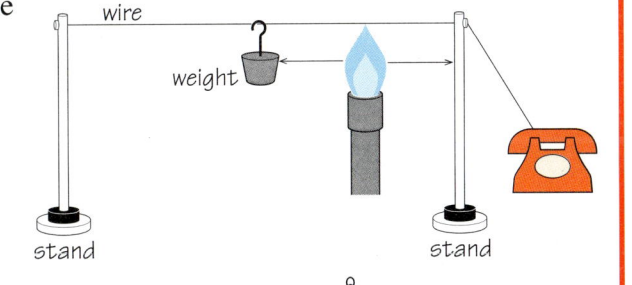

2 Hold the ball with tongs. Try to put it through the ring.
Heat the ball as shown. Find out what happens to the size of the ball.

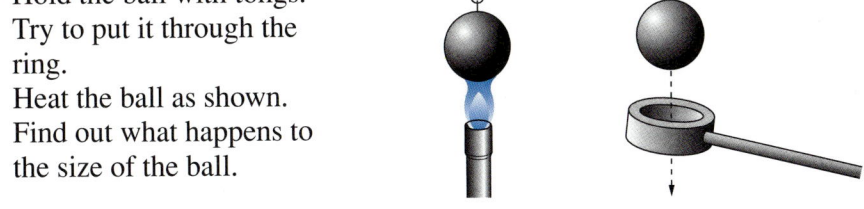

3 Your teacher will show you a third experiment.

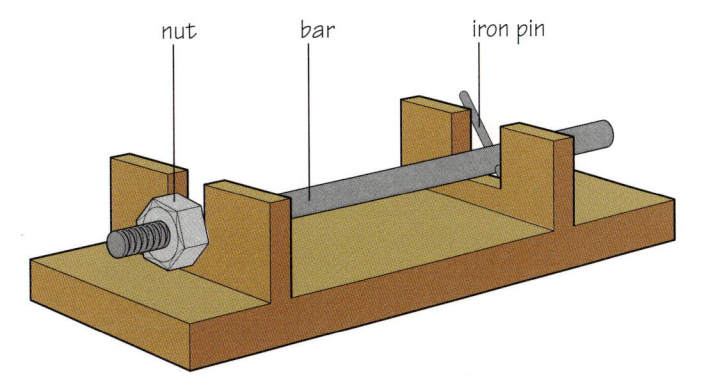

What your teacher will do:
1. Tighten the nut
2. Heat the bar
3. Tighten the nut again
4. Cool the bar

1 Write a short description of each experiment.
2 How many of your predictions were correct?

2.10 Problem

Build a fire alarm

Heat makes particles in an object move faster. When they move faster they usually get more spaced out. This means that the object expands (gets bigger).

Remember what happens when two metals that are stuck together try to expand by different amounts (see Topic 2.2). Repeat the magic-strip experiment on page 20 if you cannot remember.

Problem
You have to use a bimetallic strip to make an automatic fire alarm. The alarm should ring when there is a heat source nearby.
(Use a burning candle as a source of heat.)

Hints
- You will need the equipment shown below.

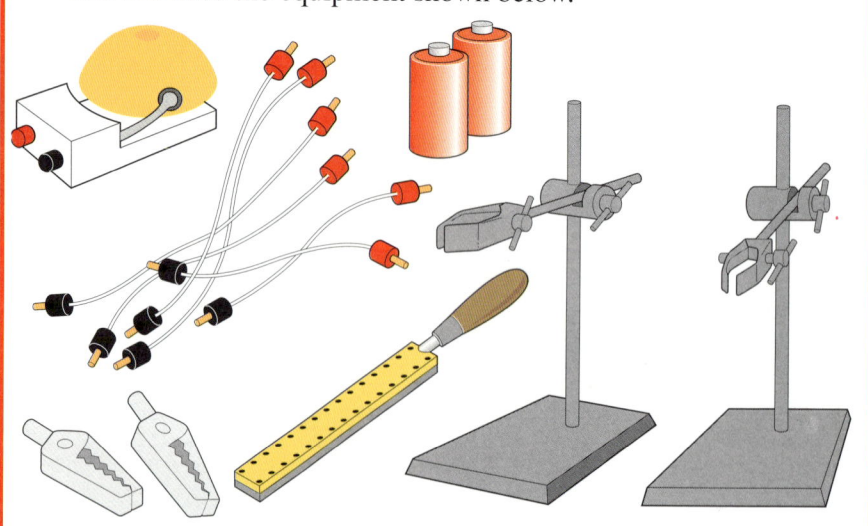

- Your teacher has clue cards to help if you get stuck. Use as few clues as possible.

Draw a diagram of your final design. Describe how it works.

2.11 Talkabout

Good questions

Look at the four pictures. Your teacher will tell one person in your group what has happened in picture A. The rest of the group have to ask this person good questions to get more information about the picture. The person may only answer **yes** or **no** to any question.

The group has a maximum of 20 questions to work out what has happened in picture A. Another person is then told what picture B is, and so on . . .

a A man walks into a bar. He says nothing. The barman takes out a toy gun and points it at him. The man says thank-you and leaves. Why?

b What was this object used for?

c What is this?

d This person always gets off at floor 3, yet she lives on floor 5. Why?

2.12 Readabout

Nicolaus Copernicus

Galileo Galilei

The Earth from the Moon

Forbidden ideas

People used to think that the Earth was the centre of the universe. The Earth stayed still and everything moved around it. Two famous scientists had other ideas: **Nicolaus Copernicus** and **Galileo Galilei**.

Nicolaus Copernicus was born in Poland in 1473. He was skilled in many things. He practised medicine amongst the poor. He designed a new money system. He even defended a castle against invaders. Copernicus was also very interested in astronomy. He studied other people's observations of the movement of the planets. These observations did not support the hypothesis that all the planets moved round the Earth.

Copernicus thought up, and wrote about, a more likely explanation. The Sun was at the centre and all the planets, including the Earth, went round it. His ideas were not liked by the authorities. It was only on his deathbed, in 1543, that he saw printed copies of his book.

His hypothesis did not die. In 1564, a very talented Italian called Galileo was born in Pisa. Galileo was also skilled in many things. He first studied medicine, but then became a professor of mathematics and a successful inventor.

Galileo was fascinated by movement. He proved that falling objects, no matter how heavy or light, take the same time to fall the same distance. In 1609 he improved the recently invented telescope and used it to observe the Sun and Moon, the planets, and the stars. Many of these observations supported Copernicus's hypothesis.

In 1632 Galileo published a book which discussed the theory of planetary motion. Unfortunately, some powerful people did not like his ideas. Galileo was tried and sentenced to house arrest. He died in 1642, a virtual prisoner in his own home.

1 From the passage, describe
   a the hypothesis that Copernicus **disagreed** with
   b the **new** hypothesis that Copernicus wrote about
   c the observations that Galileo made which supported Copernicus's ideas.
2 Use the books in the classroom or from a library to write a paragraph about Galileo, his work and his trial.

3
Good health

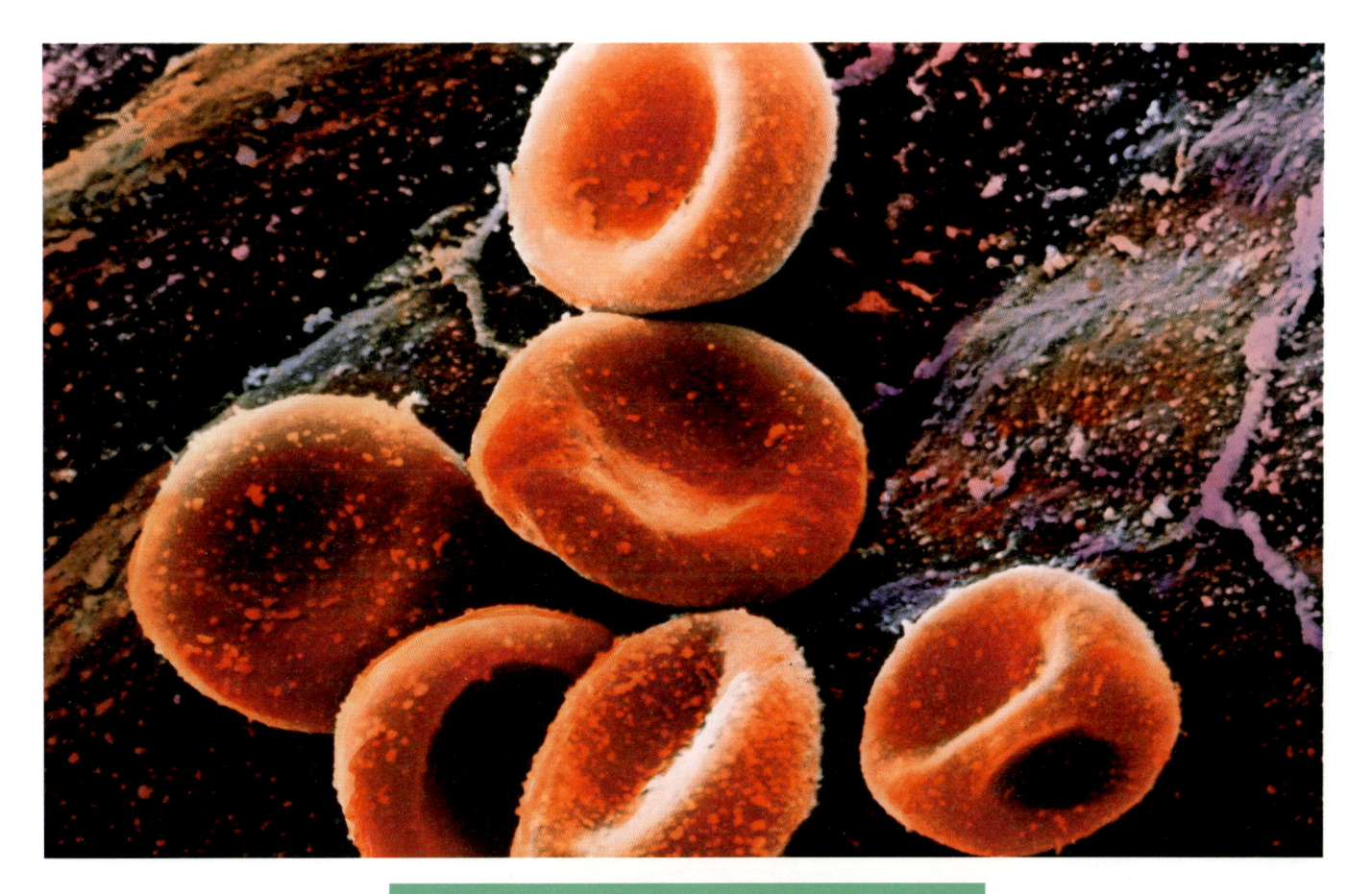

BIG IDEAS IN THIS UNIT

1 The human body is organised at four levels: cells, tissues, organs and organ systems.
2 The food in our diet contains seven types of substance needed for health and growth.
3 Food is broken down into soluble products in the digestive system.
4 Aerobic respiration releases energy from sugar in body cells.
5 The transport and breathing systems work together to exchange gases between the body and the atmosphere.
6 Smoking and the abuse of alcohol and other drugs is harmful to health.

3.1 Body systems

A Organs and systems

The human body is made up of millions of cells. Groups of similar cells form **tissues**.

An **organ** is formed from several different types of tissue. It carries out one particular job. When you are fit and healthy all the **organ systems** of your body work well together.

The cartoon locates your main organs and organ systems.

1 **Brain** – controls movement and is the centre for thinking, memory and emotions. Part of the **nervous** system.

2 **Lungs** – supply the body with oxygen. Part of the **breathing** system.

3 **Kidneys** – keep the blood clean. Part of the **excretory** system.

4 **Bones** – give support and protection and allow movement. Part of the **skeletal** system.

5 **Heart** – pumps blood round the body. Part of the **circulatory** system.

6 **Stomach** – stores and mixes food. Part of the **digestive** system.

7 **Sex organs** – produce sex cells. Part of the **reproductive** system.

Collect
- Body sheet
- Scissors
- Glue
- Stop clock

1 Start the clock. You and your partner have five minutes to learn the position, name and job of each organ.
2 Close the book when you have read these instructions.
3 Cut out the organs and the labels.
4 Discuss with your partner where each organ should go. Place the organs on the body outline and the labels around it. Draw arrows to match each label with its organ.
5 Join another group and compare your answers. When you are sure they are right stick the completed body outline into your book. Write down the job of each organ beside or under its label.

BODY SYSTEMS

Collect

- Health-hazard cards

Discuss each card with your partner.
Use your new knowledge to put the cards into four sets: cards that describe hazards to your

- digestive system
- nervous system
- breathing system
- circulatory system.

Copy and complete the table below using your card sets.

Organ system	Health hazards

B Game, set and match

Collect

- Body system card set

You can play this game in a group of three or four.
You have to collect a full set of four cards for each body system

- picture card
- system name card
- main organ name card
- job card.

Follow the instructions with the card set.
Show your teacher the complete sets.

41

3.2 Food for health

A Food

You have to eat food for three reasons

- food gives you energy for activity and to keep you warm
- food gives you substances that your body needs for health
- food gives you the building blocks for growth and repair.

A food can contain a mixture of the following seven types of substance.

Fat: to store and provide energy.
Protein: to grow new tissue, repair damage and provide energy.
Carbohydrate: to provide a supply of energy. The two main forms are sugar and starch.
Water: to carry things round the body and replace lost water.
Minerals: to make healthy blood, bones and other tissues.
Vitamins: to take part in important chemical reactions in your body.
Fibre: to keep the digestive system healthy.

A balanced diet contains the correct amount of all of the seven types of food substance.
   A simple rule is to eat something every day from each of the four food groups shown below. Malnutrition is caused by having a diet that is not balanced.

Milk and milk products

Fruit and vegetables

Bread and cereals

Meat and meat substitutes

FOOD FOR HEALTH

Collect
- Small pieces of different foods
- Clinistix
- Albustix
- Bottle of iodine
- Filter paper
- 4 test tubes and rack
- Stirring rod
- Safety glasses

Carry out these tests to find the types of substance in different foods.

1 Stir the food in warm water in a test tube.
2 Divide the liquid into the three remaining test tubes.
3 Test the liquids using tests a–c. Use a solid piece of dry food for test d.

Tests

a Starch (carbohydrate) — iodine
Starch gives a black colour

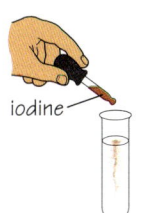

b Sugar (carbohydrate) — Clinistix
Sugar gives a purple colour

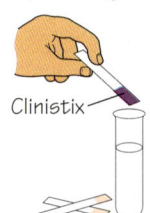

c Protein — Albustix
Protein gives a green colour

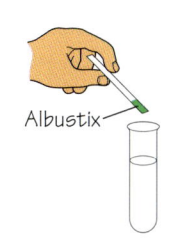

d Fat — paper
Fat leaves a greasy see-through mark

4 Collect and test another food.

1 Write a report about your findings. Include a short description of each test and your results.
2 Make a table to show what each of the seven types of substance in food does.
3 What is **a** malnutrition, **b** a balanced diet?
4 What four food groups should you eat something from each day to have a balanced diet? Which of the seven types of food substance does each food group provide?

B Food sources

Some foods contain a lot of one type of food substance.

Lots of carbohydrate   Lots of fibre    Lots of protein    Lots of vitamins and minerals    Lots of fat

Collect a copy of the buffet-table diagram and some coloured pencils. Make a colour key to show which foods contain lots of
- carbohydrate
- protein
- fibre
- vitamins and minerals.
- fat

43

3.3 The fate of food

A Digestive system

Food must be digested before it can provide energy or the materials for growth and repair. In digestion, large insoluble lumps of food are changed into soluble molecules that can enter the blood. The path food takes through the digestive system is shown below.

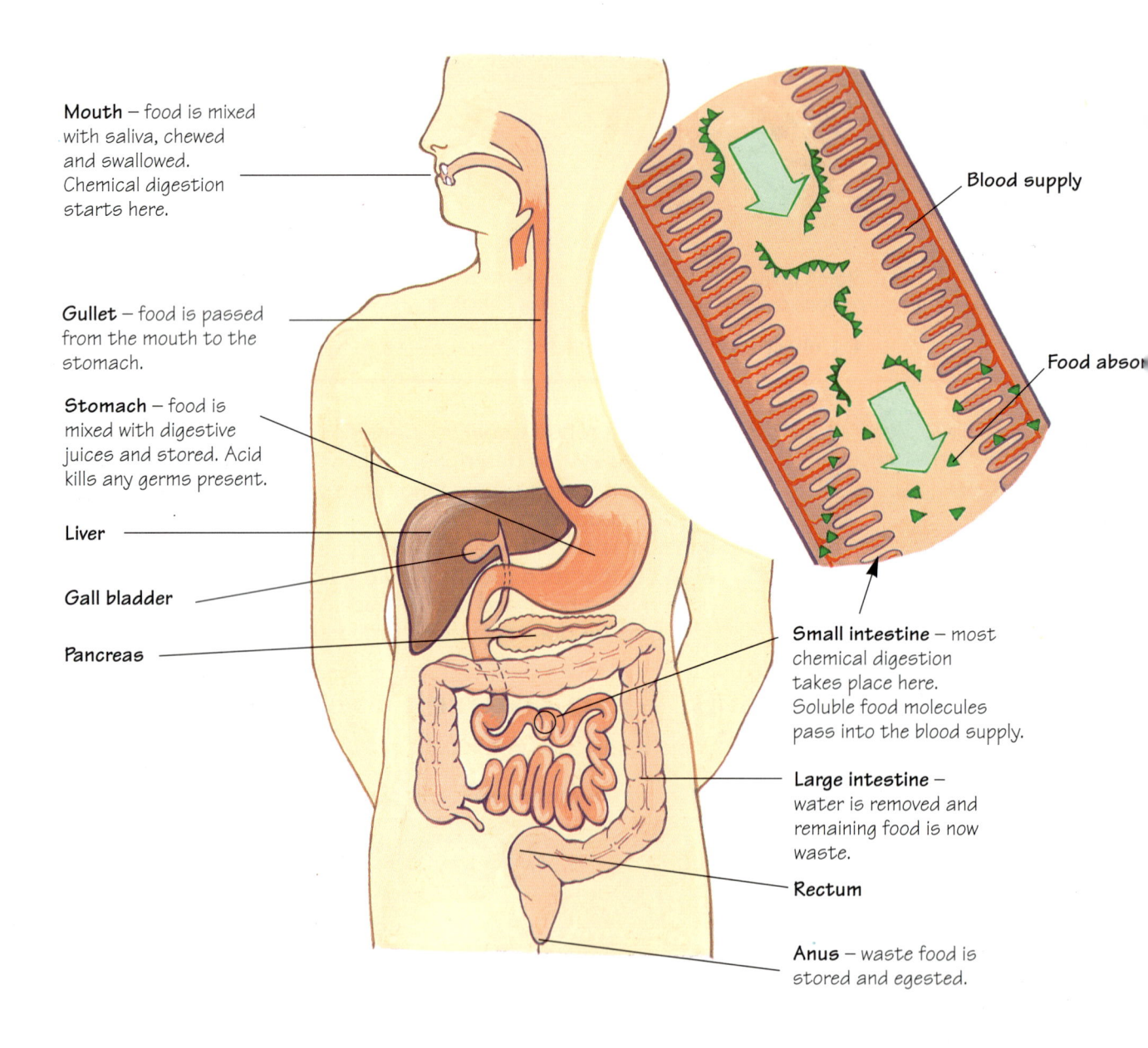

Mouth – food is mixed with saliva, chewed and swallowed. Chemical digestion starts here.

Gullet – food is passed from the mouth to the stomach.

Stomach – food is mixed with digestive juices and stored. Acid kills any germs present.

Liver

Gall bladder

Pancreas

Small intestine – most chemical digestion takes place here. Soluble food molecules pass into the blood supply.

Large intestine – water is removed and remaining food is now waste.

Rectum

Anus – waste food is stored and egested.

Blood supply

Food absor[bed]

Special chemicals called **enzymes** are involved in chemical digestion. They help to break insoluble molecules of

- fat into soluble glycerol and fatty acids
- protein into soluble amino acids
- carbohydrate into soluble sugars.

THE FATE OF FOOD

Digestion is a complicated set of processes. When things are difficult to understand it is a good idea to use a model to help explain what is going on. You will make a model of the small intestine in the next experiment and use it to study what happens **after** chemical digestion has taken place.

Collect

- 1 boiling tube
- 1 strip of cellulose tubing
- Thread
- Bottle of iodine
- Clinistix
- Spotting tile
- 2 droppers
- Bottle of glucose solution
- Bottle of starch solution
- Digestion system diagram
- Safety glasses

Bread contains a lot of starch molecules which are **insoluble**. Starch molecules are changed into **soluble** glucose molecules by the **enzyme** amylase in the small intestine.

1 Discuss the experiment shown below. Set it up when you understand the aim of the experiment.
2 Wash the outside of the tubing, then put it in the test tube of water.
3 Test the water for starch and glucose at the start of the experiment and after 20 minutes.

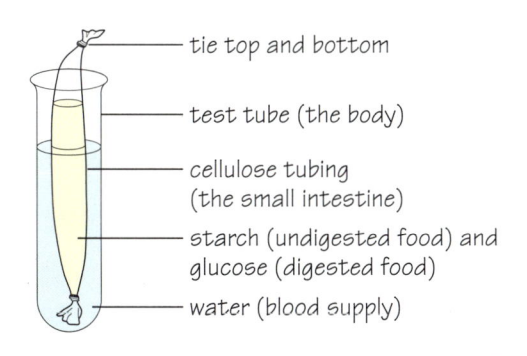

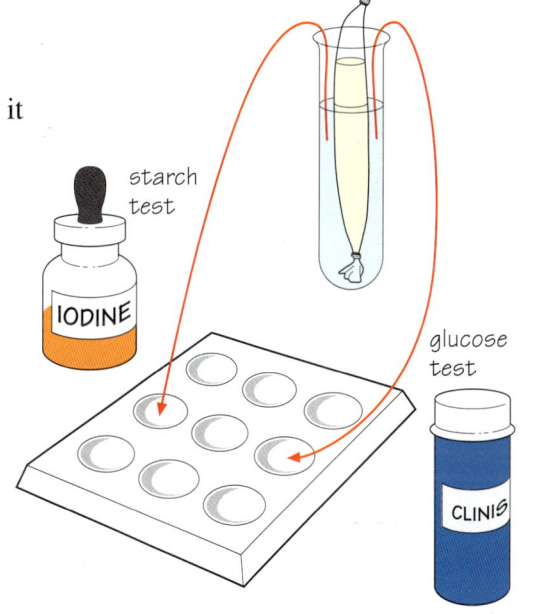

- tie top and bottom
- test tube (the body)
- cellulose tubing (the small intestine)
- starch (undigested food) and glucose (digested food)
- water (blood supply)

starch test

glucose test

1 **Collect** a digestion system diagram – label the parts.
2 Why must food be made soluble by digestion?
3 Imagine you are a slice of bread containing starch and fibre. Describe your journey through the digestive system. Say what happens to the starch and fibre.
4 Write a short report about the experiment. Include a

- title and aim
- labelled drawing
- description of what you did
- sentence describing the result
- sentence explaining the result.

B Digestion summary

Collect

- Bingo card
- Bag of bingo caller cards
- Digestion summary sheet

1 Play 'Digestion Bingo' in a group of four or five.
2 **Collect** the digestion summary sheet. Cut out the boxes. Make up a flow diagram to show the fate of food in digestion.

3.4 Food for thought

A Energy from food

Digested food is passed into the circulatory system. Blood carries it to all the cells of the body. In the cells, chemical reactions break the food down and release energy. Oxygen, also supplied by the blood, is needed for some of the reactions. Carbon dioxide and water are produced by the reactions. This process of slow and controlled energy release from food is called **aerobic respiration**. Only carbohydrates, fats and proteins provide energy. The other types of substance in foods do not.

Collect

- Food samples
- Balance
- Bunsen burner and mat
- Thermometer
- Test tube
- Tongs
- Food test equipment (see page 43)
- Safety glasses

You are organising a walk from John o'Groat's to Land's End. You will have to carry everything you need in a backpack. This includes food, so you have to choose foods that provide a lot of energy.

Your task is to use the apparatus below to find out which food would supply the most energy. You will have to design a fair test. You should repeat your experiments to check your results. You have to compare

- dry biscuits
- peanuts
- raisins.

1. Before you begin, carry out tests (see page 42) to find out what types of substance are present in the three foods.
2. Set up the apparatus as shown below. The food will burn best if it is crushed first.
3. Think about
   - which variables you need to keep the same
   - which variable you will change
   - what measurements you will have to make
   - how often to repeat each experiment.

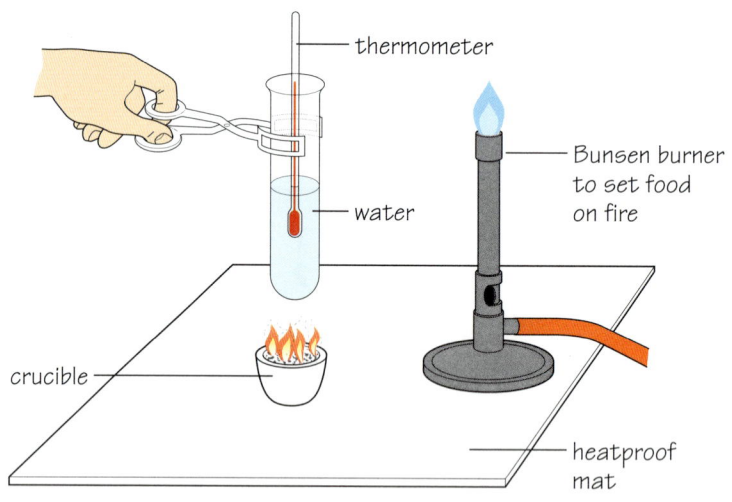

1. How does the body get energy from food? Name the process. Use the information on this page to write a word equation.
2. Draw a diagram of the apparatus you used to find out which food provides the most energy. Label the diagram to **explain** what the parts do, not just what they are. Put your results in a table and write a conclusion.
3. a Write a letter to the people going on the walk. Tell them which of the three foods to take and explain why.
   b They may not like the food you suggest. Which food group should they choose a replacement from? Explain your answer.

FOOD FOR THOUGHT

B A balanced diet

You are young, growing and active so you need lots of energy and lots of protein. The amount of energy you need depends on many things like your age, size, how active you are, and if you are a boy or a girl.

However, your weight gives a rough guide to the amount of energy and the amount of protein that you require each day. You must have

- about 170 kilojoules of energy every day for each kilogram of body weight
- about 0.6 g of protein every day for each kilogram of body weight.

Collect

- Weighing scales
- Food wrappers with nutritional information

1. Weigh yourself.
2. Work out your energy needs in kilojoules per day.
3. Work out your protein needs in grams per day.
4. Design a meal using the nutritional information on the food wrappers.
5. Calculate the total energy supplied and the total protein supplied by this meal.

1. What affects the amount of energy you need each day?
2. Why do you need a lot of protein?
3. Copy and complete this table.

My weight (kg)	Energy per day (kJ)	Protein per day (g)

4. List the foods you chose and the energy and protein supplied by each one. Show the total energy and protein supplied.
5. What would happen to your weight if your daily energy intake was
   a much less than your energy need
   b much more than your energy need?

3.5 Heart and circulation

A How they operate

The circulatory system is made up of the heart, blood vessels and blood. The human heart is made mainly of muscle. It weighs about 375 g and is about the size of an adult's fist. Your heart beats roughly 100 000 times every day.

Blood enters the heart from veins. A heart beat pumps it out at high pressure through the arteries. In a lifetime the heart will pump 300 million litres of blood. You can feel the pumping action of the heart in your arteries. This is called a **pulse**.

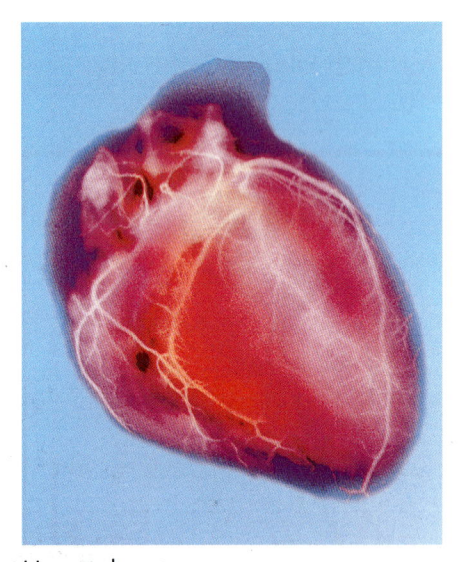

Human heart

Your teacher may show you the important parts of a sheep's heart or a model of a human's heart.

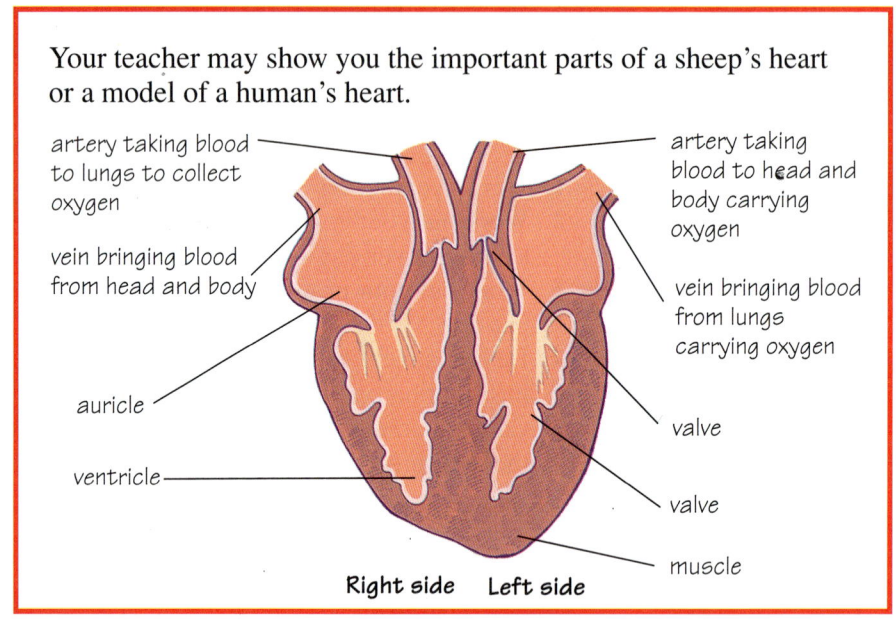

- artery taking blood to lungs to collect oxygen
- vein bringing blood from head and body
- auricle
- ventricle
- artery taking blood to head and body carrying oxygen
- vein bringing blood from lungs carrying oxygen
- valve
- valve
- muscle

Right side   Left side

Arteries carry blood under pressure away from the heart. **Veins** bring blood back to the heart at lower pressure. **Capillaries** are narrow blood vessels that connect the arteries with the veins.

Capillaries pass oxygen and food into body tissues and collect waste produced by cells.

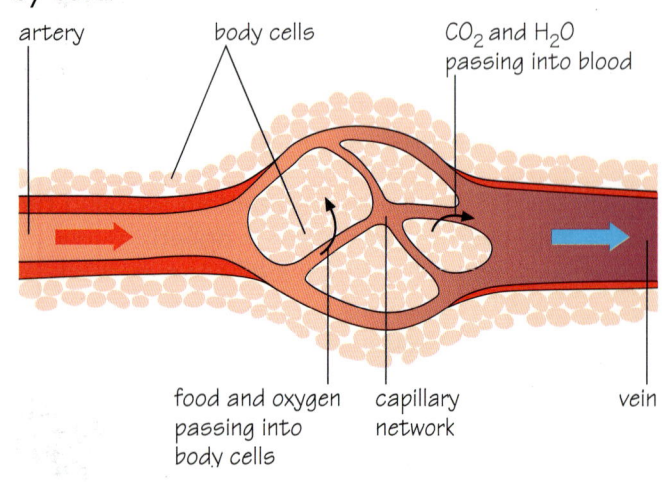

- artery
- body cells
- CO_2 and H_2O passing into blood
- food and oxygen passing into body cells
- capillary network
- vein

Capillaries collect oxygen from the lungs and pass waste gases (CO_2 and H_2O) made by cells into the lung's air sacs.

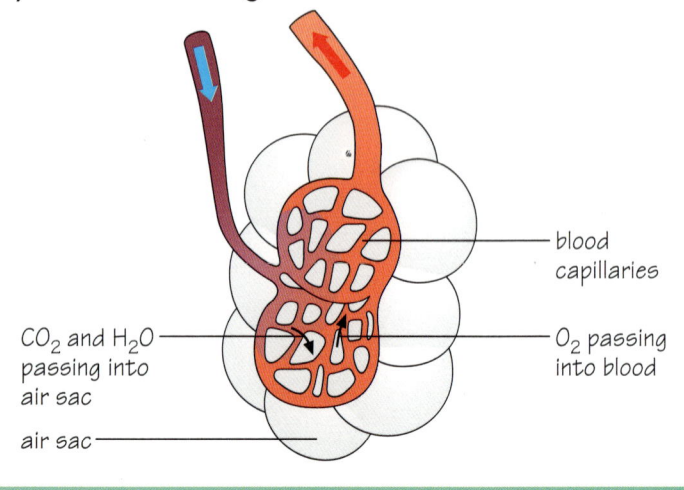

- blood capillaries
- O_2 passing into blood
- CO_2 and H_2O passing into air sac
- air sac

HEART AND CIRCULATION

Collect
- Timer
- Stethoscope
- Dropping bottle of oil
- Binocular microscope

1 Find the pulse in your wrist or your neck. Count the beats in one minute. This is your pulse rate. If there is a stethoscope use it to listen to your heart valves opening and closing.

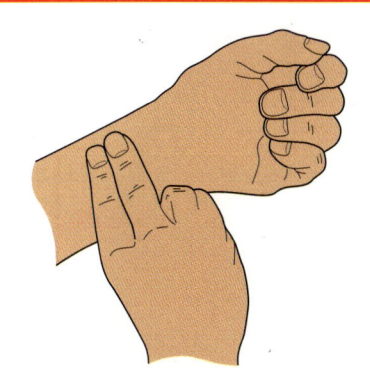

2 Put a drop of oil on the back of your finger between the nail and the first joint. Look at your finger under a low-power binocular microscope. Try to find the thin red lines of your smallest blood vessels (called capillaries).

1 **Collect** a heart diagram. Label the parts. Complete the description of how it works.
2 Write two sentences about the work that the human heart will do in a lifetime.
3 What is a pulse? What is your pulse rate when you are resting?
4 Describe the journey made by a molecule of oxygen from its starting point in the lungs.

B Get it straight

1 **Collect** the heart beat card set. You have to place the cards in the correct order to show what happens in the circulatory system.
2 Work with a partner. Shuffle the heart beat cards. Turn one up and lay it on the bench. Turn up the next card. Decide if it should go before or after the first card. Place it on the bench. Turn up the next card. Discuss where it should go – before or after the first card, before or after the second card? Repeat this until all the cards are placed. Ask your teacher to check your work when you are sure the order is correct.
3 Copy the card sequence into your book.

49

3.6 Lungs and breathing

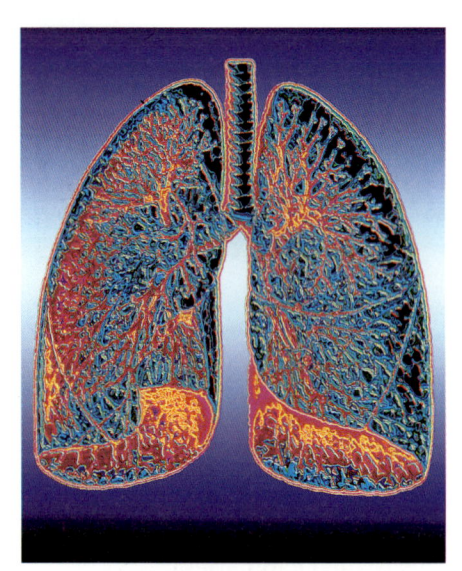

A Lung structure

You breathe air into your lungs. If you hold your ribs as you breathe in you can feel your lungs filling with air.

The lungs pass oxygen from the air into blood capillaries when you breathe in (inhale). Oxygen is then delivered to all your cells to keep them alive. Capillaries also collect carbon dioxide and water from body cells. These gases are exhaled. Healthy lungs are good at taking oxygen out of the air and passing carbon dioxide and water back into the air. Unhealthy lungs are not.

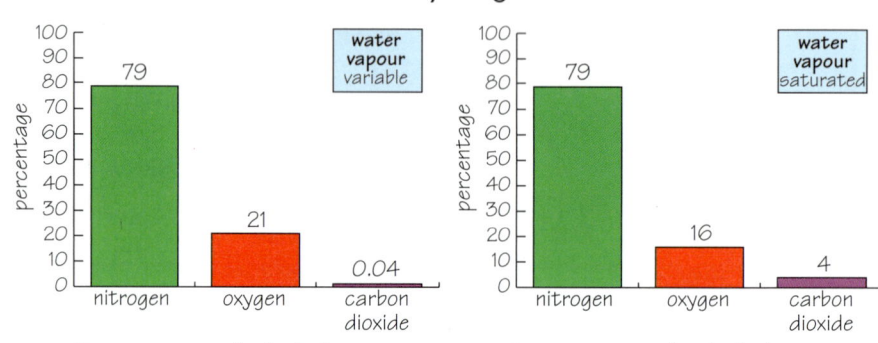

Capillary network in lungs

Composition of inhaled air
- nitrogen: 79
- oxygen: 21
- carbon dioxide: 0.04
- water vapour: variable

Composition of exhaled air
- nitrogen: 79
- oxygen: 16
- carbon dioxide: 4
- water vapour: saturated

Your teacher may show you the important parts of a sheep's lungs or a model of a human's lungs.

As you watch the dissection, find out

- what the lungs are like
  (where they are in the body, and their size, colour, texture and protection)
- the path of air through the lungs
  (name and describe each part in turn)
- how we breathe
  (what happens to the ribs and diaphragm).

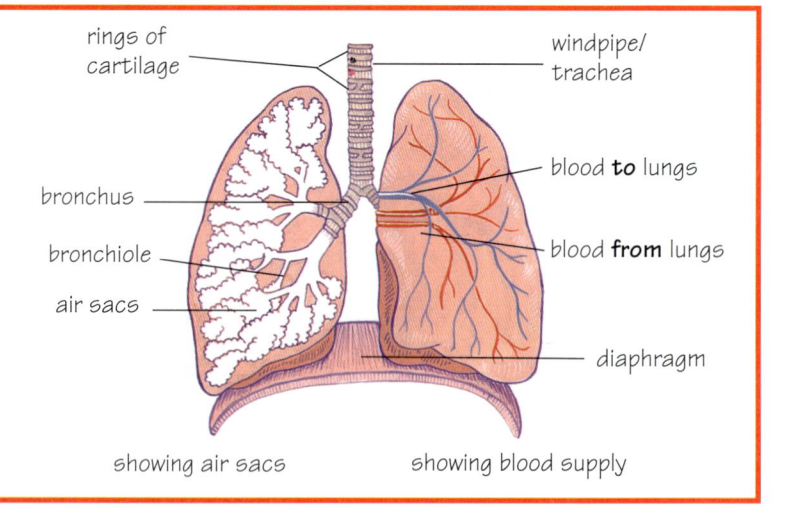

Labels on diagram: rings of cartilage, windpipe/trachea, bronchus, blood **to** lungs, bronchiole, blood **from** lungs, air sacs, diaphragm

showing air sacs   showing blood supply

Discuss what you can remember in a small group. **Collect** a 'bundling' sheet to help.

1. Write a group summary about the lungs. Use the headings *Description*, *Path of air* and *How we breathe*. Compare your summary with others in the class. Copy a correct summary into your book.
2. **Collect** a lung diagram. Label the main parts. Use a coloured pencil to show the path of oxygen through the breathing system.
3. Make a table to show the difference between inhaled and exhaled air.

You can find out about the effect of exercise on breathing rate, heart rate and rate of respiration by making some simple measurements.

LUNGS AND BREATHING

Collect

- Stopwatch
- Lime water
- 3 test tubes and rack
- 3 straws
- Lung volume kit
- Clinical thermometer
- Experiment sheet
- Record sheet
- Coloured pencils
- Safety glasses

Work in a group of three or four at the most. You will all need to co-operate to obtain good results for each other. The idea is to take some simple measurements before and after exercise and compare the results.

Five measurements are shown below. The experiment sheet explains what to do in more detail. Read this carefully before you begin.

Help each other take measurements when you are at rest. One member of the group should then exercise for three minutes. The others then take all the necessary measurements and record these. Repeat this for the second, then the third member of the group.

- **Heart rate:** by measuring pulse rate at 30 second intervals.
- **Respiration rate:** by measuring skin temperature with a clinical thermometer.
- **Depth of breathing:** by using the kit shown on the experiment sheet.
- **Breathing rate:** by counting breaths/minute.
- **Respiration rate:** by measuring CO_2 production.

4 Write a short report on the experiments, including your results. Write an explanation for the differences before and after exercise.

5 Put your results into a group or class spreadsheet. Use the computer to calculate the average change in measurements for your class. You could also produce some bar charts and make a class poster to display the results.

B Every breath you take

This is a model of the human breathing system. Your teacher will show you how it works.

1 Copy this diagram.
2 Label the diagram to
   - show what the parts represent
   - explain what happens when you breathe in and out.
3 What important part of how we breathe is missing from the model?

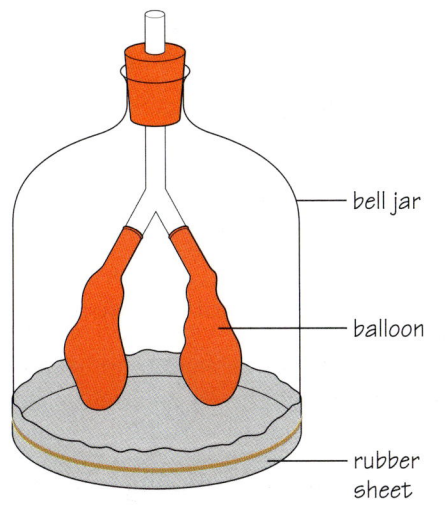

(diagram labels: bell jar, balloon, rubber sheet)

51

3.7 Fit for nothing

A Smoking and drinking

Tobacco
Tobacco smoke contains chemicals that can damage your lungs.

Tar and other substances in tobacco smoke irritate the lungs. You cough more, and more germs get into your lungs.

Nicotine is a poison. It makes the arteries narrower. Your heart then has to pump harder to push blood along.

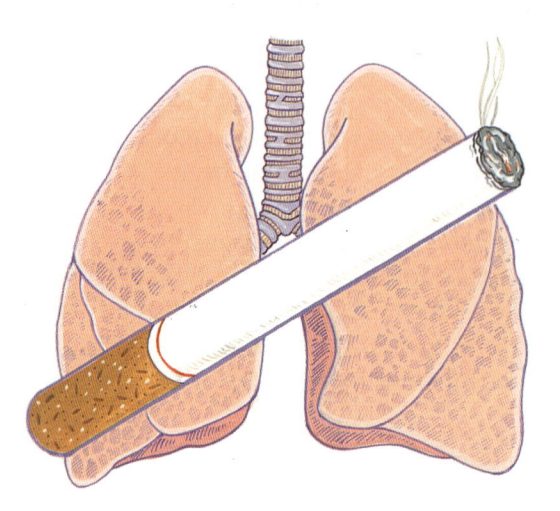

Carbon monoxide gas is quickly picked up by the blood. It prevents the blood from picking up oxygen, and so you have to breathe faster and your heart has to beat faster.

Smokers may feel that they need nicotine. They have become **addicted**.

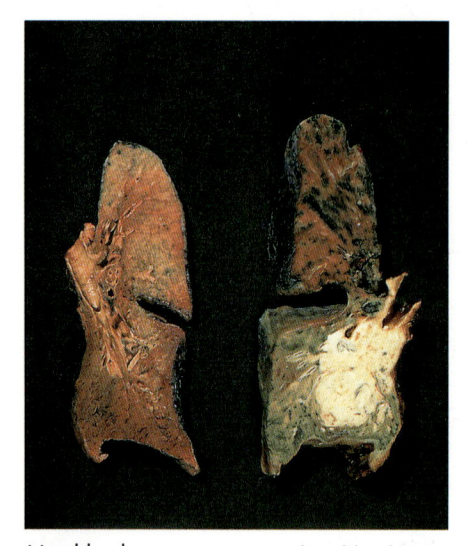

Healthy lungs   Unhealthy lungs

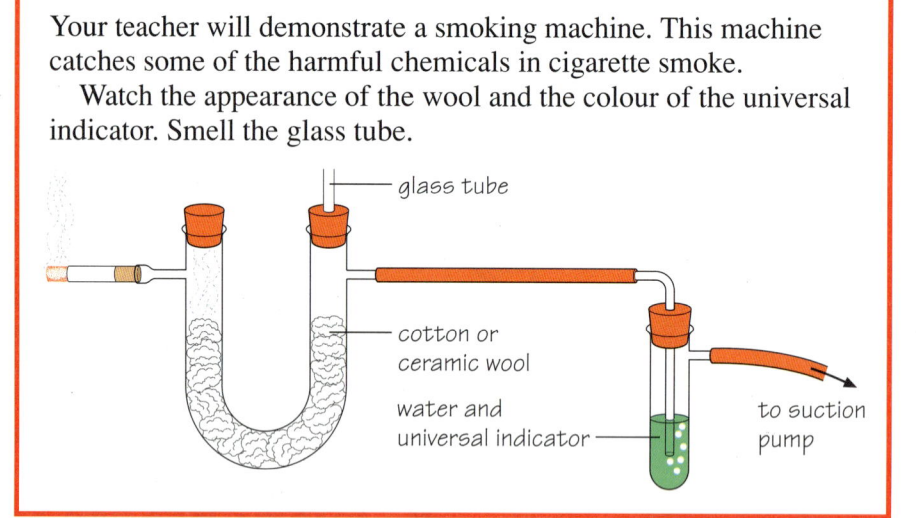

Your teacher will demonstrate a smoking machine. This machine catches some of the harmful chemicals in cigarette smoke.
   Watch the appearance of the wool and the colour of the universal indicator. Smell the glass tube.

- glass tube
- cotton or ceramic wool
- water and universal indicator
- to suction pump

Imagine that you are a doctor giving advice to a patient who smokes. You need to tell this person

- about the experiment and what it shows
- what the harmful chemicals in smoke are and what they do.

Your teacher may ask you to

- write a letter to your patient
- make a tape recording giving your advice
- draw a diagram with labels **explaining** what happens in the smoking machine.

FIT FOR NOTHING

Alcohol

Alcohol is a drug. You can become addicted to it by drinking it regularly, even in small amounts. A heavy drinker runs the risk of serious liver damage. Drinking too much alcohol in one go can kill you. Alcohol has an effect on behaviour.

Here are two important facts about alcohol to learn.

- All of these drinks contain about the **same** amount of alcohol. This is called **one unit**.

| 1 unit | ½ pint of beer | glass of wine | glass of sherry | small whisky | small vodka | small martini |

- It takes your liver about one hour to remove one unit of alcohol from the blood.

Collect

- Clipboard
- Paper
- Poster paper
- Coloured pencils

Your task is to design a survey questionnaire to find out what people in the school really think about drinking alcohol. Use the information on this page to design your questions.

Here are some suggestions to get you started.

- Be sure that *you* know the facts.
- Write questions that can be answered **yes** or **no**.
- Find out what people *know*. For example,
  Does a half pint of beer have the same amount of alcohol as a measure of whisky? **(yes)**
  or
  Can your body get rid of the alcohol in a pint of beer in less than 1 hour? **(no)**
- Find out what people *think* about drinking alcohol. For example,
  Do you think that the legal limit for driving should be lowered from 80 mg of alcohol per 100 ml of blood?

continued ▶

FIT FOR NOTHING

▶ *continued*

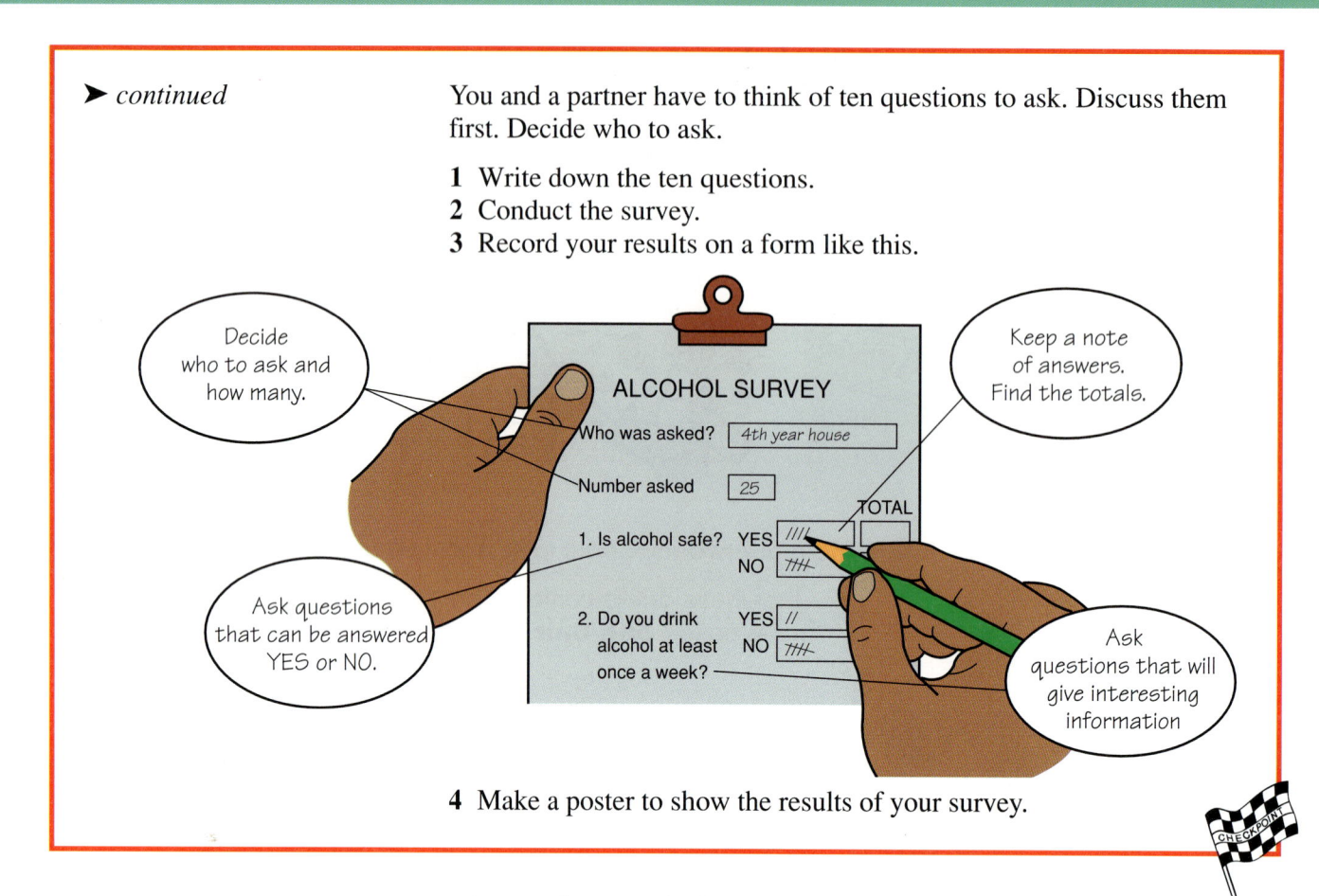

You and a partner have to think of ten questions to ask. Discuss them first. Decide who to ask.

1 Write down the ten questions.
2 Conduct the survey.
3 Record your results on a form like this.

Decide who to ask and how many.

Keep a note of answers. Find the totals.

ALCOHOL SURVEY
Who was asked? 4th year house
Number asked 25

TOTAL
1. Is alcohol safe? YES ////
   NO 7///
2. Do you drink YES //
   alcohol at least NO 7///
   once a week?

Ask questions that can be answered YES or NO.

Ask questions that will give interesting information

4 Make a poster to show the results of your survey.

B Advertising

Collect
- Advertisement
- Felt pens
- Glue
- Paper
- Stencils

Advertisements for cigarettes and alcohol usually connect smoking and drinking with something good in life. You know how dangerous they can be. Change and reword your advert so that it warns people about the dangers of smoking or drinking.

3.8 Problem

Design a game

Your problem is to design a board game which

- is fun to play
- teaches the players about healthy living **or** food and digestion **or** body systems.

Hints

Your group should decide what type of game to produce. Here are three suggestions:

Simple path game like snakes and ladders

Shaped path game

Quiz path game

- Decide on the aim of the game and the rules.
  (Games with simple rules usually work best.)
- Make a list of at least five **good health** points and at least five **bad health** points if you are designing a healthy living game. Make a list of ten points about digestion for the digestion game and a list of ten points about body systems for the body systems game.
  You must use these in your game.

1 Design and make your game.
2 Play your game to make sure that it works.
3 Try out some of the other games made in the class.

Collect

- Blank game board
- Stencils
- Coloured pencils
- Coloured paper
- Scissors
- Dice
- Plasticine

3.9 Talkabout

Smoking and health

How would you persuade someone to stop smoking? Some of the ideas that you can use are given below. You will be able to think of others.

Some survey information

A survey of more than 10 000 11–16 year olds produced these results.

Where do smokers smoke?

Should children be allowed to smoke at home?

What percentage of boys and girls started to smoke in their first year at secondary school?

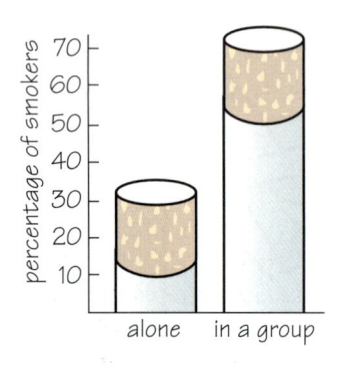

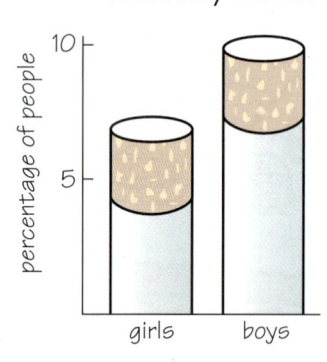

Some medical facts

- 9 out of every 10 people who get lung cancer are smokers
- If you smoke you're twice as likely to have a heart attack
- A pregnant woman who smokes may have a smaller baby than she otherwise would have
- Hot smoke damages the cells that let you smell and taste

Some advice

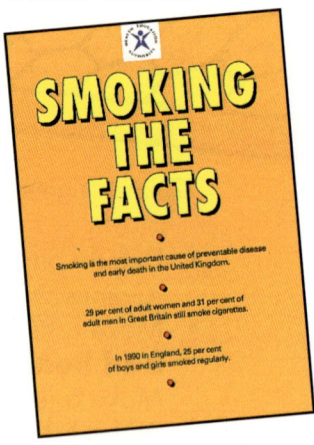

SMOKING THE FACTS

Smoking is the most important cause of preventable disease and early death in the United Kingdom.

29 per cent of adult women and 31 per cent of adult men in Great Britain still smoke cigarettes.

In 1990 in England, 25 per cent of boys and girls smoked regularly.

STOPPING SMOKING MADE EASIER

Where to get help Includes a telephone helpline

Checklist Do you really want to stop?

Will power You have more than you think

Planning ahead The simple secret of success

---

1. Work in a small group.
   Discuss the ideas shown above, and any of your own.
2. Write a script for a short play or a radio advertisement to encourage people to stop smoking.
3. **Collect** a tape recorder and a blank tape. Act out your script.
4. Play your tape to the class.

3.10 Readabout

Body defences

Even when you are fit you can wake up in the morning feeling unwell. Very often it is because you have some sort of infection. Infections can be caused by **bacteria**, **fungi** and **viruses**. These are all types of **microbe**.

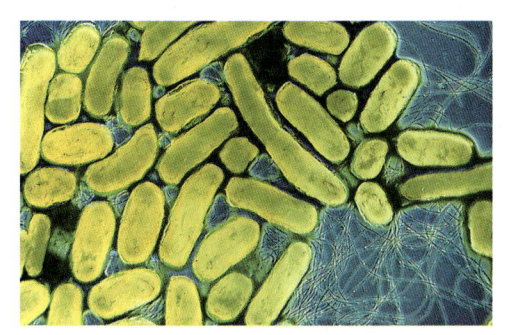

Food poisoning can be caused by salmonella bacteria [Magnified 3 000 times]

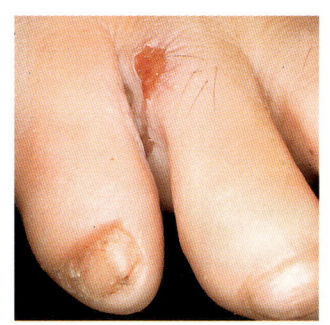

Athlete's foot is caused by a fungus

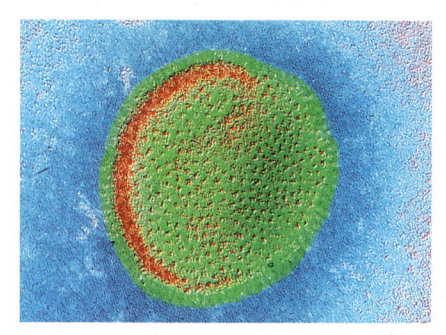

Flu is caused by a virus [Magnified 350 000 times]

Your body has a natural defence system that can fight off most infections. Your skin and blood are part of this defence system.

- Skin is a barrier that prevents microbes from entering your body. Sweat contains chemicals that stop the growth of microbes.
- When the skin is broken, blood quickly clots to seal the wound with a scab. Blood platelets start the clotting process when they are exposed to the air.
- Blood contains red and **white cells**. Red cells carry oxygen to all parts of the body. It is the job of the white cells to attack, digest and destroy invading microbes.

Your blood also carries special proteins called **antibodies**. These become attached to microbes in the blood or to the **toxins** (poisons) made by microbes. They destroy them or make them easier for the white cells to find. White cells and antibodies are part of the body's powerful **immune** system. When this system is damaged, for example by the HIV virus (which causes AIDS), it leaves a person unprotected from the mildest of infections. These can then become life-threatening.

◀ Antibodies (yellow) on the surface of a cell

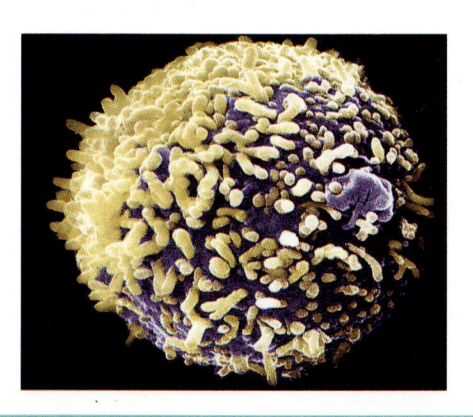

White blood cell infected by ▶ HIV (the red indicates the infection)

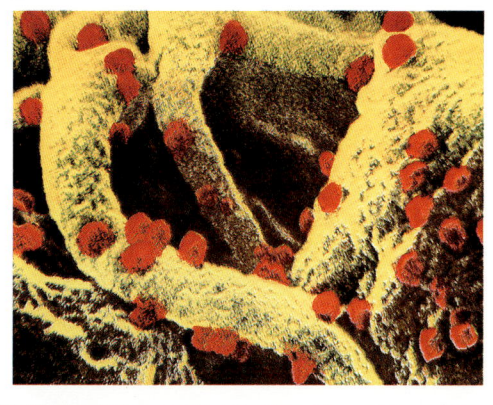

57

READABOUT – BODY DEFENCES

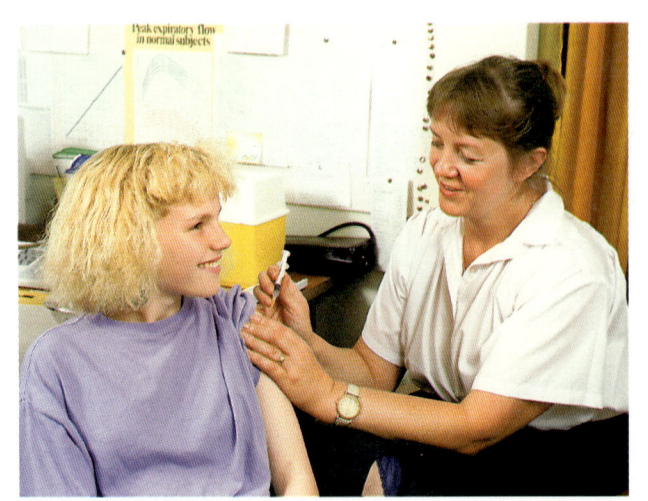

Scientists have discovered ways of improving the body's defences. Everybody now has the chance to be **immunised** against certain diseases such as smallpox, typhoid and tetanus. This is normally done by injecting a **vaccine** into the blood system. The vaccine is made from dead cells of the dangerous microbe. This tricks the body into making antibodies which are then ready if a real infection takes place.

Science comes to the rescue again if an infection does take hold or a disease develops. Medicines can be taken to cure the illness. **Antibiotics** such as **penicillin** are one type of medicine used to fight bacterial infections. Antibiotics are made by fungi. They are effective against bacteria but they don't work against viruses. Other **drugs** have also been developed to fight bacterial and viral infections. Over the last few years the drug AZT has been used to help prevent the development of full blown AIDS in people who are infected with HIV.

1 Copy and complete the flow diagram below.

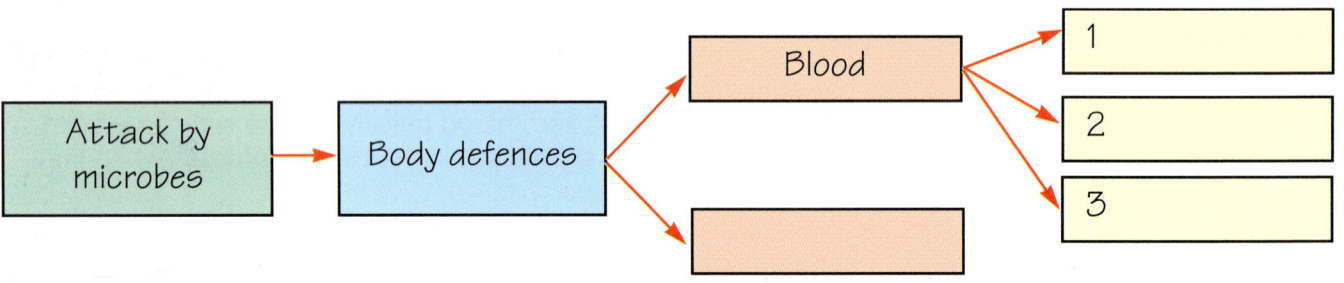

Attack by microbes → Body defences → Blood → 1, 2, 3
                                   → [ ]

2 What are the three types of microbe?
Use available books to carry out some research. Find out
   a the names of three diseases caused by bacteria

   • the symptoms of each disease
   • how each disease is treated

   b the names of three diseases caused by viruses

   • the symptoms of each disease
   • how each disease is treated

   c the name of one disease caused by a fungus, its symptoms and how it is treated.

3 Describe how immunisation and medicines help prevent and cure illness.

4 Find out who discovered penicillin. Produce a personal history file for this scientist. Include

   • nationality
   • dates of birth and death
   • three interesting facts about this scientist's life.

4 Everyday forces

BIG IDEAS IN THIS UNIT

1 There are two groups of forces – contact forces and non-contact forces.
2 Forces come in pairs when two objects interact.
3 The forces acting on one object can be balanced or unbalanced.
4 Forces can cause objects to turn around a pivot.
5 Pressure is a measure of the force acting on a unit of area.
6 Speed can be calculated from measurements of distance and time.

4.1 Describing forces

A Forces in action

Forces affect our lives every day.

Pulling or **pushing** forces can change the direction of a moving object

Pushing or pulling forces can start an object moving or stop it

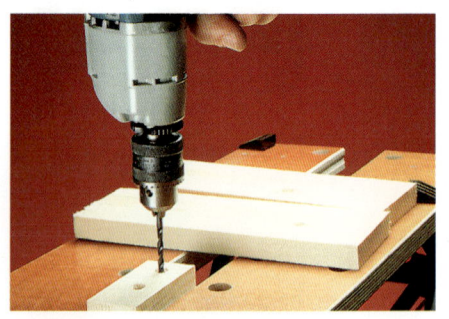

Pushing, pulling, **tearing** or **twisting** forces can change the shape of an object

Forces are measured in units called **newtons**. The name comes from a very famous scientist, Sir Isaac Newton. He was born in 1642 and studied forces and movement. His laws of motion are still used today.

Collect

- Plasticine
- Newton spring balance
- Trolley
- Masses
- Scrap paper

Using forces

Change the Plasticine into a castle by using these forces

- pushing force
- pulling force
- twisting force
- tearing force.

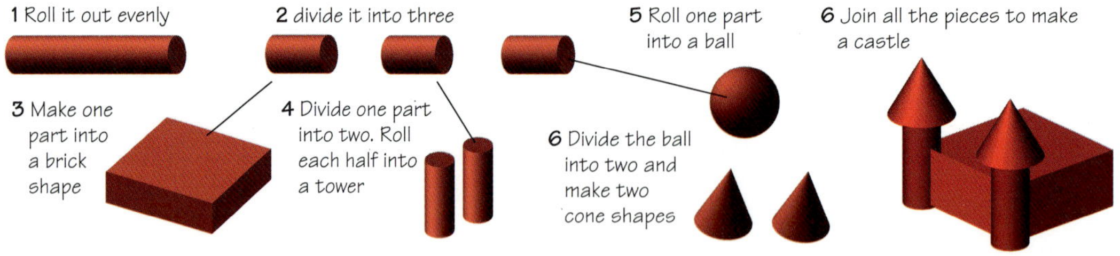

1 Roll it out evenly

2 divide it into three

3 Make one part into a brick shape

4 Divide one part into two. Roll each half into a tower

5 Roll one part into a ball

6 Divide the ball into two and make two cone shapes

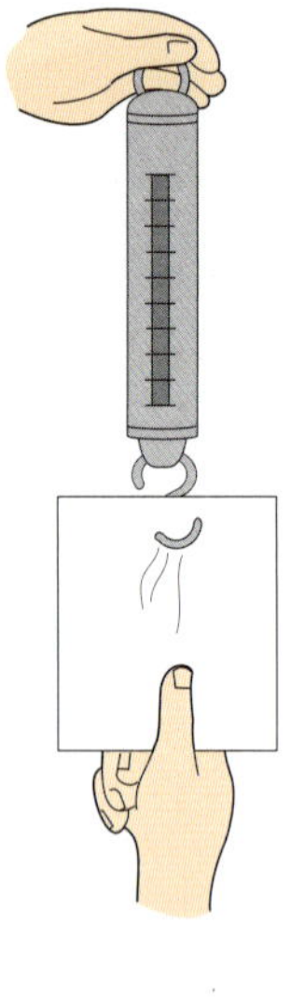

6 Join all the pieces to make a castle

Measuring forces

Use a newton spring balance to find the force needed to

- tear a piece of paper
- start a book moving
- pull a trolley along the bench
- lift some masses.

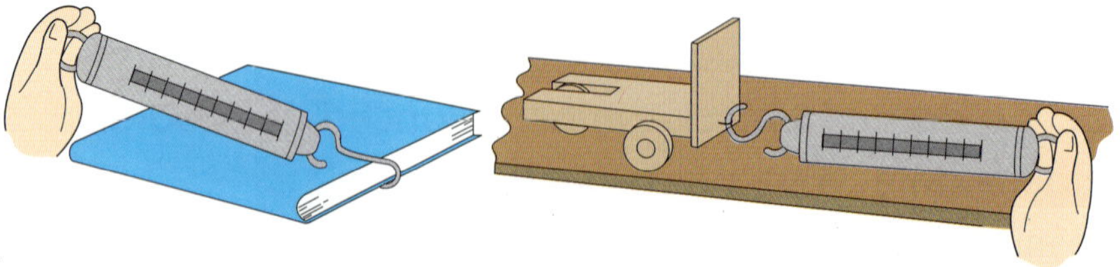

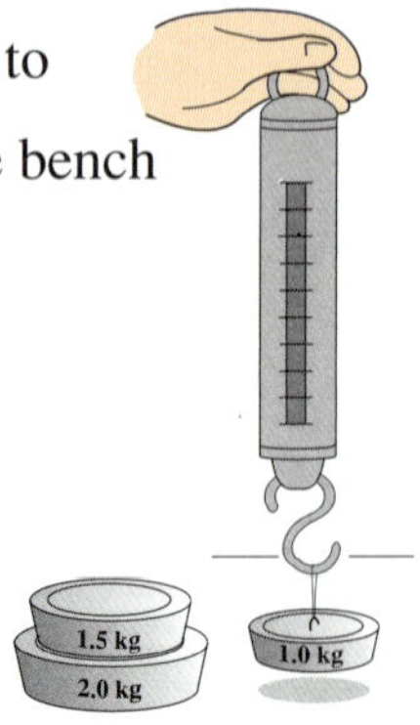

Keep a record of your results for these experiments on scrap paper.

DESCRIBING FORCES

1. Draw and complete a table with two headings: *Type of force*, and *Examples*. Working with a partner think of at least three examples of each type of force. Use today's work and also think of examples of your own.
2. Copy the castle-making diagram into your book. Under each step write down the type of force you used.
3. What instrument is used to measure force? What units of measurement are used?
4. Draw a line graph of your results for lifting the masses. Label the axes *Mass* and *Force needed*. Give your graph a title.
5. Use your graph to work out the force required to lift a mass of
   a 1.75 kg
   b 2.5 kg.
6. In the 'Good health' section you measured your own mass. How much force would be required to lift you off the ground?

B Forces everywhere

You use forces all the time. **Collect** a tray of objects. Try out each of the everyday activities shown below. Discuss whether you are using a pushing, pulling, tearing or twisting force.

Open the jar

Pick up the pen

Crumple the paper

Take off the lid

Write a poem

Put it in the bin

Make a table to record your discussions. The table should have two columns.

61

4.2 Forces at a distance

A Non-contact forces

Contact forces must touch an object before they can make something happen. Pulling, pushing and twisting are contact forces. There are other forces that can work from a distance. Three examples of **non-contact** forces are gravity, electricity and magnetism.

Collect

- Long cardboard tube
- Retort stand
- Ruler
- Plasticine

Play the three games. They will help you to understand these non-contact forces. Work with a partner.

Game 1: Bat the Ball (The Gravity Game)
An object falls because the force of gravity pulls it towards the centre of the earth.

1. Make a small ball from Plasticine.
2. Your partner will drop the ball down the tube. Try to hit the ball as it escapes from the tube. Try three times.
3. Now let your partner try.

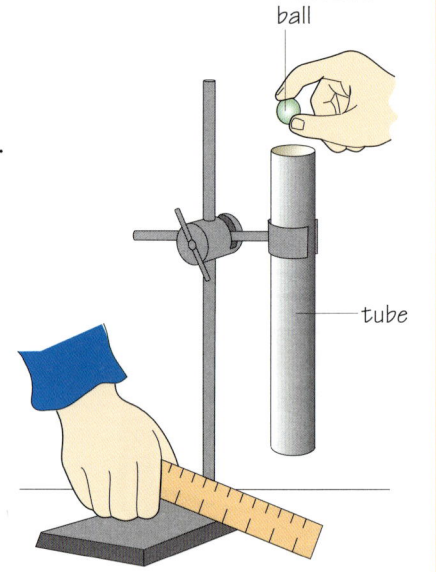

Collect

- Polystyrene ball
- Piece of cloth
- 1 plastic rod
- Timer
- Piece of filter paper

Game 2: Crazy Golf (The Electric Game)
Rubbing a plastic rod gives it an electrostatic charge. A charged rod can attract some objects.

1. Rub the rod with the cloth to give it an electrostatic charge. Time how long it takes to get the ball in the hole. You must not touch the ball with the rod.
2. Now see if your partner can beat your time.

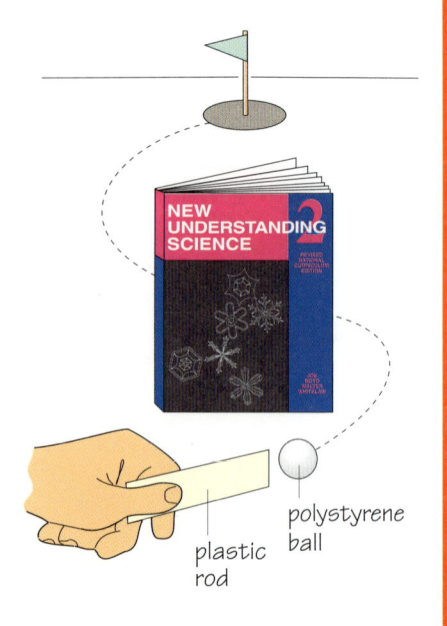

FORCES AT A DISTANCE

Collect

- Petri dish
- Face outline
- Small magnet
- Iron filings
- Timer

Game 3: Make a Face (The Magnetic Game)
Iron is attracted to a magnet.

1 Complete the face by adding two eyebrows, the middle bits of both eyes and by blacking out one tooth. Time how long this takes you.
2 Now see if your partner can beat your time.

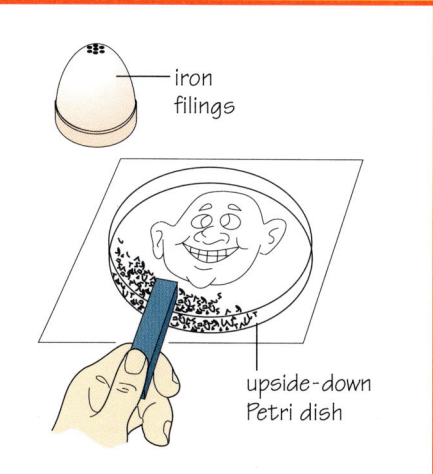

iron filings

upside-down Petri dish

1 Write down three contact forces and three non-contact forces.
2 Name the non-contact force used in each game and describe how it was used.
3 Copy and complete the table below.

Game	Force acts on . . .	Object attracted to . . .
1		The centre of the earth

B Using non-contact forces

Forces that act from a distance are used in everyday objects. Look at these pictures.

a   b   c   d

Write down the non-contact force being used in each picture.

63

4.3 Action and reaction

A Forces act in pairs

Think back to earlier lessons when you made Plasticine shapes, lifted masses off the table and moved a polystyrene ball along the bench. Could you feel the Plasticine pushing against your fingers as you shaped it? Do you remember feeling the masses pulling against you as you lifted them off the table? Did you notice how the ball seemed to push against the charged plastic rod?

You could feel these things because forces act in pairs when two objects interact. We often notice a force that seems to make something happen but usually we don't notice the other force involved. For every action force there is an equal and opposite reaction force. This is one of Newton's important laws.

Collect

- 5 experiment cards
- Bar magnet and nail
- 1 kg mass and spring balance
- Plasticine and metre stick
- Trolley
- Plastic rod and cloth

1. This is a group activity for a team of five. Each member of the team must carry out one experiment and report back to the other team members.
2. **Collect** a set of five experiment cards. Deal these out face down, so that each team member gets one card.
3. Carry out your experiment. You have five minutes to do this.

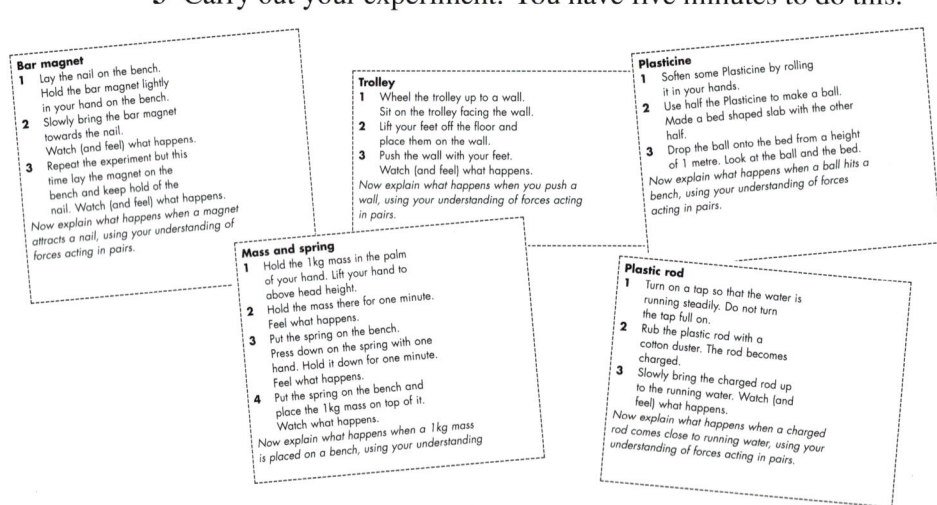

Bar magnet
1. Lay the nail on the bench. Hold the bar magnet lightly in your hand on the bench.
2. Slowly bring the bar magnet towards the nail. Watch (and feel) what happens.
3. Repeat the experiment but this time lay the magnet on the bench and keep hold of the nail. Watch (and feel) what happens.

Now explain what happens when a magnet attracts a nail, using your understanding of forces acting in pairs.

Trolley
1. Wheel the trolley up to a wall. Sit on the trolley facing the wall.
2. Lift your feet off the floor and place them on the wall.
3. Push the wall with your feet. Watch (and feel) what happens.

Now explain what happens when you push a wall, using your understanding of forces acting in pairs.

Plasticine
1. Soften some Plasticine by rolling it in your hands.
2. Use half the Plasticine to make a ball. Made a bed shaped slab with the other half.
3. Drop the ball onto the bed from a height of 1 metre. Look at the ball and the bed.

Now explain what happens when a ball hits a bench, using your understanding of forces acting in pairs.

Mass and spring
1. Hold the 1kg mass in the palm of your hand. Lift your hand to above head height.
2. Hold the mass there for one minute. Feel what happens.
3. Put the spring on the bench. Press down on the spring with one hand. Hold it down for one minute. Feel what happens.
4. Put the spring on the bench and place the 1kg mass on top of it. Watch what happens.

Now explain what happens when a 1kg mass is placed on a bench, using your understanding

Plastic rod
1. Turn on a tap so that the water is running steadily. Do not turn the tap full on.
2. Rub the plastic rod with a cotton duster. The rod becomes charged.
3. Slowly bring the charged rod up to the running water. Watch (and feel) what happens.

Now explain what happens when a charged rod comes close to running water, using your understanding of forces acting in pairs.

4. Now go back to your group. Each person in turn must describe their experiment and **explain** it to the others. Use the idea of action and reaction described at the top of this page.
5. Check one of the other explanations by trying out that experiment. Take no more than five minutes.
6. As a team discuss what to write on each card. Stick the five cards on a sheet of poster paper. Give your poster a title.
7. Pin the poster on the wall and compare what you have written with the results of the other teams. Discuss any differences.

Write a description of one of the five experiments. Explain the result of the experiment. Use the words *pairs of forces*, *action* and *reaction* in your explanation.

ACTION AND REACTION

B Spot the pair

Look at the photographs below. You have to spot the pair of forces acting in each photograph.

a Skiing

b Sprinting

c Fishing

d Lifting off

1 For each photograph
- write down the title
- state the action force
- state the reaction force.

2 Collect two of the available advertisements cut from magazines. Stick these into your notebook. Give each one a title and describe the main action and reaction forces involved.

65

4.4 Balancing act

A Getting the balance right

Several forces can act on one object. When this happens they can work together or work against one another.

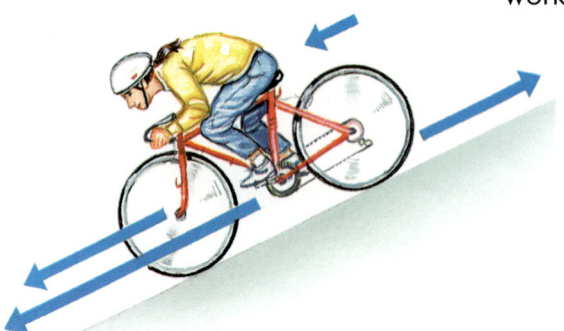

Forces on the bike acting together

Forces on the rope acting against each other

Forces acting on an object can be balanced or unbalanced. When forces are balanced an object's shape is unchanged *or* it remains at rest *or* it moves at a constant speed. When forces are unbalanced there are changes to an object's shape, or speed, or direction of movement. Think about what happens to the rope in the tug of war when the forces on each side are balanced and unbalanced.

Here is a brain teaser. There are 15 pupils in a class. 14 of them have exactly the same weight. One pupil is 2 kg heavier than the others. How could you use a see-saw to find the odd one out?
You can only use the see-saw three times.

Collect

- See-saw
- 14 coins **or** metal discs
- 1 larger coin **or** metal disc
- Ball of Plasticine
- Large beaker of water

1 Discuss and then solve the brain teaser with a partner. (There is a hint on how to start at the bottom of the next page.) Try your solution with this equipment.

BALANCING ACT

2 Here is another puzzle to solve.
How can you make a lump of Plasticine float on water?
When an object floats there must be balanced forces. The downwards push of the Plasticine is balanced by the upwards push of the water. Try to float the Plasticine on the water.
You can make it into any shape you like, but you are not allowed to throw any of it away.

1 Describe how you solved the see-saw problem. Use the words *balanced forces* and *unbalanced forces* in your answer.

2 Make a drawing to show how you solved the floating problem. Label your drawing to **explain** why the Plasticine floats. Don't just label the parts.

3 Why does a beach ball float? Use your understanding of forces in your explanation.

B Losing your balance

Look at the picture puzzles below. In one cartoon of each pair, the forces acting are balanced. In the other they are not.

Accelerate    Walk tall    Let fly

Copy the title of each cartoon pair.
Explain what is happening in each picture using the idea of balanced and unbalanced forces.

Puzzle hint: Start with seven people on each side. If the see-saw balances then the person left out is heavier. If not, the heavy person will be on the side that goes down . . .

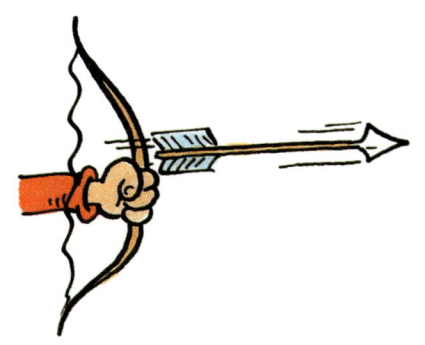

67

4.5 Turning forces

A Levers

You would have trouble trying to lift a paving slab in the school playground. You might not be strong enough to provide the force required to lift it with your hands.

This doesn't mean you couldn't do it. All you need is a **lever** and a **pivot**.

The force you apply at the end of the lever causes a turning force about the pivot, and the slab is raised.

Many simple machines and tools depend on this turning effect.

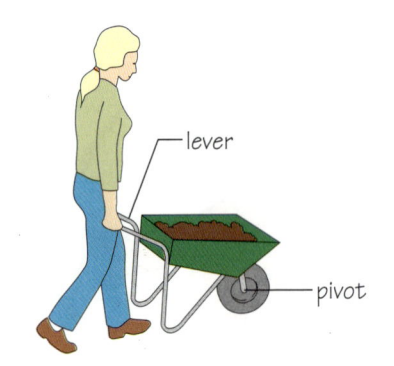

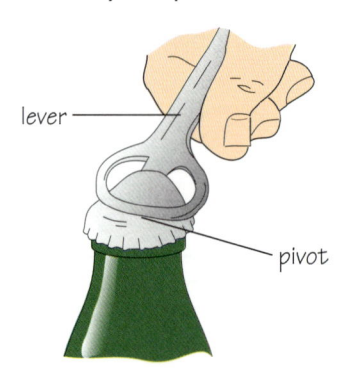

You can investigate the factors that affect the size of the turning force using a very simple lever and pivot – the see-saw.

Collect

- See-saw (made from a lever and a pivot)
- 7 small masses

1 Set up your see-saw.
2 Experiment with the lever and pivot to solve these balancing problems. There is usually more than one solution. You can place the masses wherever you like. You can place the pivot wherever you like. Try to balance the masses in piles as follows

- **4** on the left of the pivot with **3** on the right
- **5** on the left of the pivot with **2** on the right
- **6** on the left of the pivot with **1** on the right.

TURNING FORCES

1. Give three examples of a lever in action.
2. Copy and complete the table below to show the results of your experiments.

	Left side		Right side	
	Number of masses	Distance from pivot (in squares)	Number of masses	Distance from pivot (in squares)
	4		3	
	5		2	
	6		1	

3. What is the pattern in your results?
   Hint: Multiply the mass times the distance on each side of the pivot. Now you should be able to answer the question.
4. Where would you place a 2 g mass to balance the see-saw if the other side had
   a a 10 g mass 2 cm from the pivot
   b a 6 g mass 6 cm from the pivot?

B Spot the pivot

Collect
- Scissors
- Stiff cardboard

Choose *one* of these experiments to carry out and report on.

Close the door
Close the door three times by pressing your little finger against it in the three different places shown.

Cut the card
Try to make a cut in the stiff cardboard using the scissors in the three different ways shown.

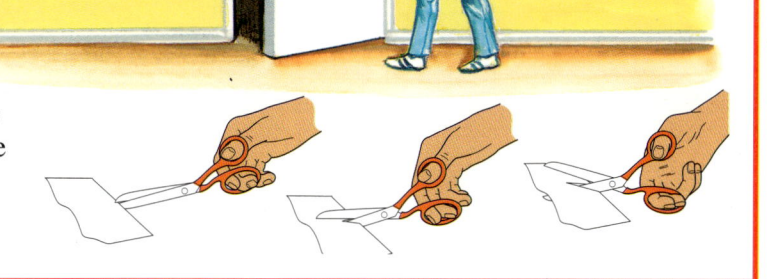

Write a report on the experiment you carried out. Include

- a title
- a drawing with labels to show the position of the pivot
- a sentence to describe when it was easiest to close the door *or* cut the card
- a sentence to **explain** why it was easy to close the door *or* cut the card.

69

4.6 On the move

A Friction

A small push can move a car. So why does it stop again? When any object moves over a surface the force of friction slows its movement. For example, with a car, friction is caused when the tyres rub along the ground. Friction is a force that opposes (acts against) motion.

Think about trying to push a heavy box along the ground. If your pushing force is less than the frictional force, then the box will not move. If your pushing force is equal to the frictional force, the box will move at a steady speed. If your pushing force is greater than the frictional force the box will move faster and faster (accelerate).

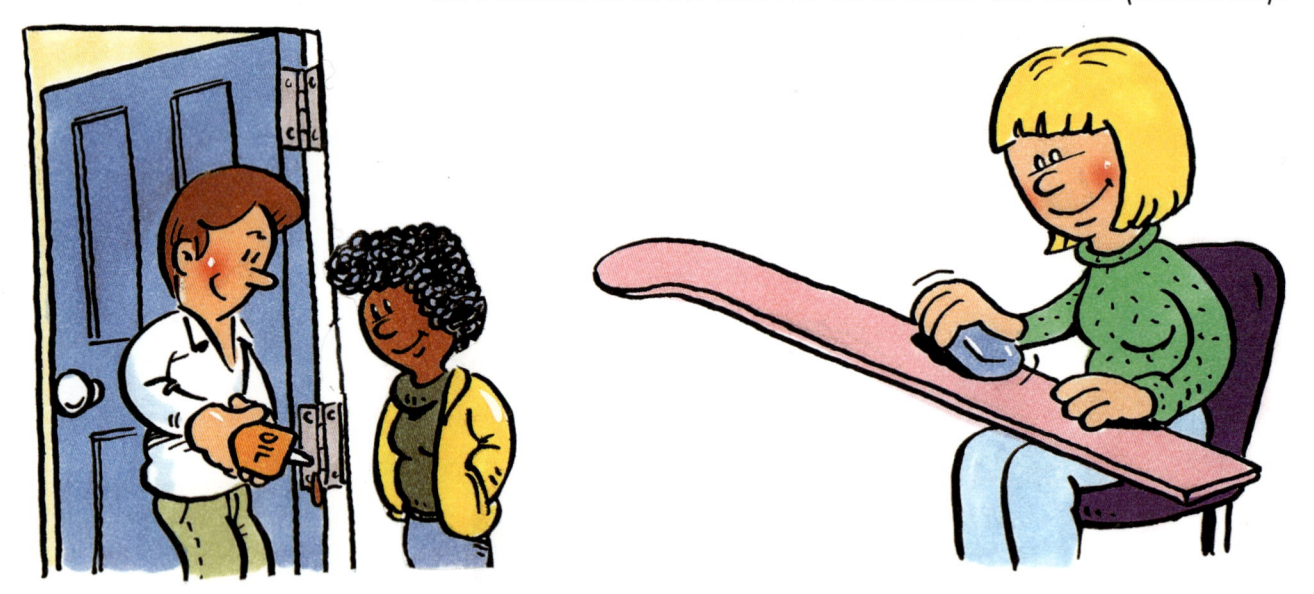

Ways of reducing friction

You can use an elastic band and coin to investigate friction. If the elastic band is pulled back the same distance each time the coin will get the same pushing force each time.

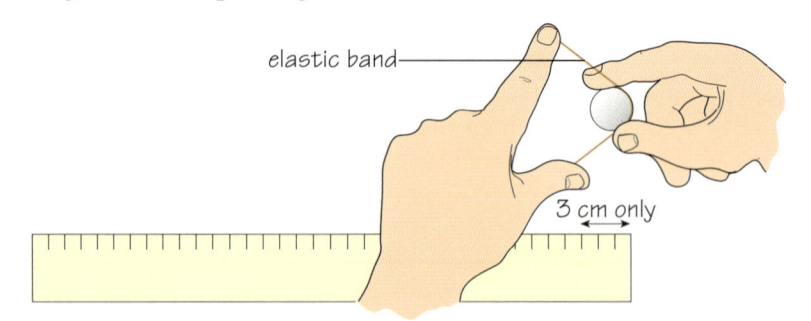

elastic band

3 cm only

Work in a group and discuss how you can make the coin move further along the bench *without* giving it a bigger push.

You will have to think of ways of reducing the force of friction between the coin and the bench.

The pictures on this page will give you some clues.

ON THE MOVE

> 1 Decide
>
> • how you will measure how far the coin goes
> • how you will make the frictional force smaller
> • how you will make your experiments fair
> • how many times you should repeat each experiment.
>
> 2 Everybody in the group should write down their ideas.
> 3 Agree on the best ideas. Write down what you need.
> 4 **Collect** the equipment you need.
>   Do as many experiments as you can.

1 How do you know when friction is acting?
2 What forces are balanced when a car is moving at a constant speed?
3 Why does a bike stop when you don't pedal, even if you do not use the brakes?
4 Write a short report on the coin experiments.
  Include a drawing with labels to **explain** why the coin moved. Make a table of your results. Remember to write down what you did to make the experiments fair.

B Using friction

Friction can be very useful. Look at these examples of how friction is put to good use.

a

b

c

d

e

Choose two of the pictures. Describe what is happening in each. Use the word *friction* every time.

4.7 Watch your speed

A Speedy measures

Lots of people like to travel fast. It is thrilling and journeys take less time. It is also more dangerous. Most vehicles have a speedometer to measure speed. Speed can also be measured if it is known how far an object or vehicle travels in a certain time. Speed is calculated by dividing distance by time.

speed = distance/time

The unit used in science for measuring speed is metres/second (m/s or ms^{-1}) but most speedometers measure it in miles/hour or kilometres/hour.

A force is needed to stop a moving object. In a car the brakes use frictional force to slow it down. The faster a car is moving the longer it takes to stop, and so the stopping distance is greater. This is important in road safety.

Stopping distances for a car travelling at various speeds on a dry level road (information from *The Highway Code*)

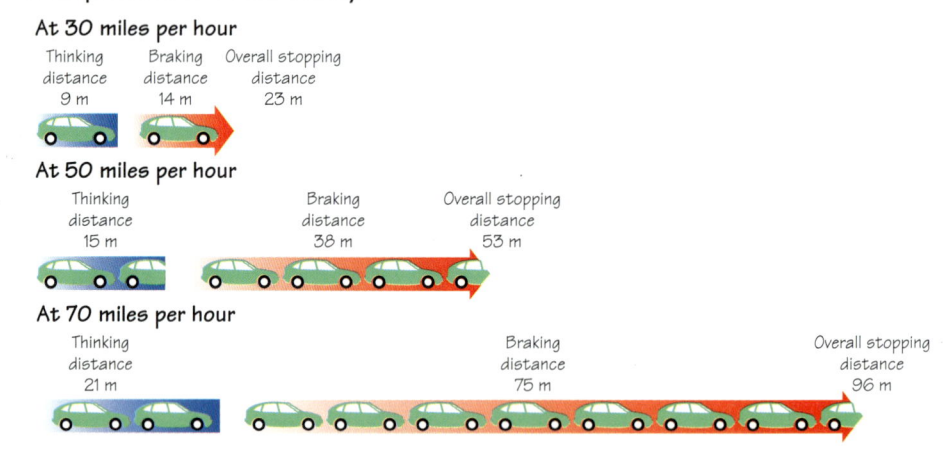

At 30 miles per hour
Thinking distance 9 m
Braking distance 14 m
Overall stopping distance 23 m

At 50 miles per hour
Thinking distance 15 m
Braking distance 38 m
Overall stopping distance 53 m

At 70 miles per hour
Thinking distance 21 m
Braking distance 75 m
Overall stopping distance 96 m

Collect

- Metre stick
- Stop clock
- Chalk
- Toys
- Graph paper

Your group has to measure the speed of some wind-up toys.

1. Choose any two of the available toys.
2. Find out which one is faster. Do this by measuring how far the toy travels in 10 seconds. Calculate the speed in ms^{-1}.
3. Repeat your time trial for each toy at least three times. Calculate the average speed for each toy.
4. Keep your speeds a secret. Have a class race – with each group entering their faster toy. Good luck!

WATCH YOUR SPEED

1 Write a short report about the experiment. You must include
   - a title
   - a description of the measurements you made
   - a sentence explaining why you repeated your measurements
   - calculations to show how you found the speed in metres/second
   - a table showing the average speed of each toy in metres/second.

2 Use the information given by the diagram on page 72 to draw a line graph of stopping distance (on the y axis) against car speed (on the x axis). Remember to put scales on the graph and to label both axes.
Give your graph a title.

3 Why do you think the stopping distance of a car in wet weather is much greater than the stopping distance in dry conditions?

B More speed

1 **Collect** the same apparatus you used in the last experiment, but choose the faster toy only.

2 You have to design a different way of measuring the speed of the toy using this same apparatus.
In the first experiment the variable you controlled was **time**. What variable could you control this time?

3 Carry out the experiment. Find the average speed from three trials.

4 If you have time try to alter the 'road conditions' to make the toy go faster.

Write out a list of instructions that a young friend could follow in order to

- carry out the experiment
- calculate the speed of a wind-up toy.

4.8 Feel the pressure

A Pressure points

You cannot push your thumb into your desk but with the same force you can push a drawing pin into the wood. The same force has different effects. This difference depends on the area on which the force presses. When the area is small, like the point of a drawing pin, the force makes a hole in the wood and we say it exerts a large **pressure**.

If you wade into a deep pond with your wellies on you are aware of the water pressing against your legs and feet from all directions. You feel the water pressure. Air presses against you from all directions too, but we are seldom aware of this air pressure.

Collect

- Squared paper
- Newton balance
- Newspaper
- Metre stick
- Tin can
- Scrap paper
- Experiment cards

Squash bottle

Watch your teacher carry out an experiment that shows the effect of air pressure on a plastic fizzy drink bottle. Take part in the class discussion to explain what happens.

Press on

Work in a group of four pupils. Find out who in your group exerts the greatest pressure on the ground. Guess who you think it might be before you start. The pressure depends on their weight and the area of their feet.

1. Draw round your shoes on cm-squared paper.
2. Count the squares to get the area of contact with the ground (only count part-squares if they are more than half).
3. Measure your weight using the newton balance.
4. Calculate your pressure using

$$\text{pressure} = \frac{\text{weight (force)}}{\text{area}}$$

5. Add your result to the group and class list.

Air pressure

There are two experiments to carry out. Work in pairs.

1. Choose **one** of the experiments. Collect the experiment card and carry out the experiment. You have 10 minutes.

Tin can

Newspaper

2. Describe or show your experiment to your partner. Now **explain** what happens.

FEEL THE PRESSURE

1 Write a short description of how you measured the pressure you exert on the ground. Show how you calculated the pressure. Enter your result in a computer spreadsheet. Program it to find the total pressure exerted by the class and the average pressure exerted by class members.
2 Draw a diagram to show the 'Squash bottle' experiment and the 'Air pressure' experiment you carried out. Label it to **explain** what happens. Don't just label the parts.
3 Watch your teacher demonstrate drinking with a straw. Draw and label a diagram to **explain** how a drinking straw works.

B High pressure problems

Look at the three situations below. Explain how you would solve *two* of the problems. Use your understanding of pressure in the explanation.

How could you get across the quicksand?

How could you cut the tree down more quickly?

How could you get the drink out of the can more quickly?

4.9 *Problem*

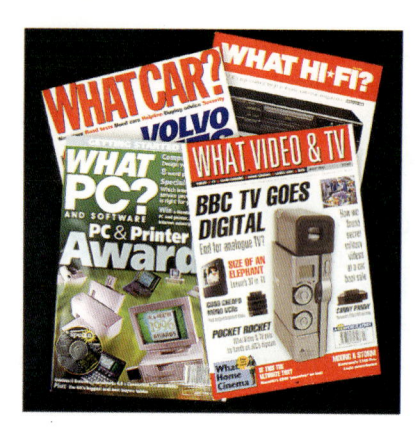

Consumer report

When you buy something you need to be sure that it will work well. There are many magazines giving advice on what to buy; there may be some in the classroom to look at.

These magazines compare different makes of a product. The product is tested in fair experiments to find out how reliable and long-lasting it is. The objects are usually tested using pulling, pushing, tearing and twisting forces. Each test is usually repeated many times so that we can trust the results.

Your task is to test three makes of one product and to prepare a report like the ones in the magazines. (These are often called consumer reports.)

Carry out tests on one of these products

- three makes of **clear sticky tape**
- three makes of **paper-clip**
- three makes of **clothes peg**.

1. Work in a group of about four people. Discuss what you want to test. Decide what type of force you should use in each test. One thing you **must** test is **strength**. **Collect** the information sheet to show how this can be done.
2. Decide what other test(s) you want to carry out. Write down a list of equipment you need.
3. **Collect** the equipment you need. Carry out your tests. Keep an accurate record of what you did. Keep an accurate record of your results.

You are going to present a report to the rest of the class. Each member of the group will speak.

- *First person:* you will say **what** tests your group carried out and explain why you thought that these were the most important tests to do.
- *Second person:* you will describe **how** you carried out each test (your methods), name the types of force acting and explain how you tried to make your experiments fair.
- *Third person:* you will present your **results**. Use tables and graphs to make these results easier to understand.
- *Fourth person:* you will **sum up**. Tell the rest of the class which make of the product they should buy.

Prepare a written summary of what **you** are going to say.

4.10 Talkabout

Good and bad design

Tools, machines and other objects are designed to prevent the forces acting on them from causing damage.

What are the design flaws in the objects below? Prepare a short talk on *good* design. Use a photograph or a real object to illustrate your talk. Think about

- the types of forces that are acting
- how the object has been designed to prevent forces from damaging it
- how the design could be improved.

4.11 Readabout

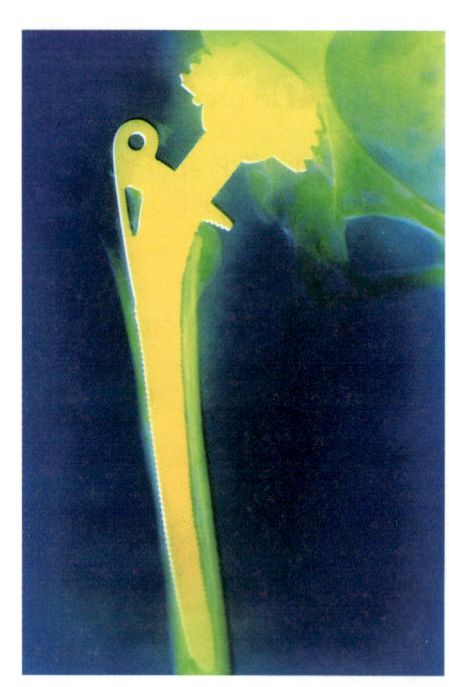

Artificial hip joint

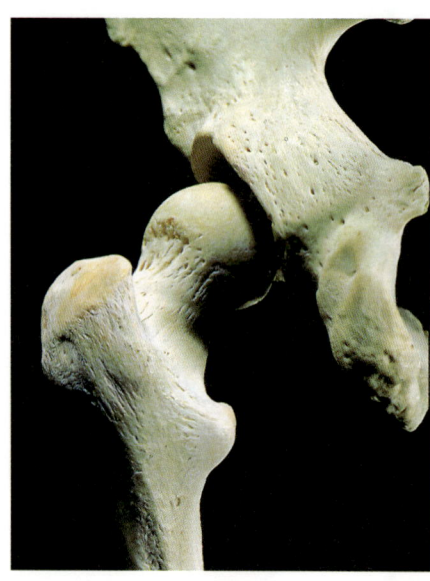

The real thing

New joints

Our skeleton has 187 joints. Forces act on our joints all through life. As we get older they move less smoothly. There is more friction between the bones and we slow down. Diseases like arthritis can make things worse. In some cases the joint becomes so damaged that any movement is painful. If this happens to the hip joint walking becomes very difficult.

A successful artificial hip joint has been designed. Every year many people who are crippled by arthritis have operations to replace their hip joints. They can then walk again.

An artificial joint has to have similar properties to a natural one. It must allow movement in the same directions. It must be lightweight, but very strong in order to withstand the forces that act on it. It must have smooth surfaces to reduce friction. It must not break up or rot in the body. It must not be made of materials that could harm the body.

Plastic and the metal titanium are an ideal combination. Titanium is light and strong, and it does not rot. It has a shiny, smooth surface. In a hip joint the titanium ball fits neatly into a plastic socket. This plastic does not wear or rot. The shape of the parts allows movement in all directions. The same materials are being used in the design of other important joints, such as knees.

1 What types of forces do you think act on the hip joint as you move? (Think about the sort of movement you have at your hip and what happens when you walk.)
2 Use available resources – books, videos or CD-ROMs to find out more about human joints.
 Find

- the names of three different types of joint
- one example of each type
- what movement each type allows
- three ways by which friction is reduced at all joints.

5
Interacting substances

BIG IDEAS IN THIS UNIT

1. Substances interact during a chemical reaction and form new substances. Energy may also be released.
2. Reaction of a substance with oxygen is called oxidation. Burning and rusting are examples of oxidation.
3. During a chemical reaction atoms are rearranged. No atoms are destroyed and no new atoms are created.
4. An acid can be neutralised by a base (such as an alkali). A salt is formed in a neutralisation reaction.
5. A word equation is a shorthand way of describing a chemical reaction.

5.1 Chemical reactions

A Chemical change

Almost all substances, including the ones in you, are made by chemical reactions. During a chemical reaction the atoms in the starting substances interact and join up in new ways. This makes new substances.

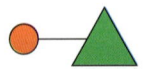

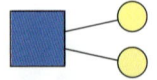

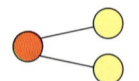

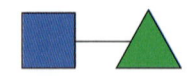

Starting substances (reactants)　makes　New substances (products)

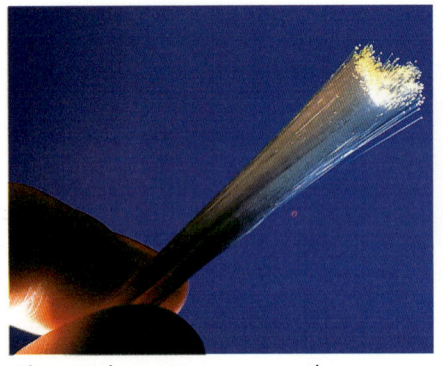

Chemical reactions can make new substances, like fibre-optic glass

Chemical reactions can give us energy

Chemical reactions are usually not easy to reverse

Collect
- Test tube
- Test-tube holder
- Bunsen burner and mat
- Splint
- Chemicals for one experiment
- Safety glasses

Do as many of these reactions as you can. Decide for each one whether
a a new substance is produced
b there is an energy change
c the change would be easy to reverse.

1 Heat the solid in a test tube.

2 Add acid to marble in a test tube.
3 Shake the bottles.
   Leave them to stand.
   Shake again.

4 Add zinc to the blue solution. Stir for a few minutes.
5 Mix two solutions in a test tube.
6 Put calcium in water.
   Test the bubbles of gas produced with a lighted splint.

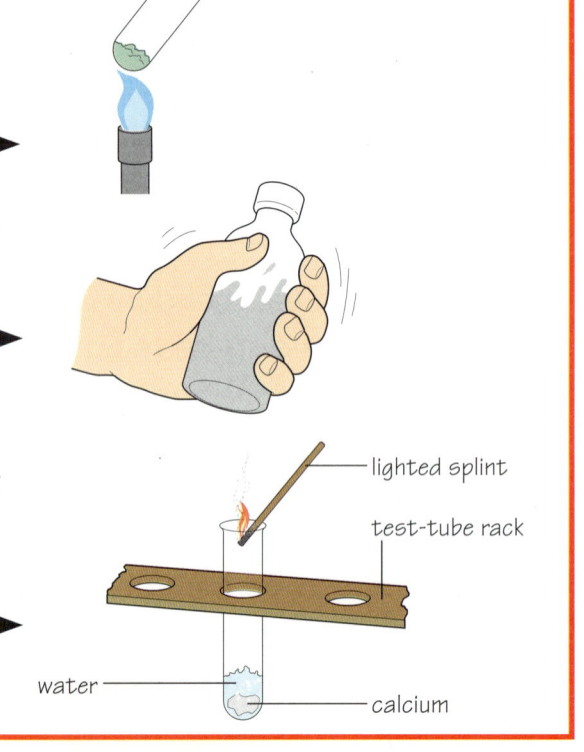

CARE

80

CHEMICAL REACTIONS

1 What happens during a chemical reaction?
2 Write down three examples of chemical reactions that happen in your home.
3 Write a full report about two of your experiments. Explain how you knew that a chemical reaction was happening.

B Spot the reaction

Discuss the following pictures with your partner.
Decide which show chemical reactions and which do not.
(Are any new substances made? Is there an energy change? Can the change be easily reversed?)

Write about your decisions.

a Mixing water and sand

b Mixing cement

c Using glue

d Boiling water

e Frying an egg

f Burning garden rubbish

81

5.2 Chemical accounts

A Oxidation

After a chemical reaction the original atoms are all still in existence somewhere. Often they have interacted and swapped partners. For example, when a candle burns on a birthday cake the wax is interacting with oxygen from the air.

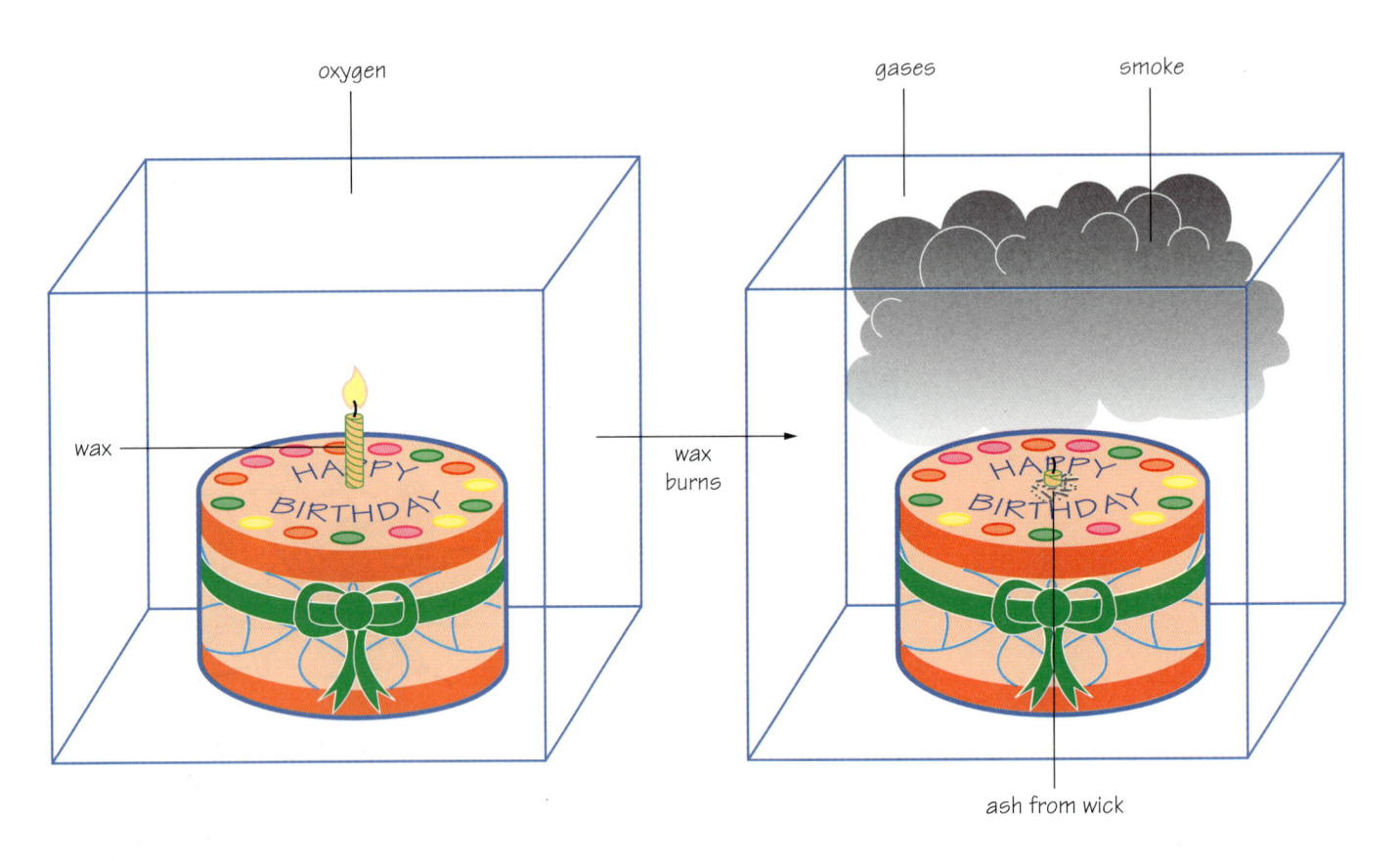

oxygen

gases   smoke

wax

wax burns

ash from wick

The number of atoms in the room before   =   The number of atoms in the room after

The chemical account for this reaction is **balanced**.

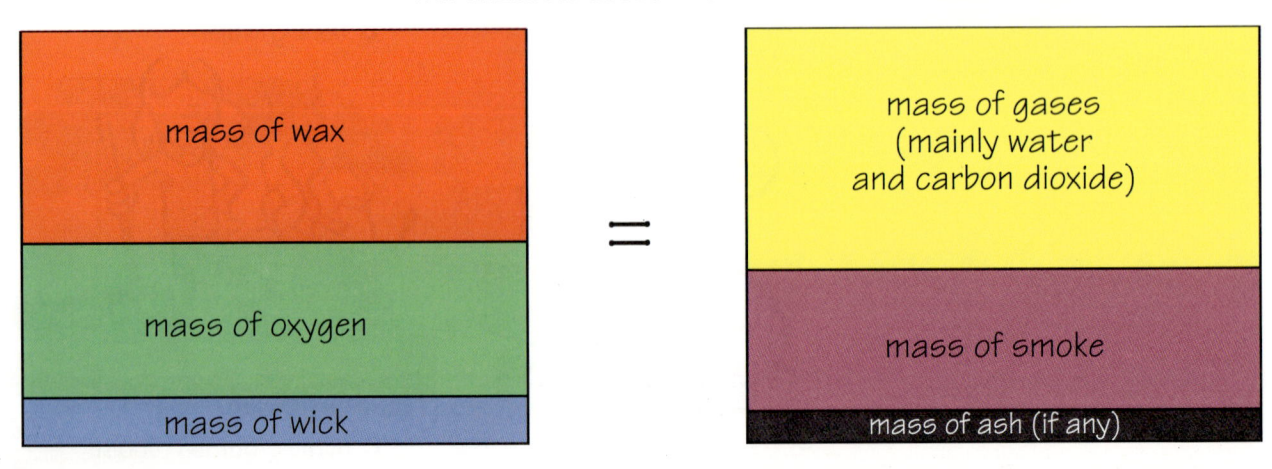

mass of wax

mass of oxygen

mass of wick

=

mass of gases (mainly water and carbon dioxide)

mass of smoke

mass of ash (if any)

CHEMICAL ACCOUNTS

A reaction in which the reactant gains oxygen is called **oxidation**. The photographs all show examples of oxidation.

reactant oxygen in the air **products** smoke, gases **reactant** metal **reactant** oxygen in the air **reactant** oxygen in the air **product** gases breathed out

reactants substances in the plant **products** substances in the ash **product** metal oxide **reactant** substances in food

Burning  Corrosion  Respiration

Collect

- Dry boiling tube of oxygen
- Iron powder
- Copper powder
- Zinc powder
- Burning spoon
- Bunsen burner and heatproof mat
- Safety glasses

1 Your teacher will show you how to fill a dry boiling tube with oxygen.
2 Weigh a spoonful of each metal powder then react each in turn with oxygen gas as shown. Look for any sign of an energy change.

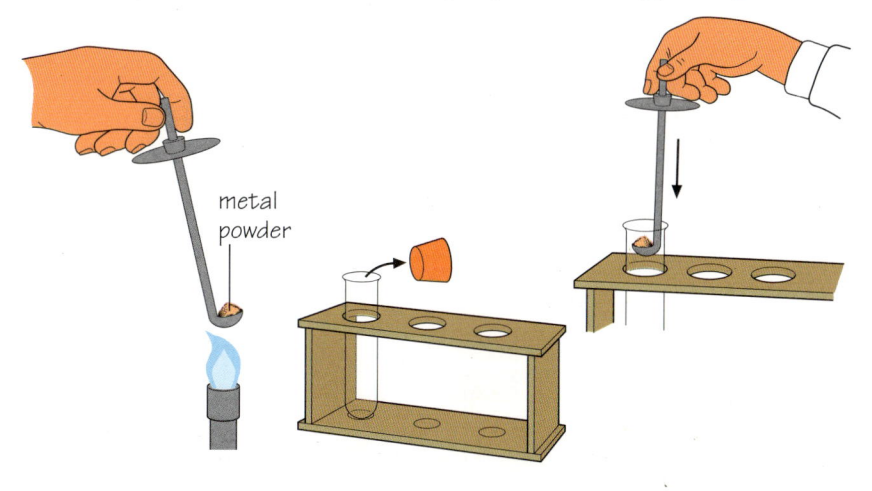

metal powder

1 Heat metal until it glows
2 Remove stopper from tube
3 Put spoon into tube

3 Weigh the metal oxide which has formed. Find some evidence that it is a different substance from the metal that you began with.

CHEMICAL ACCOUNTS

1 Choose one of the metals.
   Draw a labelled diagram of the metal's interaction with oxygen, showing the energy change and the change in appearance.
2 The reaction of zinc and oxygen can be shown as a word equation.

   zinc + oxygen → zinc oxide

   Write similar word equations for your other reactions.
3 Copy the chemical accounts below.
   Add your own results for the weights of the metal and its oxide. Calculate the weight of oxygen added to the metal.

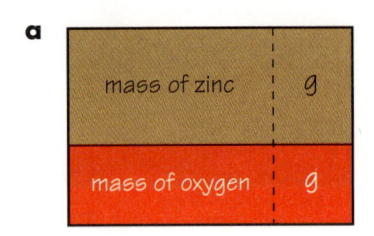

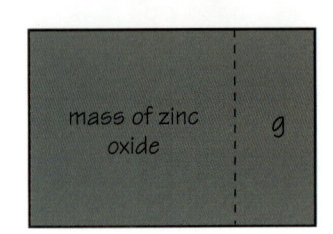

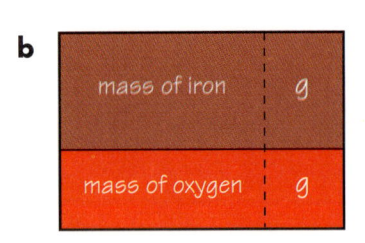

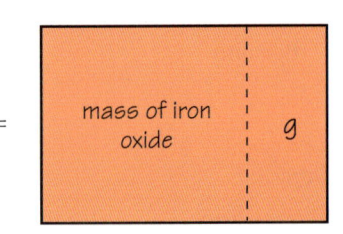

   a

   | mass of zinc | g |
   | mass of oxygen | g |

   =

   | mass of zinc oxide | g |

   b

   | mass of iron | g |
   | mass of oxygen | g |

   =

   | mass of iron oxide | g |

4 Put the metals in order of reactivity, the most reactive first.
5 Draw a diagram of an oxidation reaction that you have witnessed in your own home. Label the reactant(s) and product(s).

B Burning

During any chemical reaction the atoms are rearranged. They do not 'disappear'. New atoms are not 'created'.

Collect

- Evaporating basin
- Wooden splint
- Bunsen burner
- Heatproof mat
- Alcohol
- Dropper
- Safety glasses

CARE
1 Extinguish all flames.
2 Put 3 drops of alcohol into the evaporating basin.
3 Return the bottle of alcohol to a safe place.
4 Burn the alcohol.

84

CHEMICAL ACCOUNTS

1 What is left behind in the basin when the alcohol burns?
2 What has happened to the alcohol molecules?
3 **Explain** your observations using a chemical account. There are some hints in the diagram.

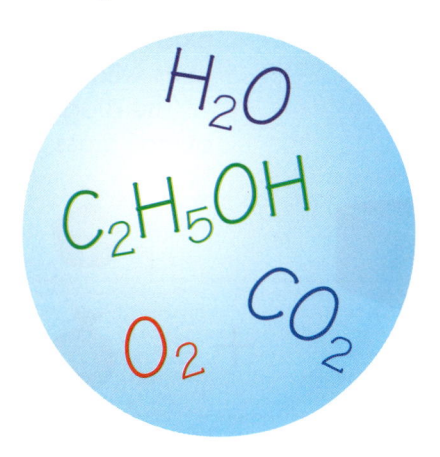

H_2O
C_2H_5OH
O_2
CO_2

4 Use the chemical accounts below to explain what happens when you burn
  a coal
  b natural gas.

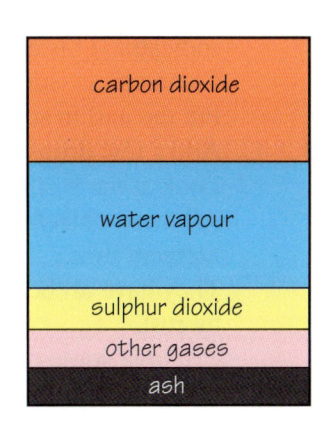

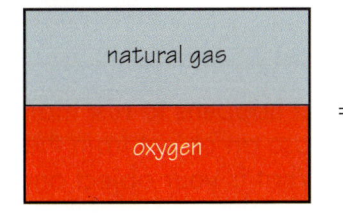

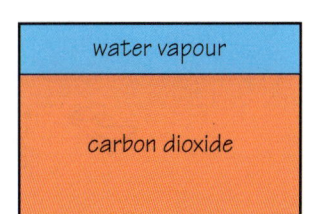

coal + oxygen = carbon dioxide + water vapour + sulphur dioxide + other gases + ash

natural gas + oxygen = water vapour + carbon dioxide

5.3 Slow oxidation

A Rust and bust

Oxygen is very reactive. Even without heating, most metals will interact with oxygen in the air to form oxides. This is called corrosion. For example, rust is an unwanted compound called iron oxide. It forms in moist places when the element iron corrodes and joins with the element oxygen.

The diagram shows that the chemical account is balanced. The overall mass stays the same when the atoms are rearranged.

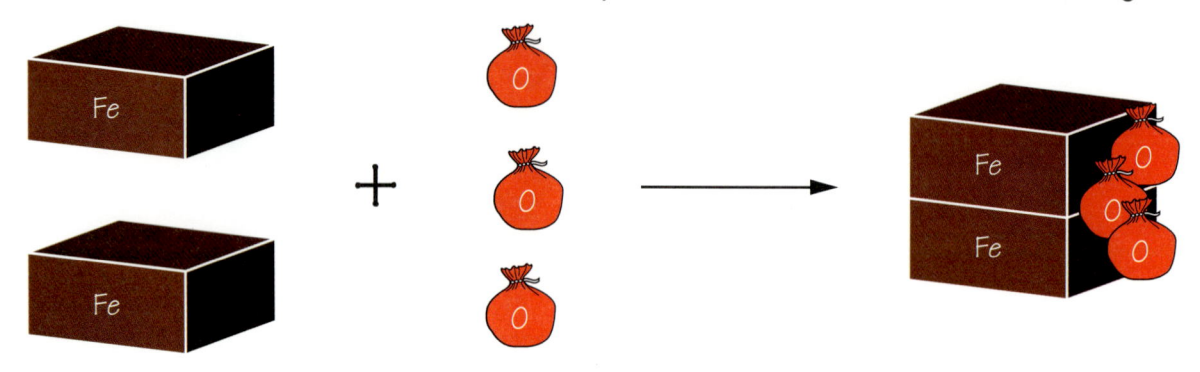

iron + oxygen → iron oxide

Collect
- Rust indicator
- Nail
- Salt water
- Sandpaper
- Test tube and rack

1. Rusting happens quite slowly, but you can show that it is happening by using rust indicator. This changes colour when iron begins to rust.
   Clean any existing rust off a nail by rubbing it with sandpaper.
   Put the nail in some salt water to speed up the rusting.
   Add a few drops of rust indicator and observe.
2. Look at the rusting display.
   All these objects contain the element iron.
   They have all been damaged by rust.
   Crumble some of the rust between your fingers.
   How do you know it is a different substance from iron?

1. What happens to rust indicator when rust is present?
2. Choose an object from the display.
   a What is your object and what is it usually used for?
   b How do you know that your object is rusting? List your observations.
   c Can the rusty object still be used safely? Explain your answer.
3. What happens to the mass of a nail as it rusts?
   Explain your answer by referring to the balanced chemical account shown above.

SLOW OXIDATION

B Stop the rot

When iron and steel (which contains iron) rust, the metal loses its strength and shape. It eventually becomes useless.

Fortunately there are ways (although they are expensive) of slowing down rusting by keeping oxygen away from the metal. If there is no oxygen then there can be no interaction.

Collect
- 4 nails
- Sandpaper
- Salt water
- 4 test tubes
- Test-tube rack
- Rust indicator
- Safety glasses

1. Clean the four nails with sandpaper.
   Use one nail in each of experiments **a**–**c**.
   a Go to the painting area. Dip a nail into paint.
      Push the nail into a polystyrene block to dry.
   b Go to the oiling area. Dip a nail into oil.
   c Go to the plastic-coating area. Heat a nail strongly.
      Push the hot nail into plastic powder.

2. Put each nail in salt water. Add a few drops of rust indicator and observe.

1. Why did you have to clean the nails first?
2. Put your results in a table of three columns.
   The headings should be *Nail covering*, *Colour of indicator*, and *Did the nail rust?*
3. **Explain** how paint, oil and plastic coating help to slow down rusting. Use the word *oxidation* in your answer.
4. Give some examples of objects that are protected from rusting by: **a** paint, **b** oil, **c** plastic coating.
5. **Collect** a cartoon sheet. Discuss the best way to protect each metal object from rusting. (You should talk about appearance, cost and how long the protection must last.) Write down the best method of protection in each case.

5.4 Acids and alkalis

A Detection

Water is a compound that contains hydrogen. Acids are also compounds that contain hydrogen.

Acids can kill living cells and can be dangerous... ...or quite safe.

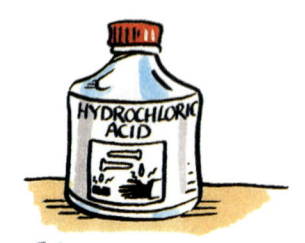

Acids are reactive. They interact with other substances like metal and stone. During this interaction the acid is **neutralised** and the other substance dissolves. Acids and alkalis are detected with indicators.

Acid gases are put into the atmosphere by people. They dissolve in rain water and cause damage

Collect

- Safety glasses
- Acid
- Alkali
- 2 test tubes
- Set of indicators
- Plant material
- 100 cm^3 beaker
- Bunsen burner and heatproof mat
- Tripod stand and gauze mat

1. Put a little acid in a test tube.
2. Put a little alkali in another test tube.
3. Add a drop of **one** of the indicators to each tube.
   Note the colour in a table.
   Your table will have three columns. The first one should be headed *Name of indicator*.

Peaty soil is acid   Sandy and chalky soil is alkaline

4. Wash the tubes. Repeat with another indicator.
5. If you have time make your own indicator by boiling plant material in water for a few minutes. Test your indicator.

ACIDS AND ALKALIS

1 What can an indicator be used for?
2 Write down the names of three different acids and describe a use for each of them. (You may use the books in the classroom to help you.)
3 Look at the photographic evidence on page 88 and in your own locality. Describe how acid gases in the atmosphere can change the environment.

B In the home

We can use a mixture of indicators to detect acids and alkalis. The mixture is called **universal indicator**. Sometimes it comes in the form of a liquid and sometimes on paper, called **pH paper**. The colours of universal indicator are shown below.

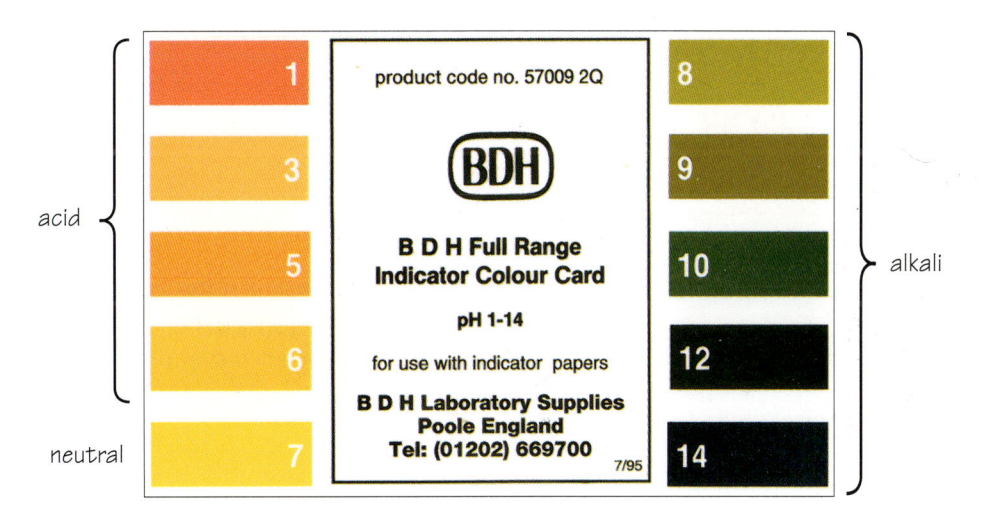

pH measures the acidity of a solution

Collect

- Spotting tile
- Pieces of pH paper
- Coloured pencils or crayons
- Safety glasses

There are a number of household liquids in the room, including tea, coffee, lemonade, bleach, baking powder solution, lime juice, water and vinegar.
Test each one separately for acidity as described below.

1 Put a drop of the liquid on a spotting tile.
2 Add a piece of pH paper.
3 a Write the name of the liquid in your book.
   b Describe the colour that the yellow indicator changes to (use a crayon if you like).
   c Write *acid*, *alkali* or *neutral* beside each liquid's name.

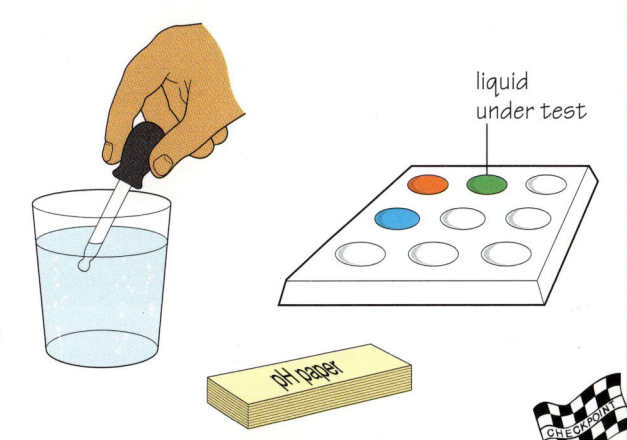

5.5 Neutralisation

A Swop partners

An acid will react with many substances (like those in your teeth for example). As it reacts, it becomes less and less acid. The substance neutralises the acid in an interaction called **neutralisation**.

Metal oxides and alkalis are called **bases** because they are good neutralisers. Some metals are also good neutralisers.

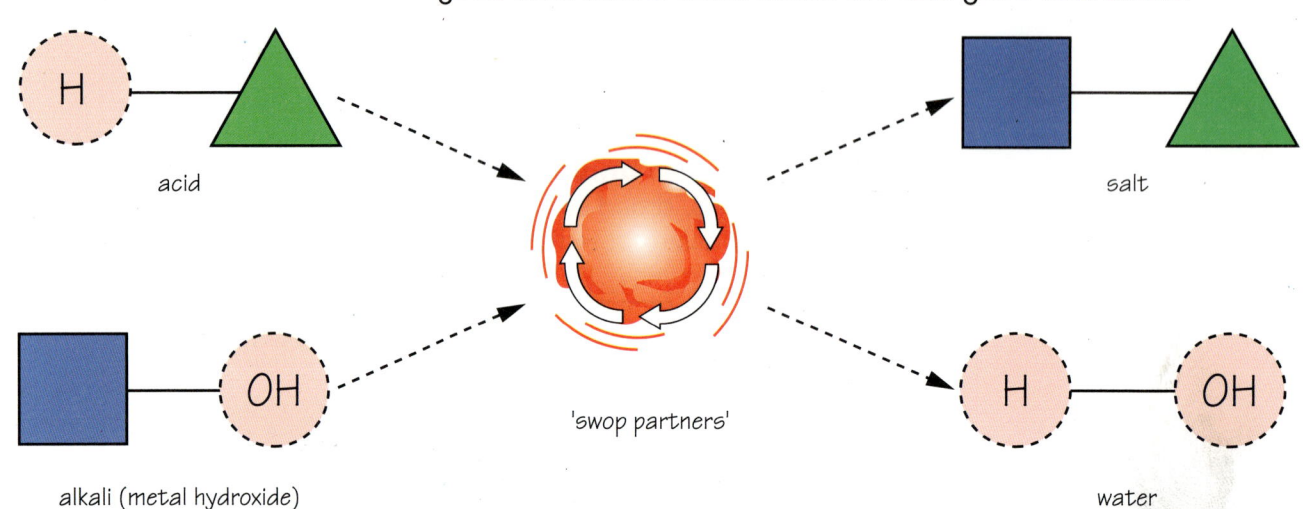

acid

alkali (metal hydroxide)

'swop partners'

salt

water

In a neutralisation reaction the acid and the other substance 'swop partners'. The hydrogen part of the acid ends up in a water molecule or a hydrogen molecule. The other part of the acid ends up in a salt. The word equation for this is

$$acid + alkali \rightarrow salt + water$$

Neutralisation is an important source of different useful salts. (We call sodium chloride 'salt' but it is not the only one!)

silver oxide	ammonium hydroxide	potassium carbonate	?
hydrobromic acid	phosphoric acid	nitric acid	?
Silver bromide is used on film	Ammonium phosphate is used as fertiliser	Potassium nitrate is used to preserve meat	Sodium chloride is used to flavour food

NEUTRALISATION

Collect
- 20 cm³ correct acid
- Correct neutraliser
- Beaker
- Filter funnel
- Filter paper
- Crystallising dish
- Heatproof mat
- Safety glasses

Use the following procedure to make copper sulphate or zinc chloride.

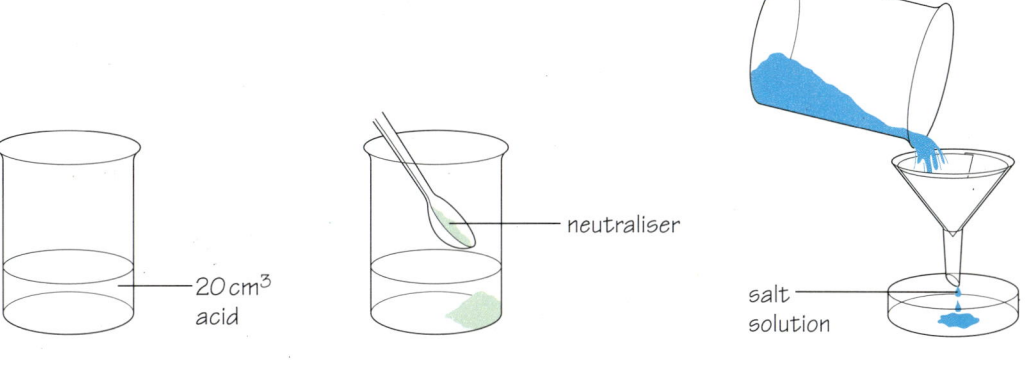

1 Put acid in beaker.
2 Add neutraliser.
3 Filter.
4 Leave to form crystals.

1 Describe your experiment using the words *acid*, *neutraliser*, *salt* and *neutralisation* in your answer.
2 Write a word equation for the reaction of
   a zinc metal and hydrochloric acid
   b sulphuric acid and copper carbonate.
3 **Explain** with the help of a labelled diagram what happened during the interaction between your chosen acid and neutraliser.

B Cancelled

The cartoons show everyday examples of neutralisation. Explain what is happening in each case, identifying any substances that are reacting.

5.6 Word equations

A chemical circle

Limestone is a sedimentary rock, mostly made from the shells of tiny sea creatures that died a very long time ago. Limestone contains the compound called calcium carbonate that can be decomposed by heat.

calcium carbonate → calcium oxide + carbon dioxide

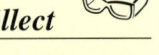

Collect
- Limestone
- Straw
- Dropper
- Filter funnel and paper
- Anything else you need
- Safety glasses

Chemical reaction 1
1 Heat the limestone piece very strongly on a wire gauze for several minutes. If you heat it strongly enough it will glow.

Chemical reaction 2
2 Leave the rock to cool. This rock is called lime.
3 Put it in a glass beaker. Add several drops of water. Listen carefully. Touch the bottom of the beaker.

Chemical reaction 3
4 Add about 20 cm^3 of water to the lime. Filter the solution into a flask. The solution is called limewater.
5 Bubble your breath into the solution through a straw. Watch carefully. The carbon dioxide in your breath is acidic and reacts with the limewater. The new substance that forms is calcium carbonate.

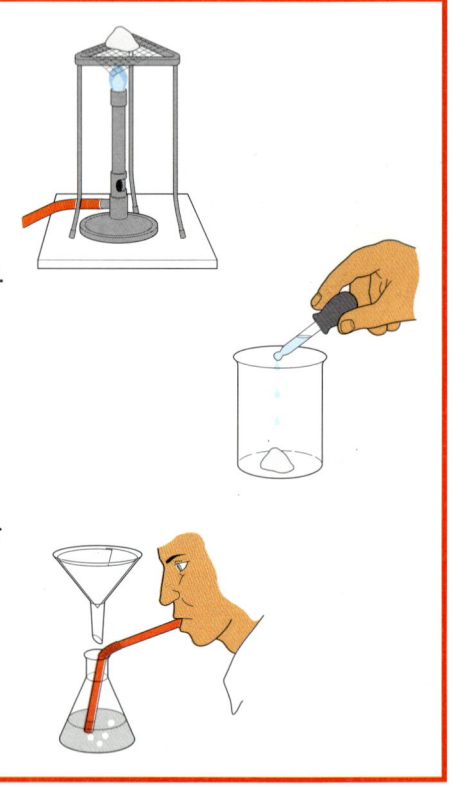

1 For each reaction explain how you knew that a chemical reaction was happening.
2 Copy and complete the diagram by writing in the names of the other reactants.
3 The chemical name of lime is calcium oxide, and that of limewater is calcium hydroxide.
   a Write word equations for reactions 1–3.
   b Identify which reaction is an example of neutralisation and which is an example of thermal decomposition.

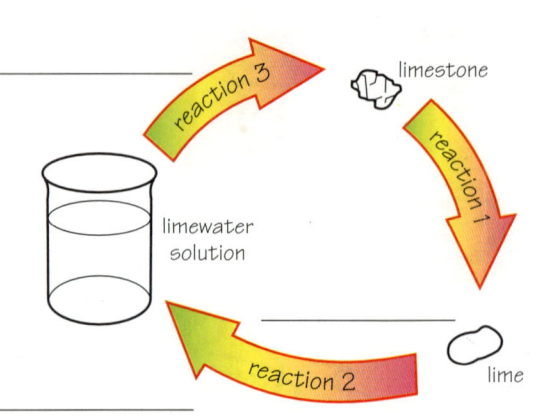

WORD EQUATIONS

B Writing word equations

A word equation is a short way of describing a chemical reaction. For example, when you heat magnesium it eventually bursts into flames and burns brightly to produce white ash. It is oxidised.

What you see
The magnesium reacts with the oxygen gas in the air and burns with a bright light. During the interaction the magnesium and oxygen atoms are rearranged to form magnesium oxide, a white solid ash.

Word equation for oxidation

magnesium + oxygen → magnesium oxide

Collect
- Tongs
- Copper foil
- Copper carbonate powder
- Stoppered boiling tube of hydrogen gas
- Zinc metal
- Hydrochloric acid
- Bunsen burner
- Heatproof mat
- Test tube
- Test-tube rack
- Splints
- Beaker
- Safety glasses

1. Heat the copper foil in a Bunsen burner flame.
2. Heat the copper carbonate powder in a test tube. Try to identify the gas released.
3. Pop some hydrogen gas in a boiling tube.
4. Add the zinc metal to hydrochloric acid. Try to identify the gas released.

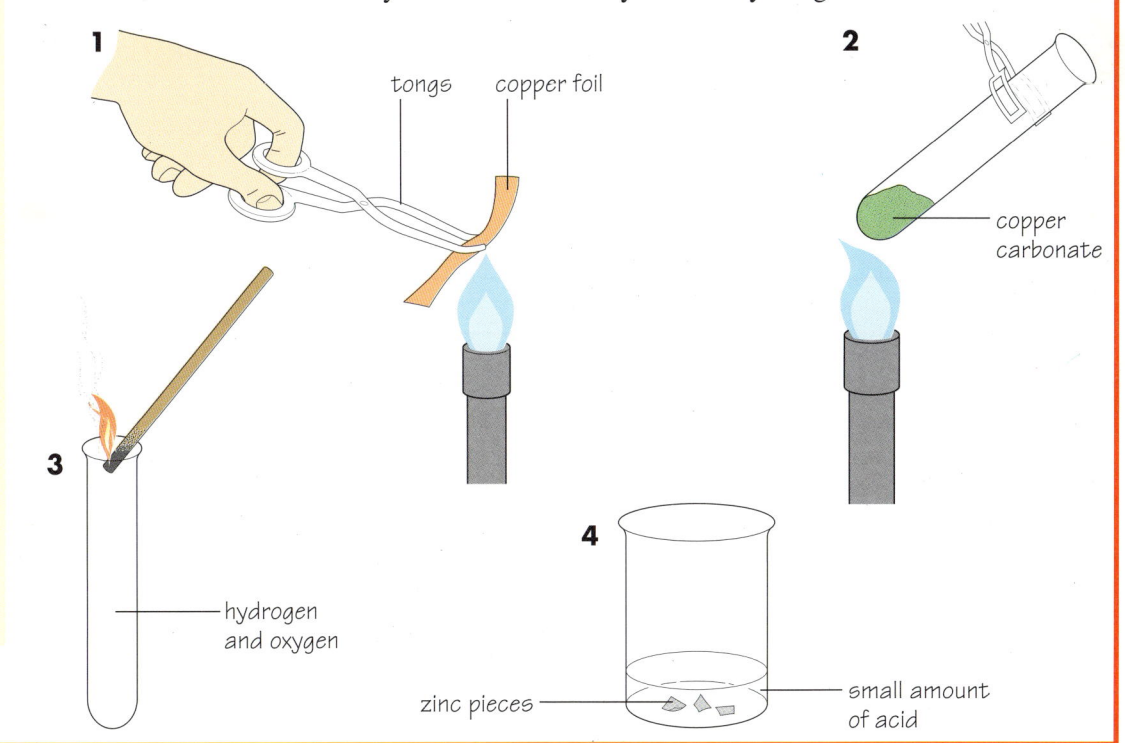

For each reaction that you complete, write a description and a word equation.

5.7 Problem

Kitchen chemistry

Some reactions happen quickly, others slowly.

fast rate ←——————————————————————→ slow rate

| Exploding dynamite | Burning upholstery | Smouldering wood | Clotting blood | Fermenting wine | Rusting car |

You can choose to investigate ways of *either* speeding up a reaction *or* slowing down a reaction.

Collect

- About 15 pieces of macaroni
- Bunsen burner and heatproof mat
- Anything else you need

Investigation 1

Sometimes you may want to speed up the rate of a reaction. For example, in the kitchen the rate of cooking can be speeded up.

Three variables have been changed in these pictures to speed up the cooking process.

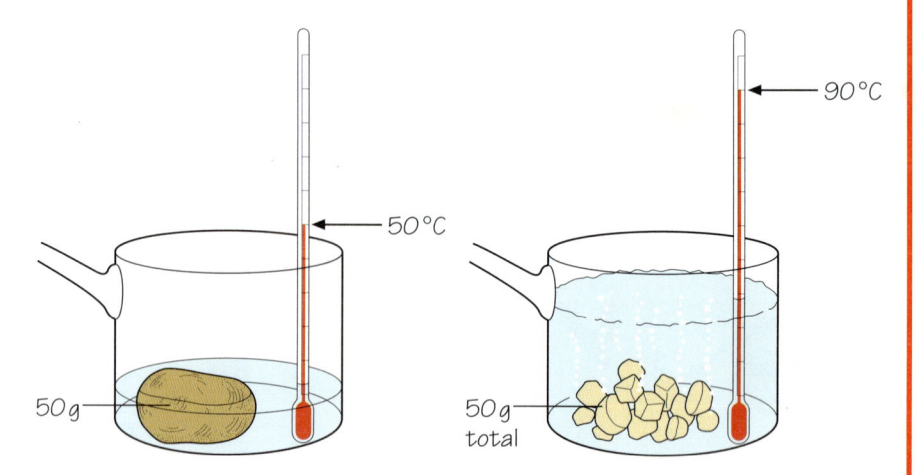

To cook a potato slowly — 50°C, 50g

To cook a potato quickly — 90°C, 50g total

Macaroni can be cooked using a Bunsen burner and some water. Plan your own individual investigation to test the hypothesis that each of the three variables in the pictures above affects the cooking time of macaroni.

You should only change **one** variable at a time. Can you think why?

PROBLEM – KITCHEN CHEMISTRY

Collect

- Avocado (or apple)
- Salt
- Syrup
- Vinegar
- Anything else you need

Investigation 2

Sometimes you may want to slow down the rate of a reaction. For example, various substances are added to food to slow down the rate of spoiling. The substances slow down the cell processes of various microbes. Three examples are shown below.

Fish preserved with salt

Fruit preserved in syrup

Gherkins preserved in vinegar

Plan your own individual investigation to test the hypothesis that each of the three substances can also reduce the rate of oxidation of avocado (or apple). (Oxidation causes these fruits to darken in colour.)

Hints for both investigations

1 You will have to decide
   a which variable to investigate first
   b how to control the other variables for a fair comparison
   c how to measure any change.
2 Write an outline of your plan in your book. Include a diagram.
3 Carry out your investigation.
4 Present your results in a suitable written form (table, chart, graph etc.).
5 Ask your teacher for help if you are not sure what to do.

5.8 Talkabout

Wishing for a new material

Imagine that you are granted *one* wish – to discover one new material with unusual properties. What will it look like? What unusual properties will it have? What could it be used for? What will you do with it?

Clothing materials – Gore-tex is a tough, waterproof material that 'breathes'

Building materials – once upon a time iron was new

Imaginary materials – Aladdin's magic carpet can fly
© Disney

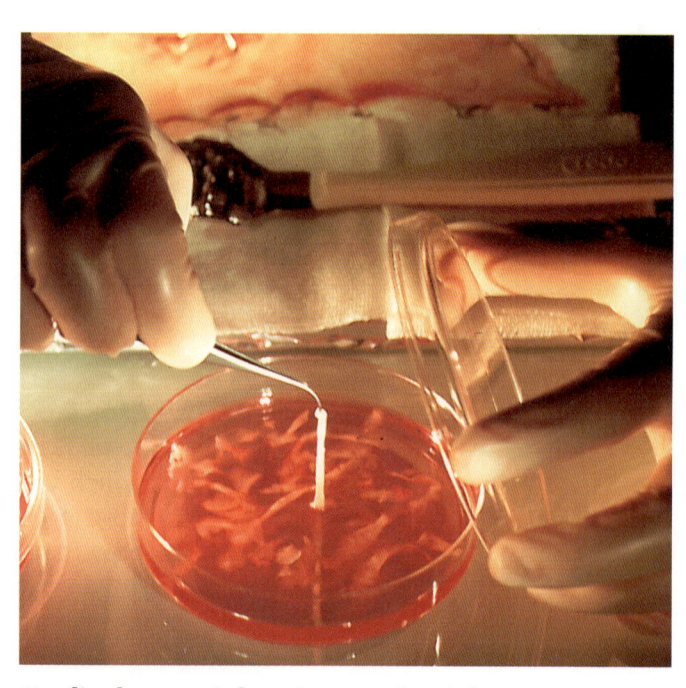

Medical materials – this is artificial skin

5.9 Readabout

Time travellers

Some substances have allowed objects to travel down through time to us. This iron pillar has stood in Delhi for about 1600 years. Iron was smelted in India from about 1000 BC and Hindu metal workers were skilled enough by the 4th century AD to cast this huge iron pillar. It is over seven metres high and about 35 cm in diameter. It weighs over six tonnes and would have been impossible to make in Europe until over a millennium later. What is really amazing is the lack of rust. The pillar has not corroded, probably because the original treatment formed a permanent protective layer of magnetic iron oxide on the surface.

Early Chinese chemists were interested in preserving the human body after death. The 'Lady of Tai' died around 186 BC and yet when first discovered her body was similar to that of a person who has been dead for only a few days. For instance, you could press the flesh and it would spring back into shape. Investigators have discovered that the body had been preserved in various substances to keep it airtight and waterproof. The temperature of the chamber was also kept at 13°C.

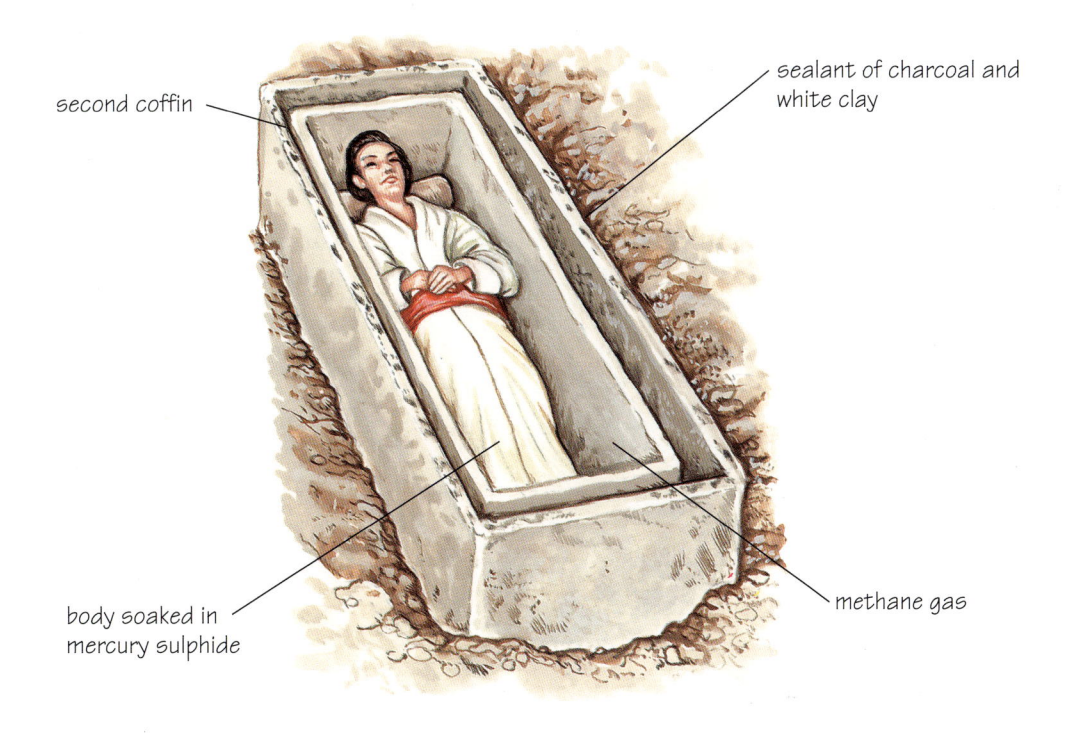

Iron pillar of Delhi

- second coffin
- sealant of charcoal and white clay
- body soaked in mercury sulphide
- methane gas

The Lady of Tai

READABOUT – TIME TRAVELLERS

Sometimes objects have been preserved from damage accidentally. The clothing and personal belongings of this Tyrolean man survived on a mountain for about 5300 years because of the very low temperatures. His body was discovered in 1991. It is thought that his remains were freeze-dried by the dry, cold wind and the ice on the mountain.

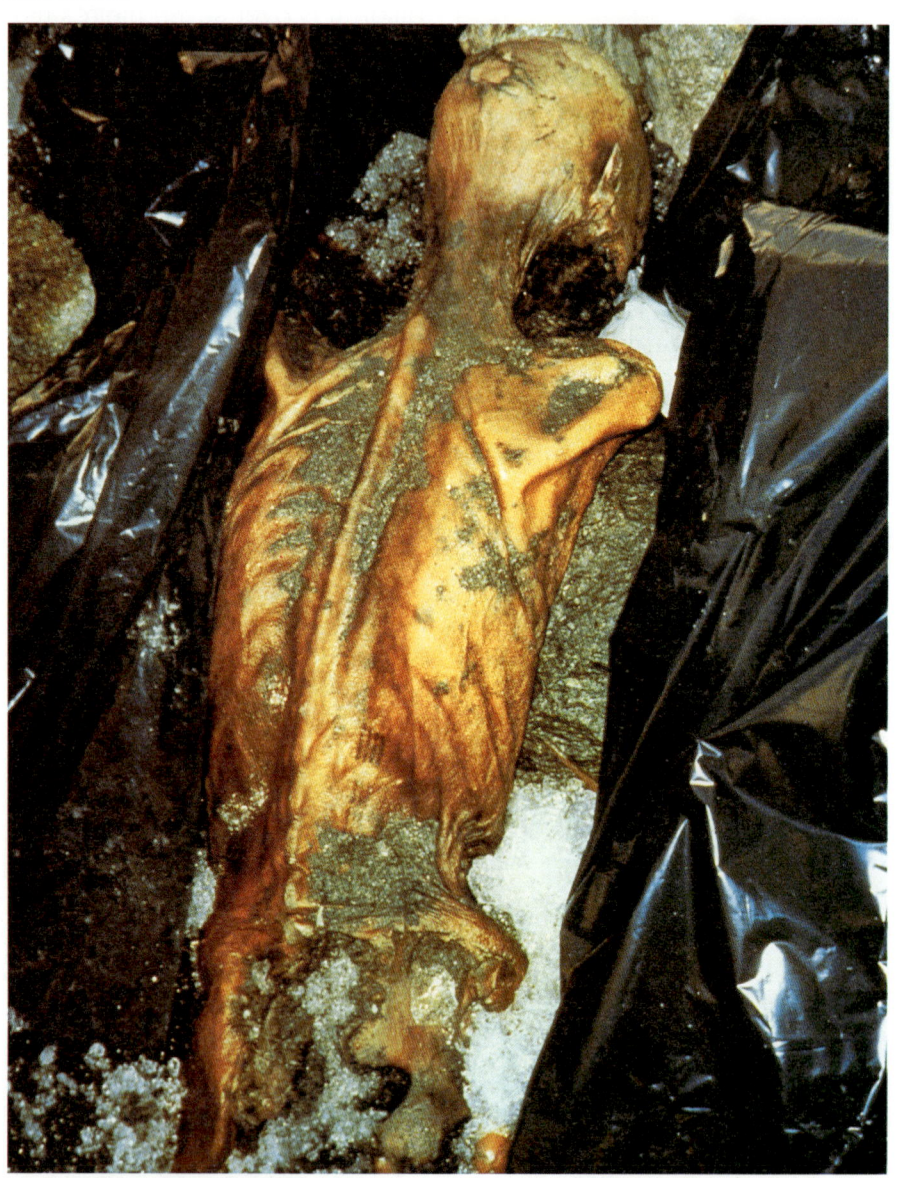

Similaun man

1. Draw a timeline to show the ages of the examples given on pages 97 and 98.
2. Use books in the classroom, books from a library or information from IT sources such as CD-ROMs and the Internet to discover more about time travellers. Key words to look up are Similaun man, bog bodies, Egyptian mummy, Iron Pillar of Delhi, Honan excavation, Taoist immortality.

Use your information to write a story titled *I am a time traveller*.

6
Science in use

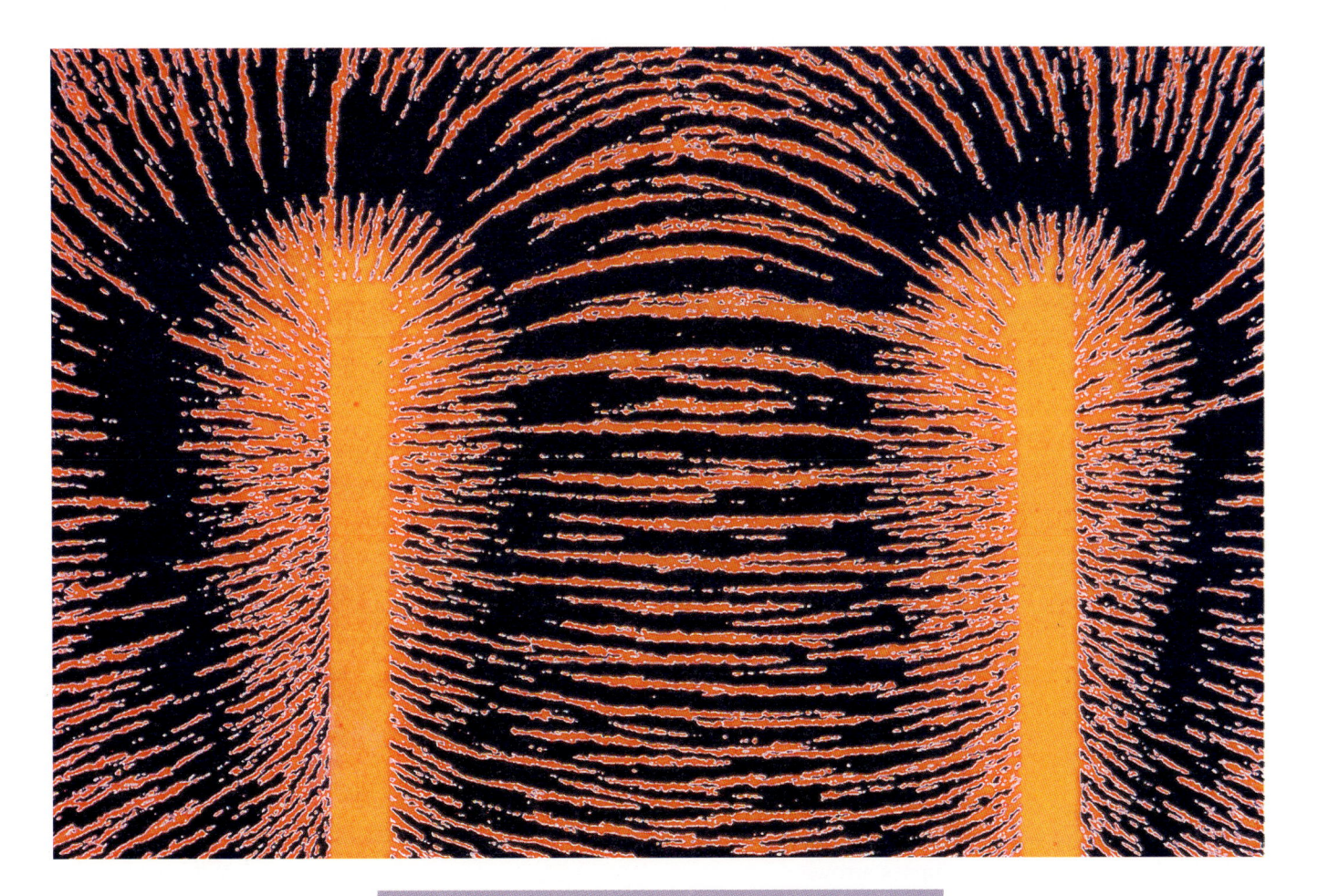

BIG IDEAS IN THIS UNIT

1 Physics is the study of physical processes like magnetism.
2 Magnetic materials produce a magnetic field.
3 Biology is the study of life processes like respiration, and living things like microbes.
4 Respiration can occur in the absence of oxygen.
5 Chemistry is the study of materials like fuels, and their properties like flammability.
6 A fuel is burned in a controlled way to provide heat energy.

6.1 The physics of magnetism

A Magnetic fields

A magnet can exert a force on magnetic materials. Iron and steel are examples of magnetic materials. Objects that are made of iron and steel will be moved by the invisible force field around the magnet.

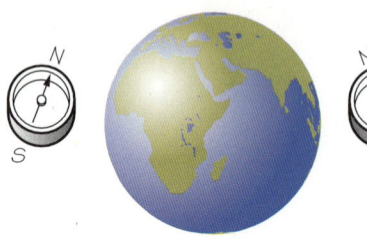

Magnetic footballer – unlike poles attract

Electromagnet – current in a coil

Earth as a magnet

Collect

- Plotting compass
- Bar magnet
- Electromagnet
- Paper

Find the shape of the magnetic field around

- a bar magnet
- an electromagnet
- the Earth (use a reference book).

Bar magnet

1. Put a piece of paper in the magnetic field. Choose a starting point and mark with a dot.
2. Put the tail of the compass over the dot. Make a new dot at the point of the compass arrow.
3. Continue until you can join the dots in a line.
4. Follow other lines of force by starting the dots at different places. Try to find out if the magnetic field also exists above and below the piece of paper.

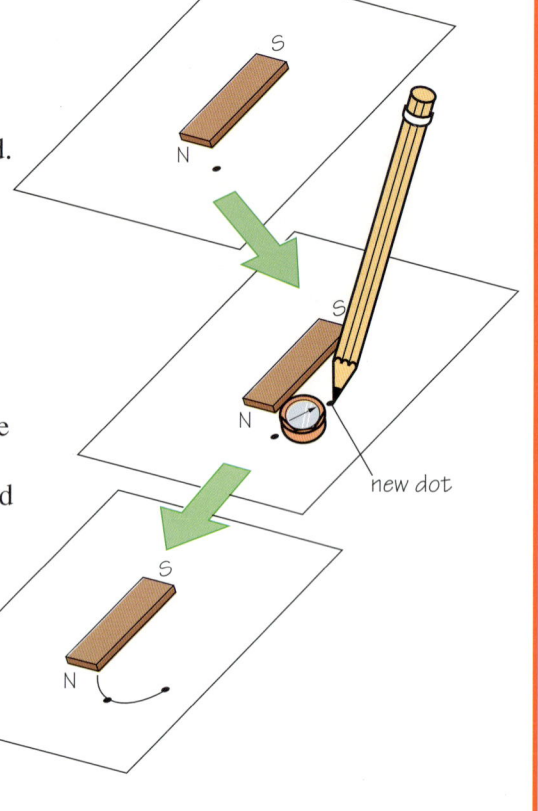

THE PHYSICS OF MAGNETISM

1. What are magnets and magnetic objects made of?
2. Describe how you used a compass to discover the magnetic field around the electromagnet.
3. Stick the drawings of magnetic fields in your book.
4. **Explain** how you found out if the magnetic field was present above the piece of paper.

B Attract and repel

Magnetism is a force that acts at a distance upon magnetic materials. The strength of the magnet does *not* depend on its size.

Predict what will happen to the reading on the balance in each case.

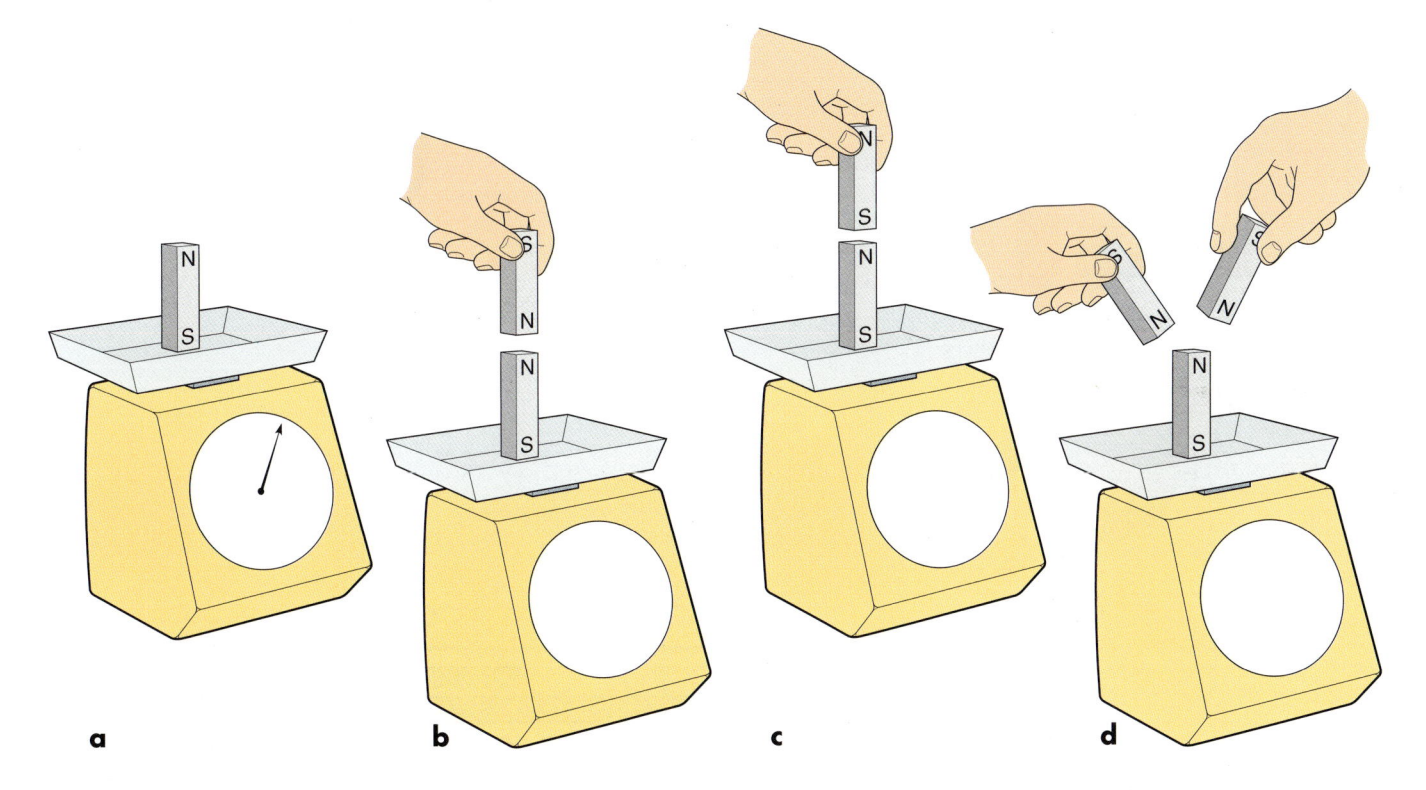

a   b   c   d

Collect

- 3 magnets
- Balance
- 2 iron pins
- Thread

1. With your teacher's help try the experiment above to check your predictions.
   Describe and explain the results of your experiment using words like *attract*, *repel*, *force* and *acts at a distance*.
2. Make your own small magnets by stroking two iron pins with a powerful magnet. Attach these magnets to thread and investigate and report on magnetic attraction and repulsion.

Problem

Electromagnets

Iron is a metal that can be magnetised. It can be made into a strong magnet when an electric current flows in a wire around it. When the current stops so does the magnetism. This type of temporary magnet is called an electromagnet and it has many uses.

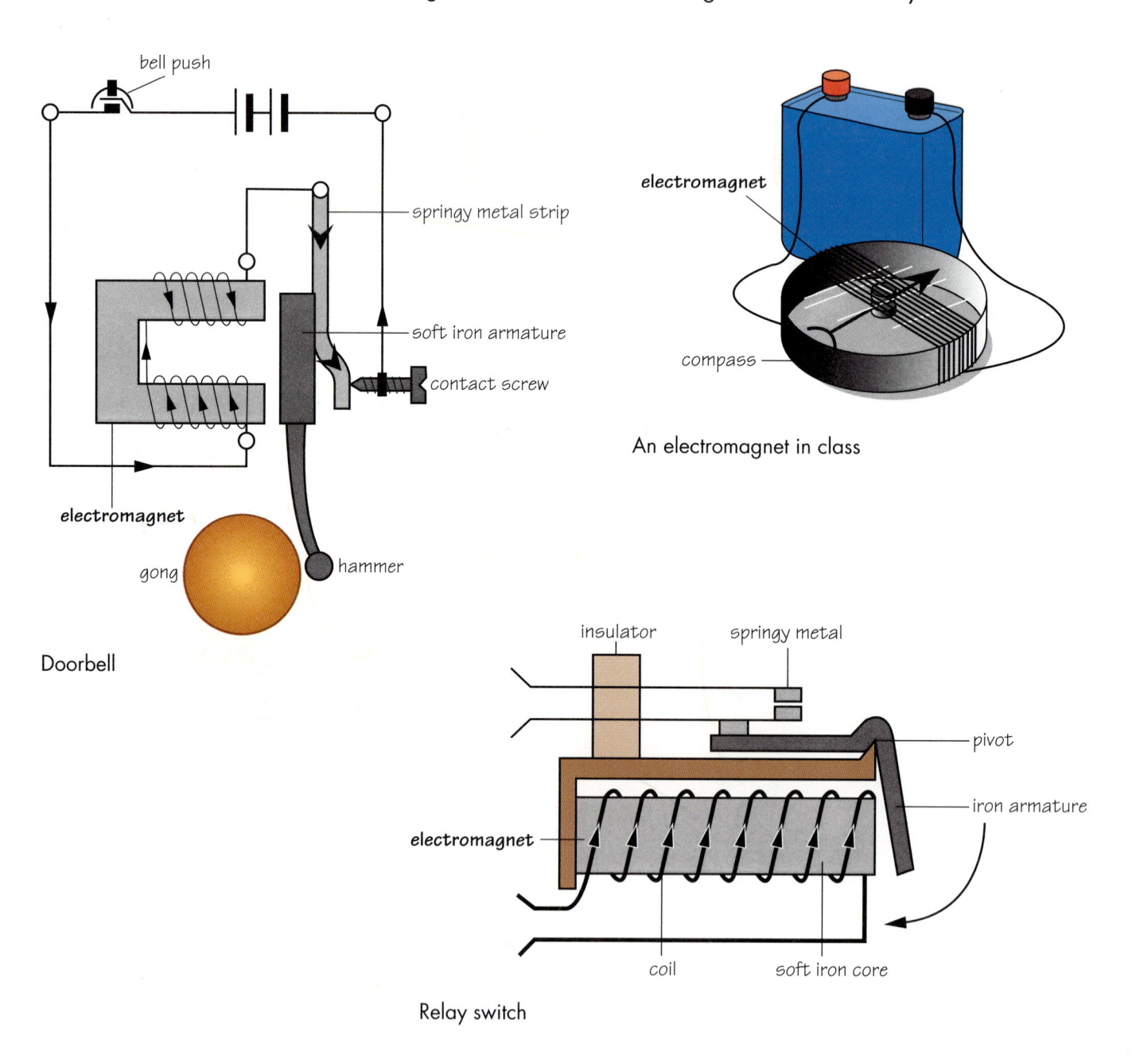

An electromagnet in class

Doorbell

Relay switch

PROBLEM – ELECTROMAGNETS

Many household gadgets contain electromagnets.

Collect
- Steel key
- Muddy water
- Iron nail
- Insulated wire
- Power supply
- Switch

Problem
You have dropped a steel car key down a drain into muddy water. Use the equipment supplied to rescue the key.

Hints
You can increase the strength of an electromagnet by changing the arrangement of the wire.

Write a full report to explain how you solved the problem.

6.2 Microbe biology

A Food from respiration

Living things are useful in technology. For example, very small **microbes** (which are usually just a single cell) can be used to make food, medicines and fuels. The two most useful types of microbes are bacteria and moulds (fungi).

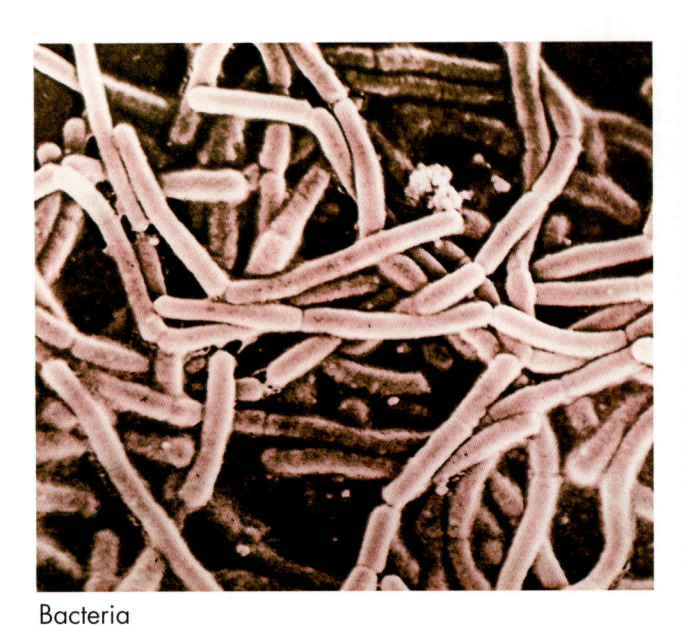

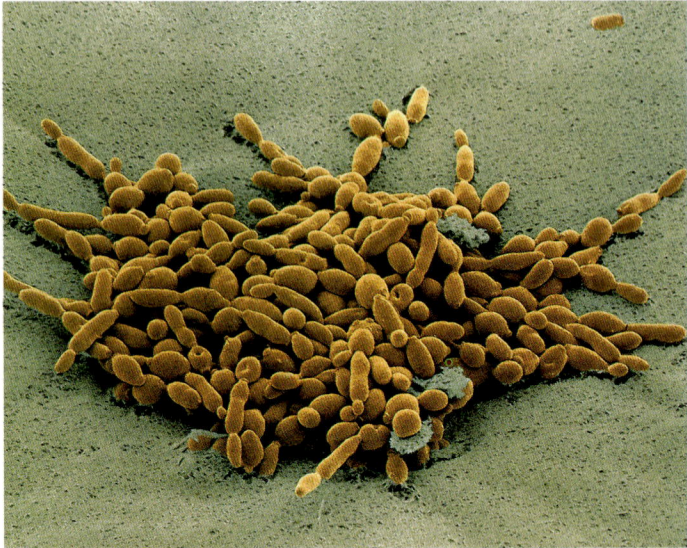

Bacteria

Yeast (single-celled fungus)

Beer has been brewed for 5000 years. Wild yeast, a single-cell fungus found on the surface of some cereal seed, turns the sugars in the seed into alcohol.

Bread making is another ancient industry. Bakers' yeast is added to the dough. It changes the sugar into alcohol and the gas carbon dioxide. The gas makes the dough rise. When the bread is baked the alcohol is boiled away.

Nearly five hundred years ago the Aztecs of South America made **cakes** from microscopic one-celled plants that they collected from shallow lakes.

As people learnt more about microbes, new technology was invented so that they could be used to produce a wide range of products. Today the **food industry** uses many different microbes.

Bacteria turn milk into cheese. Certain moulds give blue cheese its special flavour

Bacteria change beer into malt vinegar

Quorn is a type of protein made from mould. It is used to replace meat in some foods

Bacteria turn milk into yoghurt

104

MICROBE BIOLOGY

When microbes are used to make foods the process often depends on the **respiration** of the microbe.

For example, during respiration **without** oxygen (anaerobic respiration)

- some bacteria use up the sugars in milk and make acid, changing the milk into yoghurt
- some fungi, like yeast, use up the sugars in grape juice and make alcohol, changing the grape juice into wine.
This form of anaerobic respiration is called **fermentation**.

Collect

- Thermos flask
- Small tin of evaporated milk
- Teaspoonful of live yoghurt
- Plate
- Kettle

Making yoghurt

1 Sterilise the flask with boiling water.

2 Add the contents of the tin plus an equal amount of boiling water.

3 Add one spoonful of live yoghurt.

4 Close the flask. Shake it. Leave it for one day.

5 Pour the contents into a dish. Eat!

MICROBE BIOLOGY

Collect
- Bubble trap
- Boiling tube
- 0.5 g of brewers' yeast
- 2 g of glucose
- Limewater

Making alcohol

1 Mix the yeast and the glucose.
2 Dissolve the mixture in warm water in the boiling tube.
3 Half-fill the bubble trap with limewater as shown and stopper the tube.
4 Look at the boiling tube after about 5 minutes. Smell the contents after an hour.

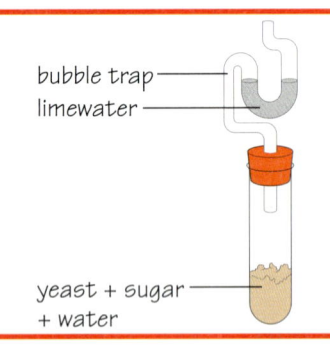

bubble trap
limewater
yeast + sugar + water

1 Draw a flow diagram to show the stages in
   a the yoghurt-making process **and/or**
   b the alcohol-making process.
2 In each case write down the observations that show that a chemical reaction has occurred.
3 Look up the meaning of the word *respiration* given elsewhere in this book. (Use the index to help you.)
   Explain what microbes do during respiration without oxygen.
4 Copy and complete this word equation for fermentation.

$$glucose + yeast \longrightarrow \rule{1cm}{0.4pt} + \rule{1cm}{0.4pt}$$

B Build a fermenter

Microbes are often grown in a fermenter. The diagram below shows a batch fermenter for growing brewers' yeast. In this fermenter, the more bubbles that are produced the faster the yeast is growing. (The bubbles are carbon dioxide gas.)

Collect
- Fermenter
- Bubble trap
- Limewater
- 2 g yeast
- Anything else you need

Choice 1
Add a spatulaful of plant nutrient **or** no plant nutrient
Choice 2
Add boiled airless water **or** warm air-full water **or** cold air-full water
Choice 3
Add a spoonful of glucose **or** a spoonful of sucrose

1 Make the three choices above and set up your fermenter.
2 Leave the fermenter for 10 minutes.
   Count how many bubbles are produced in 2 minutes.
3 Record your three choices and your bubble count.

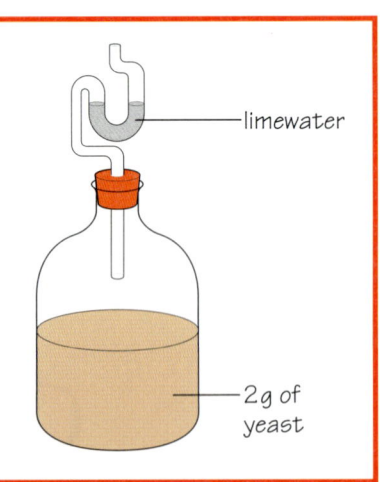

limewater
2 g of yeast

1 Draw and describe your experiment.
2 Compare your results with others in the class. Which three choices help the yeast to grow fastest? Can you explain this by using the idea of respiration?

Problem

Biological washing powder

Enzymes are substances that help a specific chemical reaction to take place. Biological washing powder contains enzymes that have been produced by microbes. These help to remove protein stains like gravy from clothes by encouraging the big protein particles to break up.

Collect
- Tray of apparatus
- Milk agar petri dish
- 3 or 4 types of washing powder

You are going to design an experiment to compare three or four washing powders to see which works best.

Think about how to
- use the agar plate
- use the washing powder
- make the experiment fair.

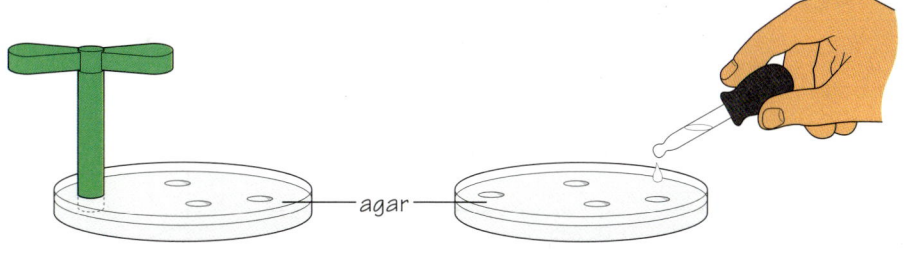

Note: The milk agar in the petri dish is white to start with, but if the protein in the milk is broken down the agar will go clear.

1. Write a short report about your investigation. Include two diagrams: one to show how you designed your experiment and one to show the result.
2. How could you have made the experiment work more quickly?

6.3 Fuel chemistry

A Fuels

When substances interact during a chemical reaction there is often a transfer of energy. Some substances interact quickly with oxygen and burn to transfer a lot of energy. We can use some of this transferred energy to heat our homes and power our machines. The energy story of coal is shown below.

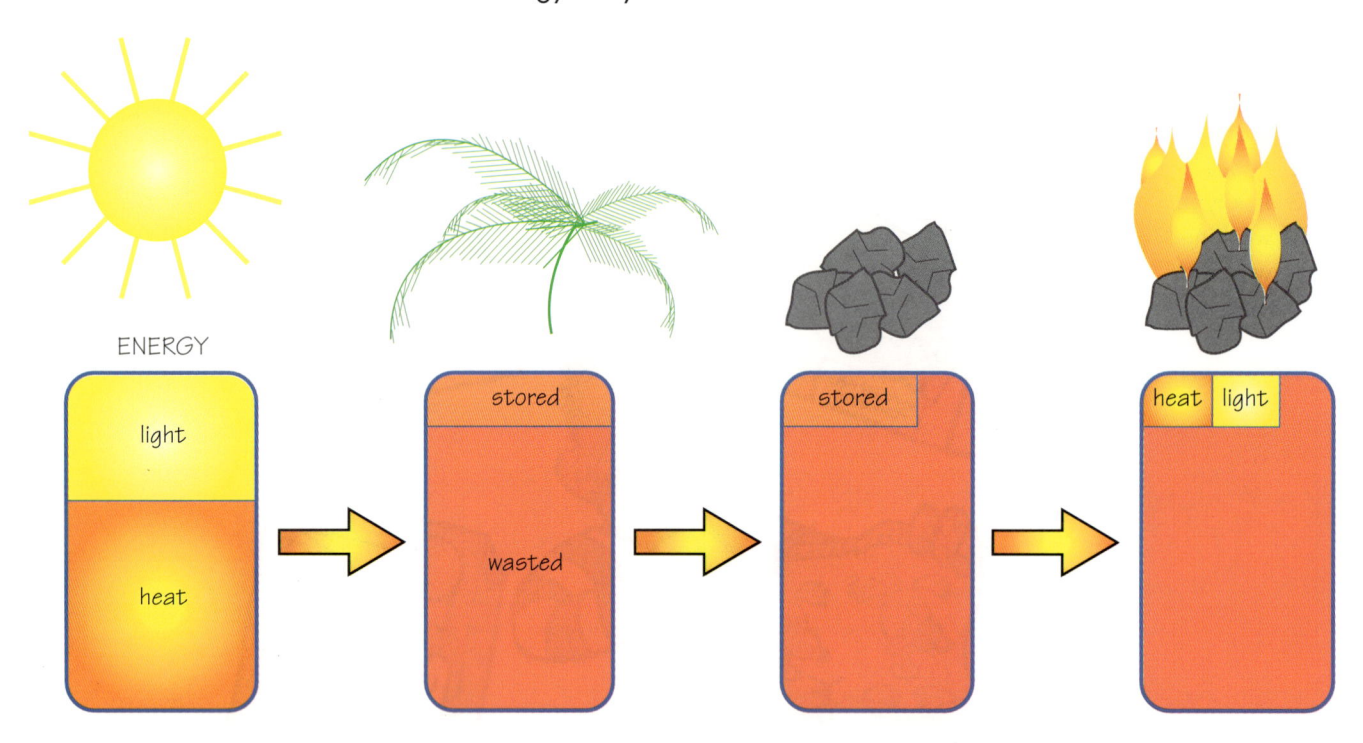

Coal is a good fuel: it is a concentrated source of energy. Other useful common fuels are petrol, kerosene, methane (natural gas) and charcoal. Your teacher may demonstrate how well a fuel like petrol can burn. Think about the following question as you watch: how can we control this reaction and use it as a source of energy?

Collect
- Boiling tube
- Water bath
- Tin
- Tripod
- Splint
- Safety screen
- Safety glasses

1. Collect methane in a boiling tube and then investigate the following properties of methane gas
   - appearance
   - pH
   - how it burns.

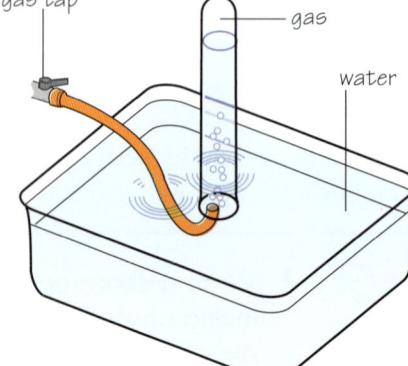

108

FUEL CHEMISTRY

2 This is a picture showing the results of a major gas explosion.

A small group may demonstrate the following experiment.
a Collect a tin with two holes.
b Allow gas to flow into the tin for 10 seconds. Switch the gas tap off.
c Stand the tin on a tripod and light the gas at the top hole with a burning splint.
d Stand back behind the safety screen and **wait**.

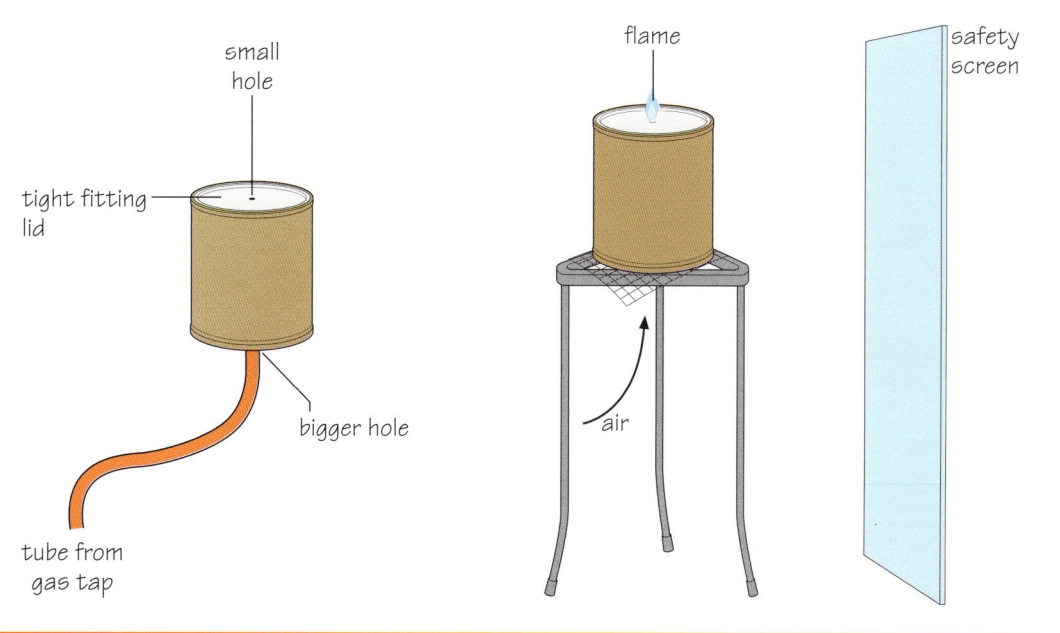

CARE

Labels: small hole, tight fitting lid, bigger hole, tube from gas tap, flame, air, safety screen

1 Draw an energy story and write an energy account for natural gas from its original energy source (the Sun) to its combustion in your school laboratory.
2 What properties does pure methane gas have?
3 Describe and explain the result of burning gas in the tin.

109

FUEL CHEMISTRY

B The fire triangle

A fuel will only burn with flames when it is hot enough and when it can interact with oxygen. Fire needs three things – fuel, oxygen and energy. The fire triangle shows this – if any side of it is removed the fire will go out.

Collect

- Bunsen burner
- Wire gauze
- Wax taper
- Clamp and stand
- Beaker
- Boiling tube and holder
- Safety glasses

1 Light the Bunsen burner by holding a lit taper above the gauze. Observe the burning gas.

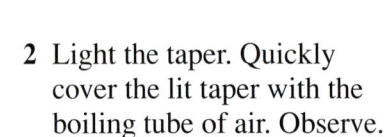

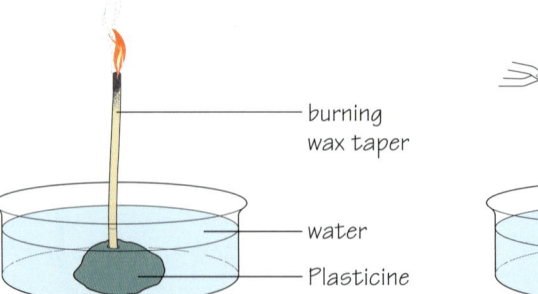

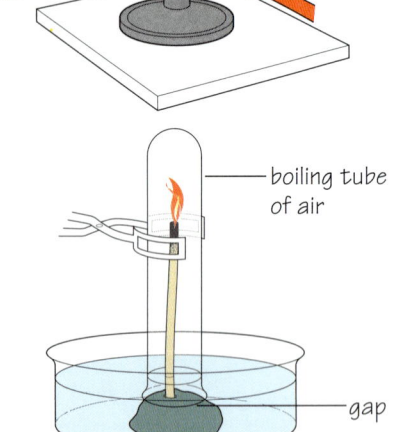

2 Light the taper. Quickly cover the lit taper with the boiling tube of air. Observe.

1 Describe the two experiments. Use the fire triangle to explain the results.
2 Wax is a substance that is separated from crude oil. Draw an energy story and an energy account for wax, from its original energy source (the Sun) to its combustion in your school laboratory.

Problem

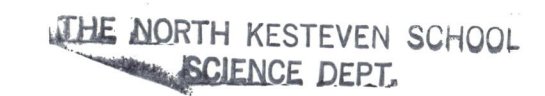

THE NORTH KESTEVEN SCHOOL SCIENCE DEPT.

Fire and smoke

Many materials are **flammable**; they can be set on fire. Once on fire, a material will produce a lot of heat energy. It will also react and **decompose**, which means that the molecules of the material will break up into smaller molecules. For example, some materials burn to produce a lot of smoke which can suffocate a person. Many synthetic materials decompose in a fire to make poisonous gases which can kill in minutes.

Synthetic material	Used in	Produces poisonous
Polyurethane foam	Some furniture	Hydrogen cyanide
Polystyrene	Ceiling tiles/insulation	Carbon monoxide
Rubber	Carpet lining	Sulphur dioxide
PVC	Chair coverings/tiles	Hydrogen chloride

The two photographs show how quickly a smouldering object can produce an inferno of heat, thick smoke and poisonous fumes.

After 30 seconds

After 3 minutes

In house fires it is much more likely that a person will be overcome by smoke and gas than by flames. This is why all firefighters say that you should have a smoke alarm in the house.

> 1 **Collect** and examine a smoke alarm. Read the instruction booklet and find out how this sensor works.
> 2 Design a **safe** experiment to test the alarm.
>   Show your design to your teacher.
>   Test your design, using a fume cupboard if necessary.
> 3 If you have time investigate how sensitive the alarm is. Use a small syringe and smoke from a wax taper.

1 Describe your investigation of the smoke alarm. What is your opinion of the alarm?
2 Apart from an alarm, what other precautions should people take to protect themselves against fire in their homes? (You will find some ideas and information in the leaflets/books in class.)

6.4 Talkabout

Technology

Prepare and deliver a two minute talk on one of the following topics. Describe how technology in that area has changed recently and give information about exciting new developments. Use reference books, magazines, newspapers and electronic media for ideas.

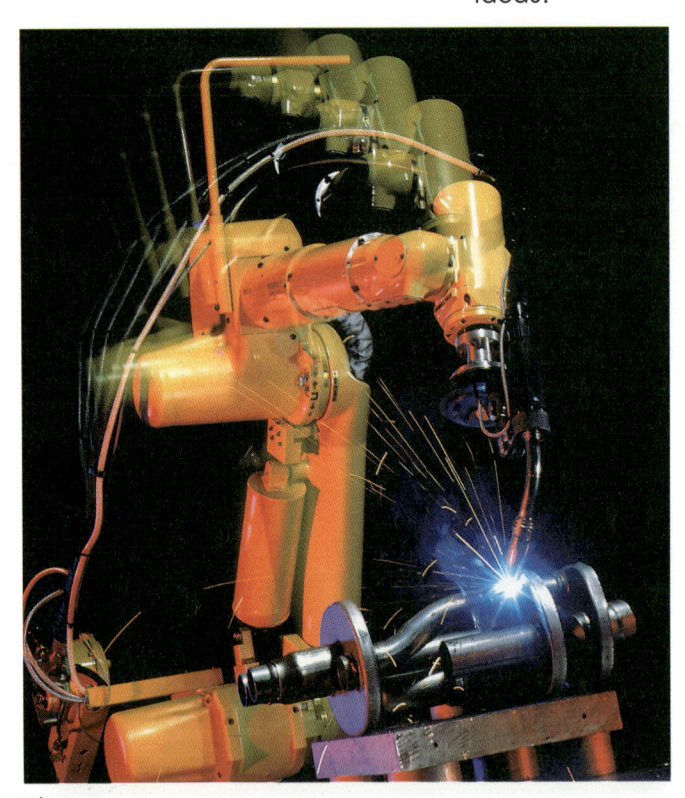

Electronics

Materials

Microbes

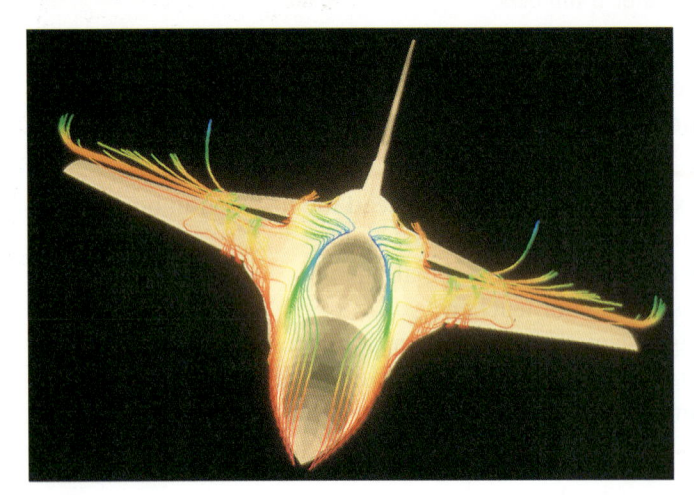

Computers

Telecommunications

Fuels

6.5 Thinkabout

Your future

Scientific knowledge and skills play an important part in many jobs today. Here is a selection.

HILL HEALTH AUTHORITY
NORTH PARK HOSPITAL

Technician
Pharmacy Production

We are looking for a technician with 'A' levels, HNC/HND or similar in a life science subject for this interesting and varied job.

This position offers an opportunity to develop a career in pharmaceutical production. Enthusiasm and commitment are more important than experience as full training will be given. The department is very well equipped and is taking on an expanding role. The successful applicant would become involved in all aspects of the department's work which includes cytotoxic reconstitution, ampoule production and preparation of IV feeding solutions.

North Park Hospital is situated within easy access to central London via the Metropolitan line. The working conditions are excellent and accommodation is available if required.

Materials Scientist
Kettering, Northants

F.O.O.T. is the world's leading research and technology organisation for the footwear industry with 1,100 members in 60 countries. We are a successful and expanding company with an impressive financial record. We have an opportunity for a Materials Scientist to join our Polymer and Environmental Research team which is working on applied science research topics and providing consultancy in polymer-based materials, adhesion and environmental issues.

The role will suit someone with a degree or equivalent qualification in applied physics, materials science or similar discipline. You will have a confident approach in presenting technical work to non-specialists and will be familiar with simple, computer-based data and word processing systems. The post offers excellent career prospects and benefits include a non-contributory pension and life assurance scheme, flexible working hours and subsidised dining facilities.

Game Conservancy Trust Upland Research Unit

Two full-time posts are available to work with our team of red grouse biologists. One will be based in the North Pennines, the other in North Wales. Both posts will involve monitoring of grouse populations, their habitats and their responses to improved management.

Suitable applicants should hold a degree or equivalent qualification and full driving licence. Personal communication skills are important for both posts, a Welsh speaker will be advantageous in Wales. Experience of fieldwork in an upland environment, basic computer skills and use of dogs would be of benefit.

WORKS CO-ORDINATOR

Person aged 18–25 years required from Engineering background to compile mechanical drawings and then co-ordinate projects through to final invoicing. Some purchasing of plant equipment will also be required.

Salary: dependent on age and experience.

SALES TRAINEES

HNC/BSc in a Biological Science? Work experience, preferably in a lab? Positive, outgoing and communicative? Aged 22–30, are you ambitious and highly motivated, do you crave success?

If you fit this profile you could have a successful career in technical sales.

Your rewards will include an enticing salary package with car + bonuses.

SCIENTIFIC PUBLISHING

The highly acclaimed review journal *Opinion Now* in Structural Biology needs an In-House Editor. You should be a graduate/post-graduate with a sound grasp of basic Biochemistry (some knowledge of Structural Biology preferred) and a good command of written English. You should also be good at dealing with people, meticulous, organised and have word processing skills.

> Find and cut out 10 advertisements for jobs likely to need some scientific knowledge and skills. Use these to make up a newspaper page.

1. What kind of job would you like to do in the future?
2. How do you think science will help you in the future, even if you do not use it at work?

6.6 Readabout

Electronic processing

An understanding of science can often lead to ways of solving real problems in the world. For example, scientists have helped to develop the electronic technology that is now used in many devices.

Data handling

Measurement

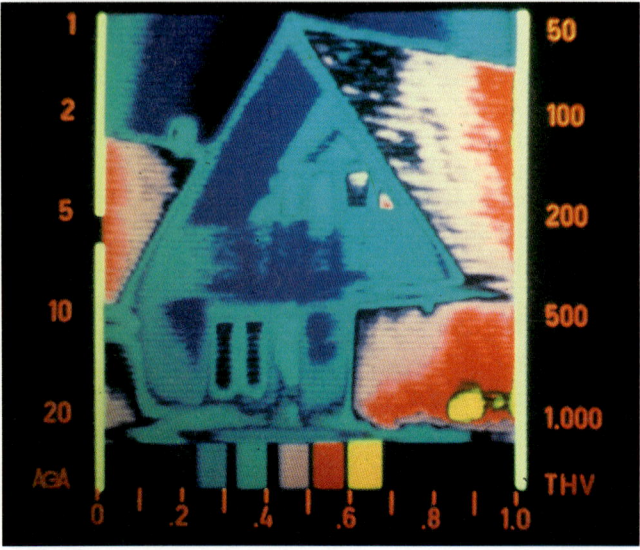

Detection

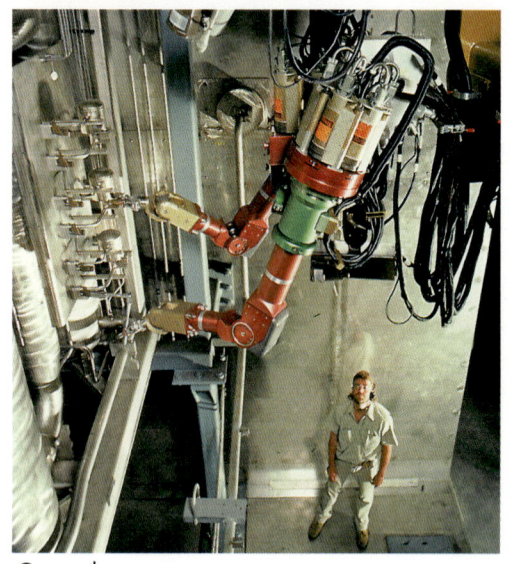

Control

Most electronic circuits are complicated. However, they make use of some basic ideas.

1 A current of electricity is made up of particles called **electrons**.
2 The electrons move (flow) around a circuit.
3 The flow of electrons can be

- stopped
- started
- increased
- decreased.

READABOUT – ELECTRONIC PROCESSING

Electronic circuits are built up from parts called components. Some important components are:

15 **Switch:** stops and starts current

Resistor: alters the current by a fixed amount

Variable resistor: alters the current by a changeable amount

Thermistor: resistance is changed by heat

Photocell or light-dependent resistor (LDR): resistance is
20 changed by light

Diode: allows current to flow in one direction only

Transistor: fast acting, sensitive switch

More complicated circuits can be made by etching (marking) tiny
25 components onto a thin piece of silicon, called a **chip**. Such circuits are complete and yet very small. They are called **integrated circuits**.

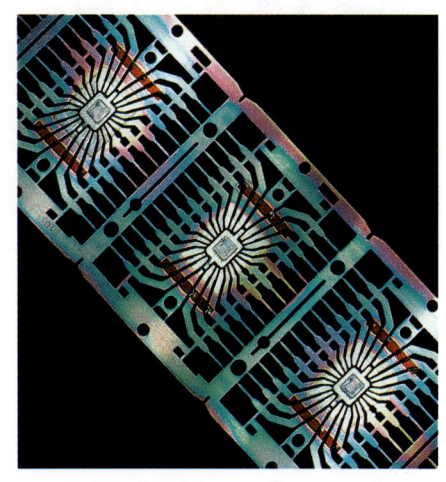

30 Separate microelectronic circuits are used to build up **electronic systems**. A system is a collection of circuits that are designed to work together to do a particular job. The job that the system is to do is called the **output**. What you need to put into it is called the **input**. The electronics in the middle do the **processing**.

input → processing → output

continued ➤

115

READABOUT – ELECTRONIC PROCESSING

continued ▶

1. You can **scan** a passage to find certain facts quickly. Each line of the passage on electronics is numbered. Which line or lines mention
   a silicon
   b output
   c electrons
   d components?

2. A **table** is a good way of presenting some types of information. Each column in a table has a heading. This heading describes the kind of information in the column. Make a table of three columns to present the information in the electronics passage about common electronic components. The table should show the symbol as well as the job that each component does.

3. An electronic system is described in the passage. It has three parts, called input, processing and output.
   In a word processor the input is your typing. The output is what appears on the screen or printer.

   Find a newspaper article or advertisement about an electronic device. Label the input and output and stick the article/advertisement into your book.

4. Your teacher will show you how to use the word processor(s) in the classroom.
   a Type in a summary of the passage about electronics. The summary should have five sentences: one sentence for the main idea in each paragraph.
   b Use the word processor to improve your summary.
   c If possible, print out the final version and stick it into your book.

Extensions

1.1 Extension

Map measurements

Some measurements of the environment have been made already by scientists and used to make maps.

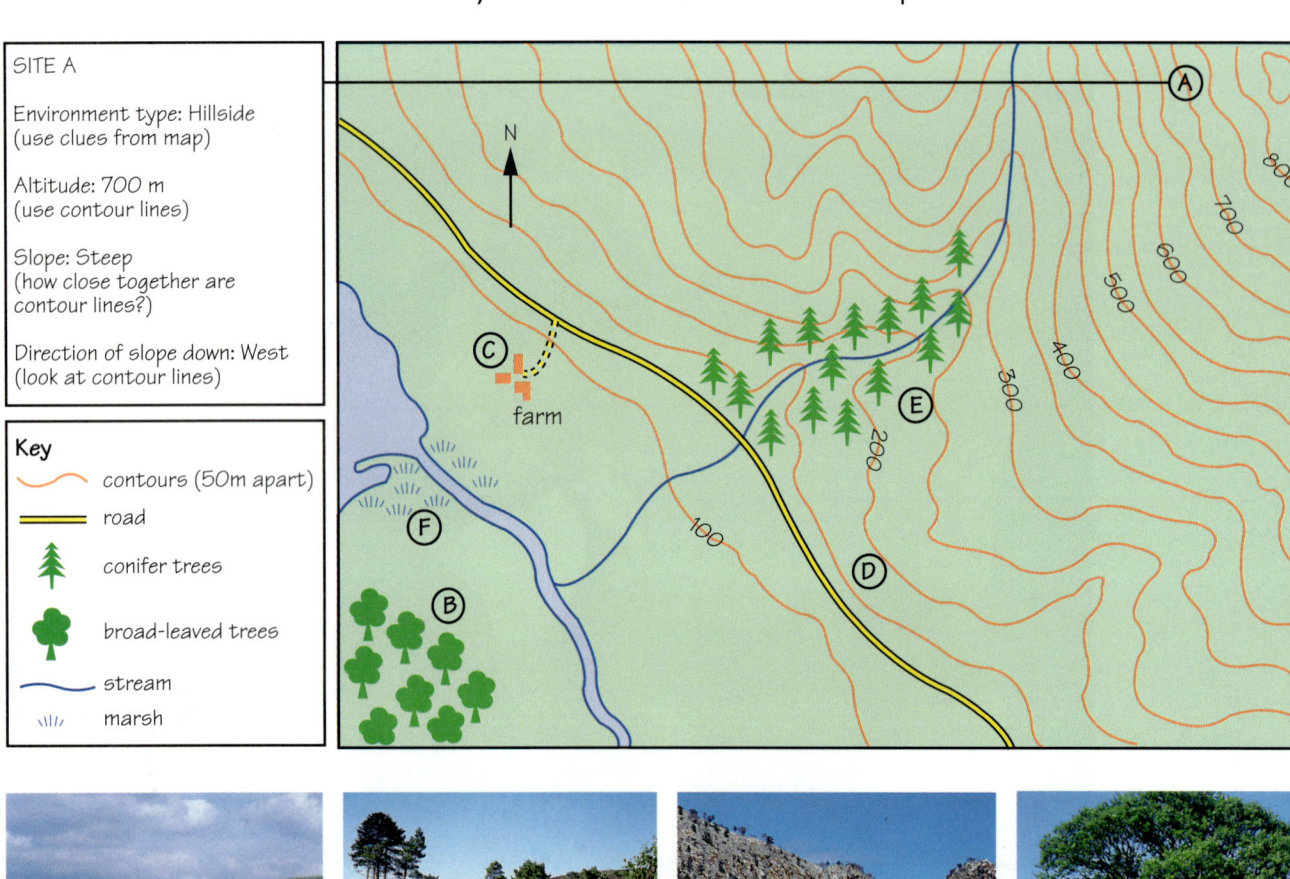

SITE A

Environment type: Hillside
(use clues from map)

Altitude: 700 m
(use contour lines)

Slope: Steep
(how close together are contour lines?)

Direction of slope down: West
(look at contour lines)

Key
- contours (50m apart)
- road
- conifer trees
- broad-leaved trees
- stream
- marsh

1 2 3 4

1. The photographs show environments A, B, C and D on the map. They are not in the correct order. Match each photograph of the environment to the correct site on the map.
2. Describe the environments marked E and F on the map above. Include measurements of altitude and direction of slope. Note the steepness of the slope.
3. If an Ordnance Survey map is available then describe your school's environment in the same way as you did for E and F.

118

1.2 Extension

Key questions

When you find a plant or an animal it is easy to find out which main group they belong to. It is also useful to be able to name them. The names we give living things tell us what **species** they are. Species names are given in latin but luckily common British species also have a common name in English.

This is a flowering plant. The common name for this species is dead white nettle

This is an arthropod. The common name for this species is hoverfly

Keys can be used to help you name an unidentified plant or animal. There are several ways to write a key, but **paired statement** keys are often found in identification books. A paired statement key for some seagulls is shown below. The labels describe how it is designed.

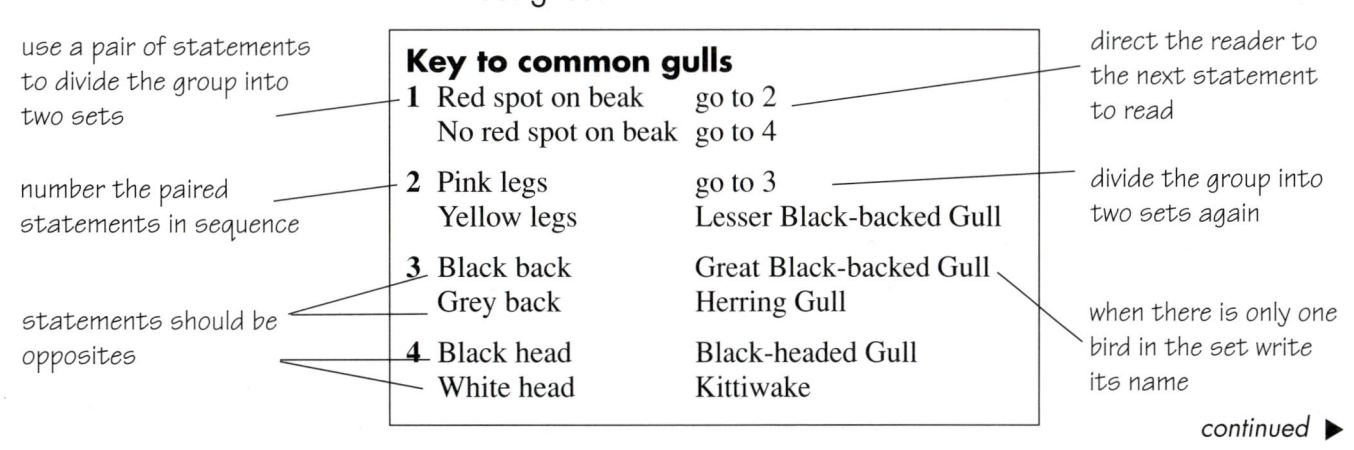

use a pair of statements to divide the group into two sets

number the paired statements in sequence

statements should be opposites

Key to common gulls

1	Red spot on beak	go to 2
	No red spot on beak	go to 4
2	Pink legs	go to 3
	Yellow legs	Lesser Black-backed Gull
3	Black back	Great Black-backed Gull
	Grey back	Herring Gull
4	Black head	Black-headed Gull
	White head	Kittiwake

direct the reader to the next statement to read

divide the group into two sets again

when there is only one bird in the set write its name

continued ▶

1.2 Extension

continued ▶

A

B

1. Name birds A and B using the paired statement key.
2. Make up your own paired statement key to identify the birds drawn below.

Great Tit

Blue Tit

Coal Tit

Crested Tit

Marsh Tit

3. There may be some books of keys in the class. **Collect** one of these and use the key to name some of the plants or animals on display.

120

1.3 Extension

Growth pattern

Living things, or **organisms**, are adapted to their environment. An organism survives best in a particular kind of habitat. On the other hand it may not be able to survive at all in other kinds of habitat.

This is *Pleurococcus*. It is a common green alga. You can find it growing on trees, walls and large rocks. However, it does not grow everywhere

Collect

- Measuring instruments
- Poster paper
- Coloured pencils

Investigate the distribution of *Pleurococcus* in the school's grounds. Look for a pattern. Think about moisture, the direction that it faces, type of surface, height, and other variables. Make any measurements that you can. Suggest a likely explanation for the distribution you observe. Test your ideas by looking for *Pleurococcus* in

- places you expect to find it
- places you do not expect to find it.

Think about any necessary changes to your ideas.

Produce a report on your survey of *Pleurococcus*.
Describe the places where it grows, giving any measurements you took.
Explain why you think *Pleurococcus* can live in these places but not elsewhere.

1.4 Extension

Animal numbers

The animals in an environment are difficult to count. They move around and they often collect in groups. They are not usually spread evenly around the area. They may also be difficult to see, because they are small, timid or camouflaged. The scientist can try to catch a sample of the animals in the environment. The sample is always set free afterwards.

Two useful animal traps are the flowerpot trap and the pitfall trap.

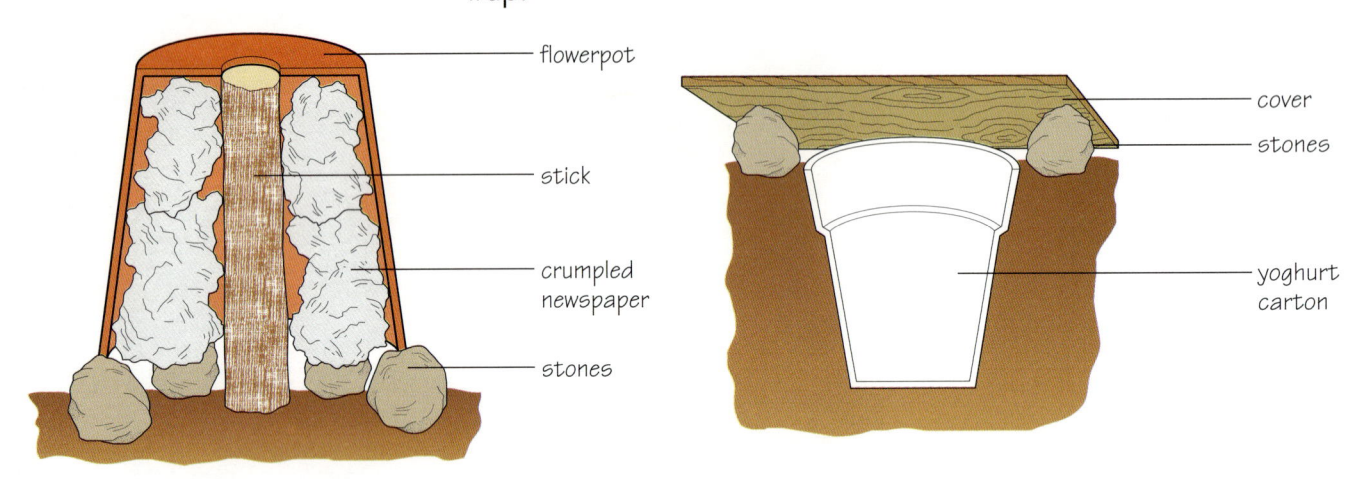

Flowerpot trap — flowerpot, stick, crumpled newspaper, stones

Pitfall trap — cover, stones, yoghurt carton

Collect

- Flowerpot
- Newspaper
- Stick
- Yoghurt carton
- Cover
- Trowel
- Tray
- Hand lens
- Animal identity sheet

1 Build an animal trap in two different places in the school's grounds (or in a nearby park). Hide your traps from bigger animals such as dogs (and people!).
2 Leave the traps for one day. Remember where they are!
3 Empty the traps onto a large tray. Count the animals.
4 Try to identify some of the animals using the identity sheet (or use a key if one is available).

1 Describe the two places where you set your traps.
2 Make a table of results for each place or draw a bar graph. Use the headings *Name of animal* and *Number*.
Give any animal that you cannot identify a letter and draw it underneath the table.
3 Choose one animal from each place. **Explain** why you think it can survive well in that place.
4 Do you think this way of counting animals in an environment is good or poor? Give your reasons.

1.5 Extension

Thermal pollution

You may have seen cooling towers at power stations and steel mills. They cool water (heated up in the industrial process) before it is returned to a river.

Your task is to find out how warm water could pollute a river by changing the amount of oxygen in it.

Collect

- Apparatus shown in the diagram
- 50 cm^3 of cold water
- Bottle of chemical A
- Bottle of red dye
- 10 cm^3 of chemical B
- Stirring rod
- Thermometer
- Safety glasses

1. Set up the apparatus as shown in the diagram. Note the scale reading at the start. Note the temperature of the water sample.
2. Slowly add chemical A from the burette. Gently stir the liquid in the beaker.
3. When the red colour suddenly disappears stop adding chemical A. Note the final burette scale reading. The more of chemical A you add to the liquid in the beaker the more oxygen is present in the water.
4. Repeat the experiment with other water temperatures.

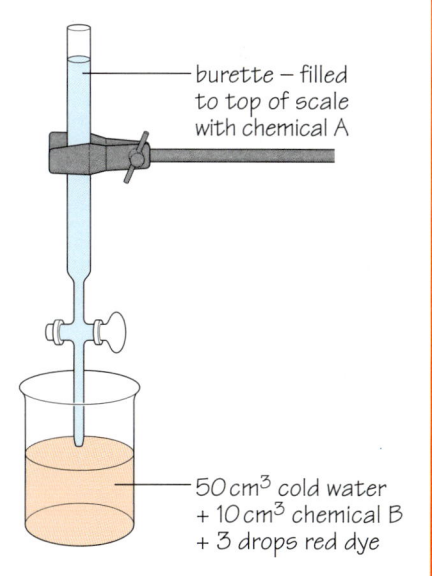

burette – filled to top of scale with chemical A

50 cm^3 cold water + 10 cm^3 chemical B + 3 drops red dye

1. Draw a line graph of volume of chemical A (amount of oxygen) against water temperature.
2. What happens to the amount of oxygen in water as its temperature rises?
3. Some insect larvae, such as mayfly larvae, use gills to breathe in water. Why will their gills beat faster in warm water than in cold water?
4. Why do you think this experiment is called *Thermal pollution*?

2.1 Extension

Use the clues

It is sometimes difficult to explain an observation. You have to think about it for a long time. You may work out different ways of explaining it. Eventually you will decide on a **likely** explanation.

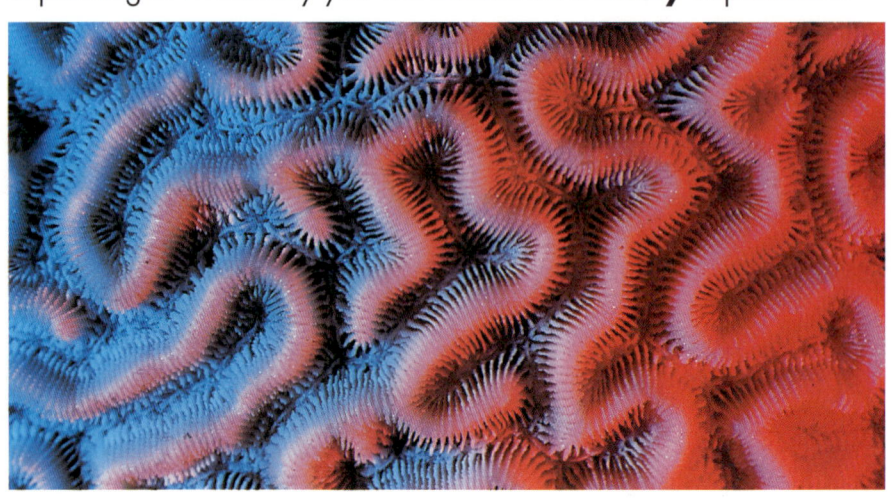

What caption would you give this photograph? What is it showing?

Collect

- Clue cards for the game of Inspector Cluedo

In the following game you have to study a set of cards. Each card contains a clue about the terrible murder that happened in the farmyard.

Your group has to work out a likely explanation which answers **all** the following questions.

- Who was murdered?
- What weapon was used?
- Where did the murder take place?
- When did it take place?
- What was the motive for the murder?
- Who did the terrible deed?

Hint: Look for a pattern in the clues.
You must **not** let another group hear any of your ideas.

1. Write down a likely explanation of the murder at the farmyard which answers all the questions.
   Give reasons if you can for each of your answers.
2. Look at the **right answer** card in the envelope.
   What is the right answer?
   Why is this answer surprising?
3. You can give a good explanation if you find a pattern in the clues.
   a What does the word *pattern* mean here?
   b Why is it useful to find a pattern in the clues?

2.2 Extension

Coloured compounds

It is not easy to find a pattern in things that are new to you. If there are a lot of objects or observations then the pattern is even more difficult to find. It is then useful to look at two or three bits of information first.

For example, some coloured compounds are shown below. The name of each compound is made up of two words; so *sodium chloride* is made up of *sodium* and *chloride*.

1 Sodium chloride
2 Copper chloride 
3 Sodium chromate 
4 Potassium permanganate 
5 Copper sulphate 
6 Potassium chloride 
7 Ammonium dichromate 
8 Nickel sulphate 
9 Potassium chromate 
10 Nickel chloride 
11 Ammonium sulphate 
12 Cobalt sulphate 

1 What colour do you think **sodium** is linked with? (Look at compound 1.)
2 What colour do you think **chloride** is linked with? (Look at compounds 1 and 6.)
3 What colour do you think **copper** is linked with? (Look at compounds 2 and 5.)
4 Find other patterns in the colours of these compounds and report the patterns in a table.

Word in the name	Colour

Work out what colour the following compounds will be. Write your ideas down. Then go and check your answers by looking at the compounds.

- Cobalt chloride
- Ammonium chloride
- Sodium dichromate

2.3 Extension

Asking questions

In many situations it is easier to work out the likely explanation if you know how to ask good questions. Some problems can be solved by asking questions that seek **important** details.

Look at the drawings below. Each one shows a very unusual situation. Your teacher knows what has happened in each case. The class have to try to work out what has happened. Put your hand up to ask questions. Your teacher can only answer **yes** or **no**. The class that asks good questions will solve the puzzles.

1 How was the elephant hurt?

2 How did I change the light bulb?

3 This woman is about to jump through an open window on the seventh floor of a high rise building. She will be completely unhurt – why?

4 Nobody put these on the lawn – how did they get there?

5 Cleopatra is asleep in bed. Mark Anthony is lying dead on the floor. There is some broken glass and water near him. How did he die?

126

2.4 Extension

Joining atoms

The same kinds of atoms can be joined together in different ways. Each different structure is a different substance.

The substances have different properties *because* the atoms have been joined in different ways. (Your teacher may allow you to investigate some of these properties.)

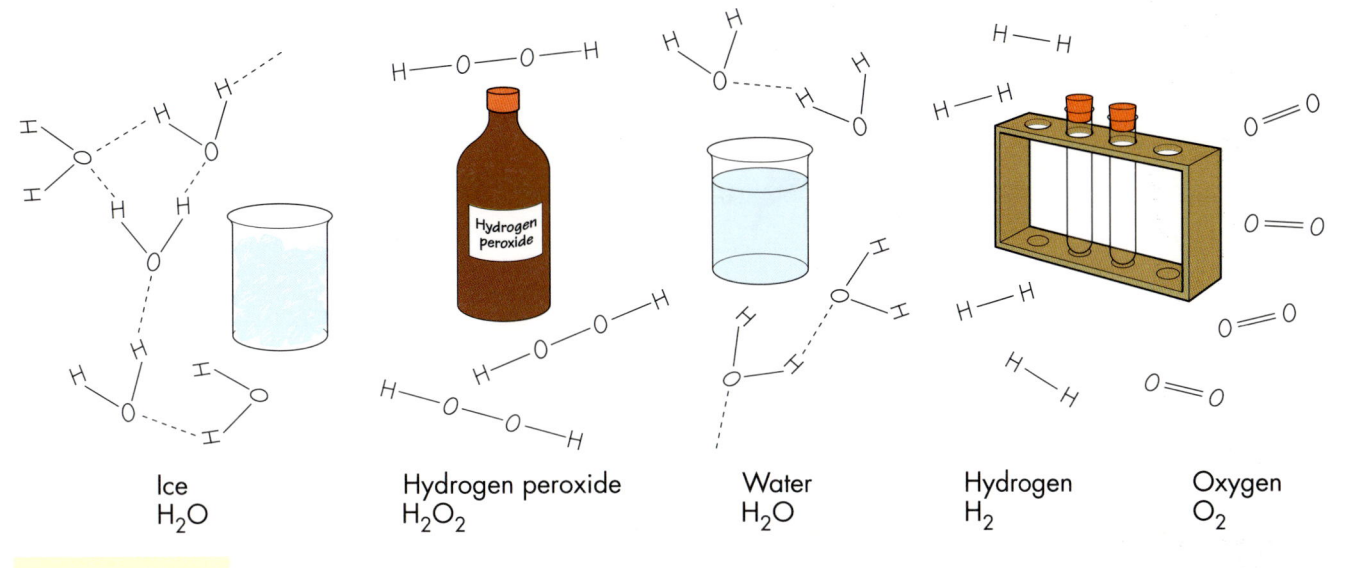

Ice
H_2O

Hydrogen peroxide
H_2O_2

Water
H_2O

Hydrogen
H_2

Oxygen
O_2

Collect
- Model-making kit

1 Make a model of a molecule of hydrogen, oxygen, water and hydrogen peroxide. (The symbol for water is H_2O because there are two hydrogen atoms (white) joined to one oxygen atom (red).)

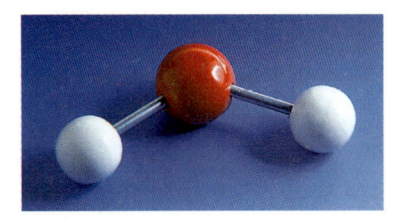

2 Make models of the following substances.

Substance	Formula
Ethanol	C_2H_5OH
Methane (North Sea gas)	CH_4
Ammonia	NH_3
Carbon dioxide	CO_2

1 What is an atom?
2 What is a molecule?
3 Draw two of the molecules that you built. Write the name and symbol beside each one.
4 Imagine that you are a water molecule inside a kettle. Describe what happens to you when the kettle is switched on and left to boil dry.

127

2.5 Extension

Ammonia on the move

Ammonia can be detected by using pH paper. The paper changes colour when ammonia molecules touch it.

Collect

- Bottle of dilute ammonia solution
- Small piece of cotton wool
- Tweezers
- Marker pen
- 5 small pieces of pH paper
- Boiling tube
- Heatproof mat
- Timer
- Safety glasses

Use the diagrams below to design an experiment to measure how fast ammonia molecules can move through air.

Conduct your experiment, remembering to record all your results.

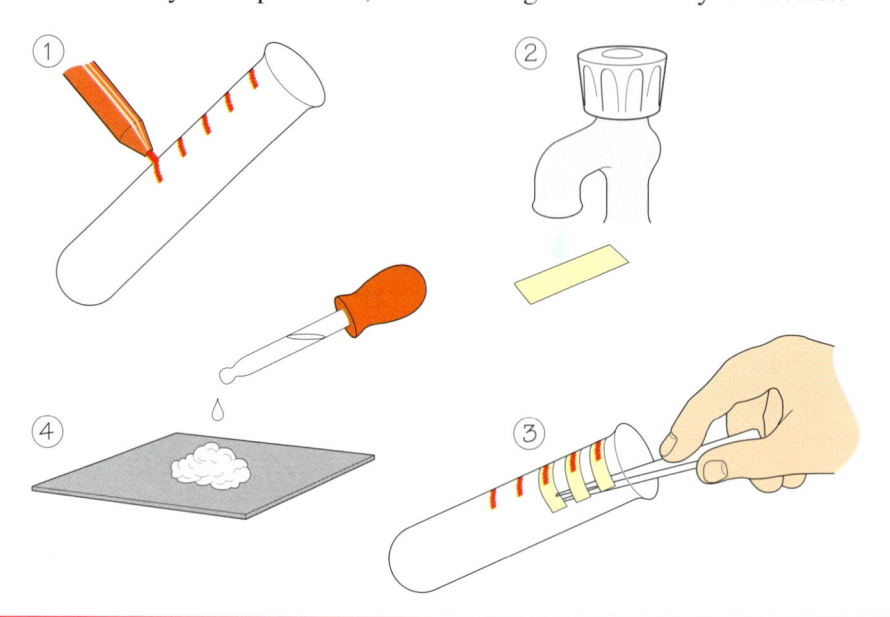

1. What colour does wet pH paper change to when ammonia touches it?
2. Present the results of your experiment in a suitable format.
3. Copy the pictures below in the correct order to show what happened in your experiment. Write a suitable caption underneath each picture to explain what is happening.

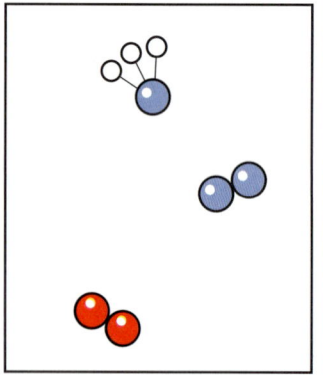

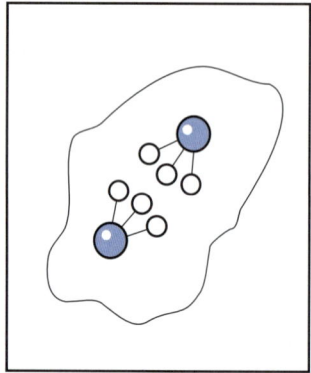

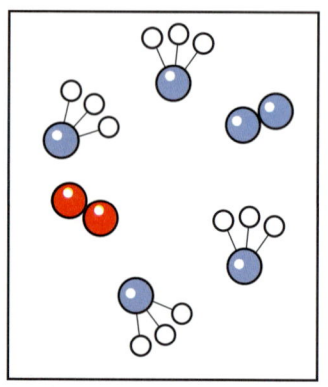

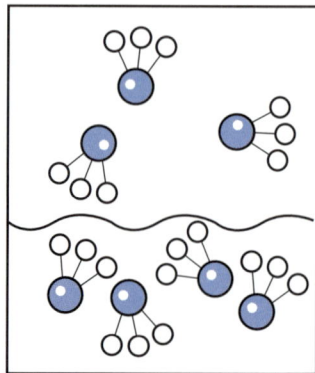

Key: ammonia molecule — nitrogen molecule — oxygen molecule

2.6 Extension

Bumped!

Diffusion is the word that describes how particles of one substance move through another substance. Particles travel in a straight line until they bump into another particle. Therefore they gradually zigzag from a place where there are many particles to one where there are fewer.

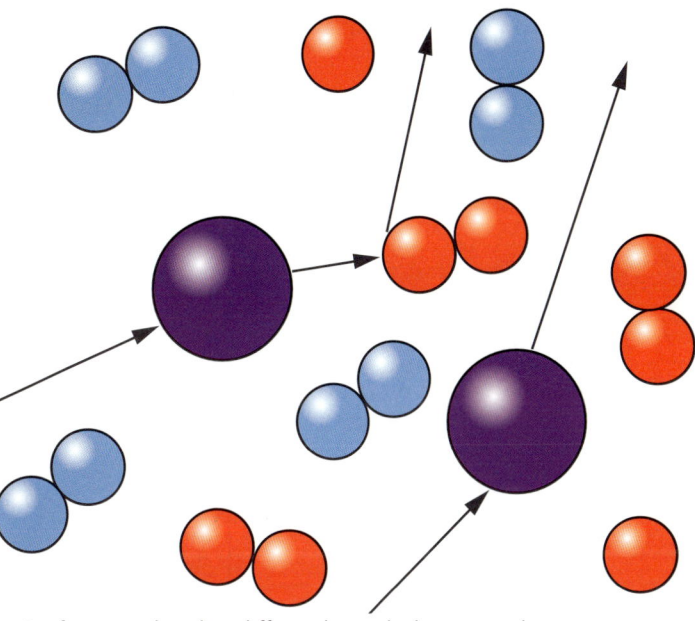

Perfume molecules diffuse through the air in the room

Collect

- 1 crystal of iodine
- 1 crystal of potassium permanganate
- 2 test tubes
- Test-tube rack

1. Fill the test tubes with water. Put them in the test-tube rack.
2. Drop the iodine crystal into one tube and the potassium permanganate crystal into the other.
3. Watch what happens. Do not disturb the test tubes for several minutes.

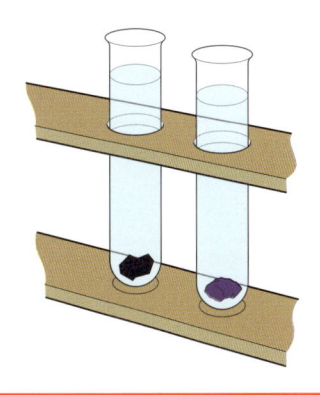

! CARE

1. Write a report about your experiment. Include a diagram of the results.
2. Which substance is best at diffusing through the water?
3. Write down any reasons that could explain why some particles can diffuse through water faster than others.
4. If there is time, your teacher may show you how fast a gas called bromine can diffuse. (**Note:** Bromine is **dangerous**.) Describe this experiment.

The Solar System

You can make a hypothesis whenever you need to explain something.

Astronomers have studied the size and densities of all the planets in the Solar System. The data is given below.

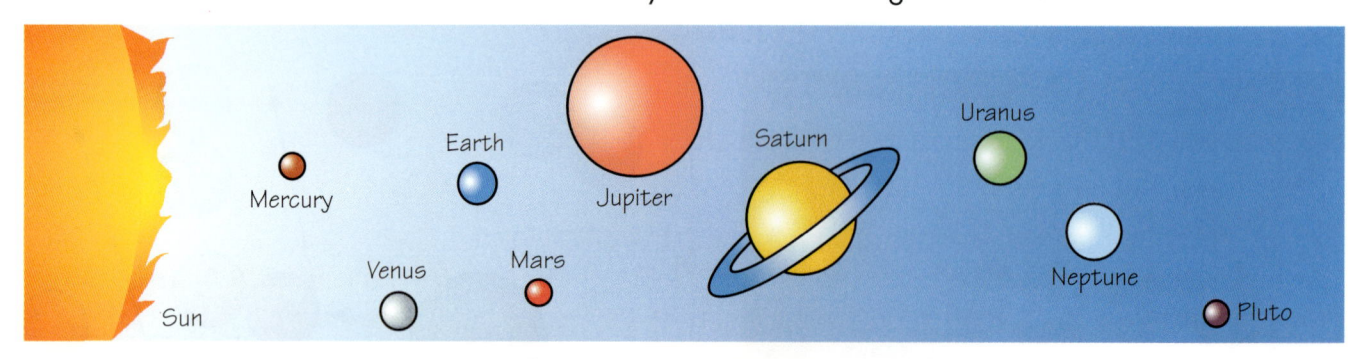

Planet	Size (relative to earth)	Density (kg per m^3)
Mercury	0.4	5400
Venus	0.9	5300
Earth	1.0	5500
Mars	0.5	3900
Jupiter	11.2	1300
Saturn	9.5	700
Uranus	4.0	1300
Neptune	3.9	1600
Pluto	0.2	2100

1. Draw bar graph(s) to show the sizes of the planets and their densities.
2. Use your bar graph(s) to look for patterns.
   a. How many groups can you divide the planets into?
   b. Write down a hypothesis that describes a connection between the size and density of a planet.
3. Which planet does not fit your hypothesis?
4. One of these photographs is of Jupiter and the other is of Mars. Predict which is which and give reasons using your hypothesis from question 2b.

Fortune teller

When you make a prediction you describe what you think will happen. It is a sort of forecast about the future. A prediction will be more accurate than a guess if it is based on good information and good thinking. A hypothesis can be used to make predictions.

A hypothesis about gravity could lead to this prediction and this guess

PREDICTION
THE APPLE WILL FALL WHEN I LET IT GO

GUESS THE APPLE WILL BREAK INTO 3 BITS WHEN IT HITS THE GROUND

Use the hypotheses below to make predictions.

Hypothesis 1
We can forecast the future if we know what star sign a person has.

Hypothesis 2
A tossed coin will show heads 50% of the time.

Hypothesis 3
Gravity causes any two balls to fall from the same place at the same speed.

Collect a horoscope. Read your horoscope. Predict what is going to happen to you next week **if hypothesis 1 is correct**.

Toss a coin ten times and count the heads. Predict how many times it will be heads in 30 throws **if hypothesis 2 is correct**.

Collect two different balls. Predict which ball will fall most quickly **if hypothesis 3 is correct**.
Design and do an experiment to find out if the hypothesis is correct. (Think about the fairness of your experiment.)

Describe your opinion of each of the three hypotheses.
(**Hints:** Is the hypothesis a good one? Do you agree with it? Do many people agree with it? Do you think your predictions will be correct?)

2.8 Extension

131

2.9 Extension

Expansion

A substance usually gets bigger when it is heated. This is called **expansion**. The opposite of expansion is **contraction**. Substances expand because the particles get more energetic when they are heated. They move more and so the spaces between them get bigger. The particles do not get bigger.

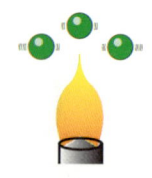

Liquids, including water, contract when cooled. Water is unusual because at its freezing point it expands again

Water expands when it is heated

Collect

- Conical flask
- Long glass tube and stopper
- Marker pencil

1. Fill the flask with water. Stopper it as shown. Make sure that the water level just shows above the stopper. Mark this level.
2. Place the flask in hot water. Leave it for 2 minutes.
3. Mark the new water level.

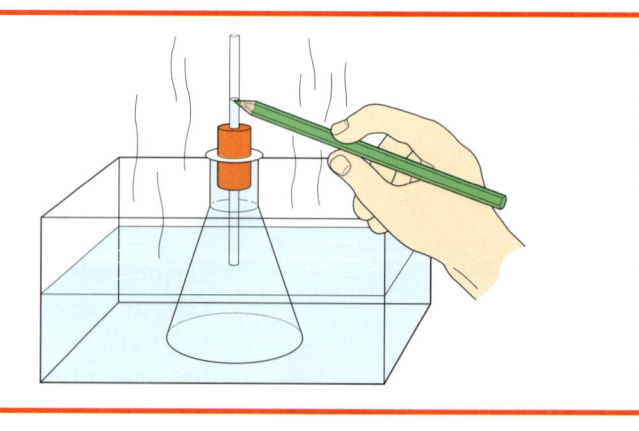

---

1. Use a dictionary to find and write down the meanings of the words *expand* and *contract*.
2. Write a report about your experiment. Include a description of what happened to the water level in the flask when the water was heated.
3. Write a likely explanation for your observations.
4. Describe an experiment that you could do to find out if gases expand more or less than liquids do when heated. Try out your experiment.

3.1 Extension

Cells and tissues

A group of cells all carrying out the same job or **function** is called a tissue. The cells have adaptations that enable them to carry out their job. Usually these adaptations are visible when you look at the cells under a microscope.

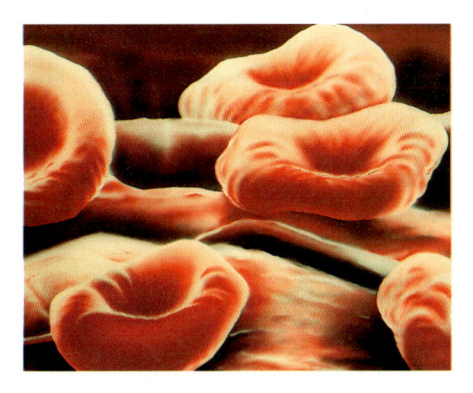

These red cells are part of blood tissue. They carry oxygen. Why do they have this shape?

These ciliated epithelial cells are in the lining tissue of the windpipe. Why do they have those tiny hairs?

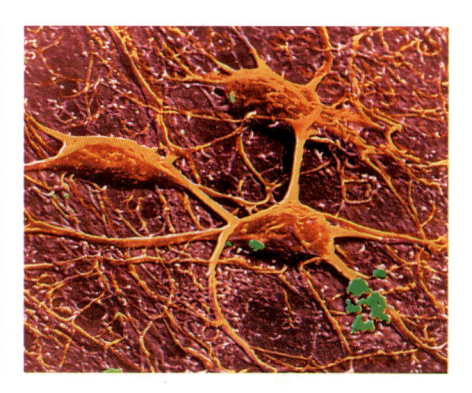

These nerve cells are part of the nervous tissue of the brain. Why do they have so many connections?

Collect

- Microscope
- Prepared slides
- Reference books

1. You have to find answers to the questions above. If prepared slides are available look at the cells. Think about their structure and their function.
2. Use the available reference books to help find answers to the questions.
3. Look at the prepared slide marked X.
   Decide on what questions you should ask about its structure.
   Find a link between the structure and function of these cells.

1. Rewrite the phrase 'Cells have adaptations that enable them to carry out their job' in simple English.
2. For each of the cells you studied
   - make a large drawing of one or two cells
   - give the drawing a title
   - label the cells to **explain** how the structure of the cell helps it to carry out its function.

3.2 Extension

Investigating vitamin C

Vitamins are a group of chemicals that we need for general good health. A balanced diet provides the small amounts required. When they were first discovered scientists did not know their molecular arrangement, so they were named with letters of the alphabet – vitamins A, B, C, D, E and K.

Vitamin C (ascorbic acid) keeps your skin, the lining of your mouth and your gums healthy. A lack of vitamin C results in **scurvy**. The symptoms are bleeding from the gums and slow repair of any skin damage.

Collect

- Bottle of DCPIP
- Dropper
- 5 cm^3 syringe
- Test tubes
- Test-tube rack
- Range of fresh food
- Balance
- Thermometer
- Bunsen burner
- Mat
- Tripod
- Beaker
- Pestle and mortar
- Safety glasses

You have to investigate

- which foods are good sources of vitamin C *or*
- the effect of heating on vitamin C.

The basic test procedure is described below. The chemical DCPIP changes colour from blue to colourless when vitamin C is present. You can compare the amount of vitamin C in different foods by counting the number of drops of liquid food needed to cause the colour change. The fewer the drops the more vitamin C present (the higher the **concentration** of vitamin C).

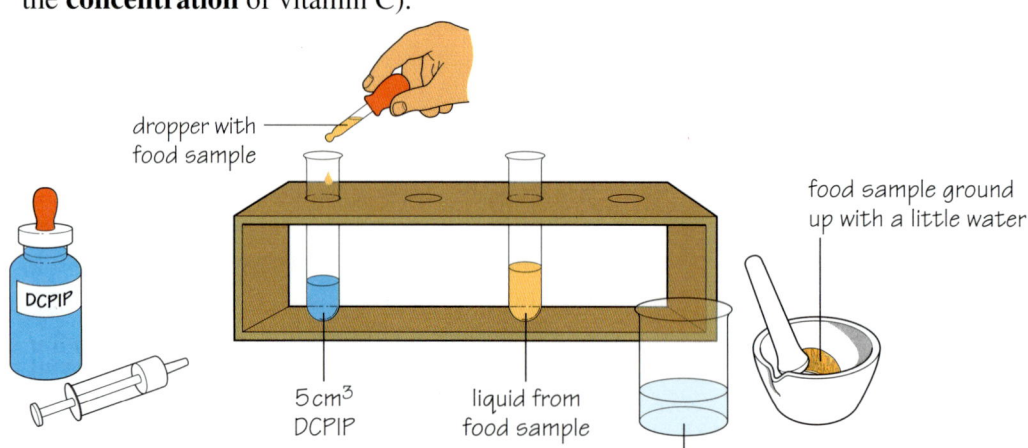

Labels: dropper with food sample; 5 cm^3 DCPIP; liquid from food sample; water; food sample ground up with a little water

- Compare at least five food sources. Make sure your comparisons are fair.
or
- Investigate the effect of heating on vitamin C using one food (your teacher may suggest which food to try). Compare at least two temperatures.

You have to prepare a report to the head of school meals. The report must

- explain the importance of vitamin C
- describe the test for vitamin C
- include a bar chart showing *either*
  a the amount of vitamin C in at least five foods *or*
  b whether fresh or cooked foods are better sources of vitamin C.

Discuss with your teacher how to produce your report.

3.3 Extension

Digesting fat

All food substances are broken down and made soluble by special biological molecules called **enzymes**. Enzymes help chemical reactions take place in living cells. **Lipase** is an example of a fat-digesting enzyme. The word equation below shows that two new substances are formed.

$$\text{fats (insoluble)} \xrightarrow[\text{enzyme}]{\text{lipase}} \text{fatty acids (soluble)} + \text{glycerol (soluble)}$$

If lipase is added to milk, which is rich in fats, you can't see anything happening. If you add lipase to a mixture of milk and universal indicator you can see something happening. (The universal indicator detects fatty acids.)

Collect

- Bottle of milk
- Bottle of lipase
- Bottle of universal indicator
- Beaker of warm water
- Two 5 cm³ plastic syringes
- Two test tubes
- Marker pen
- Safety glasses

1. Put 5 cm³ of milk into two test tubes labelled 1 and 2, using one syringe.
2. Put 10 drops of indicator into both test tubes. Shake the tubes.

3. Place both test tubes in the beaker of warm water.
4. Add 2 cm³ of lipase to test tube 1 with the other syringe.
5. Look for a change after 15 minutes.

1. Write a report about your experiment.
   Explain what has happened. The information at the top of this page should help you.
2. If you have time, design and carry out a fair experiment to find out how temperature affects the speed of this reaction.

3.4 Extension

Cramping your style

When you exercise hard you need more energy. To release more energy your muscle cells increase their rate of aerobic respiration. To do this they need more oxygen.

When not enough oxygen reaches the cells a different form of respiration takes place – **anaerobic respiration**. The product of anaerobic respiration in humans is **lactic acid**. When lactic acid builds up in the cells it causes cramp.

$$glucose \xrightarrow{anaerobic\ respiration} lactic\ acid + energy$$

When you finish exercising you gasp for breath. The extra oxygen you continue to take in switches your muscle cells back to aerobic respiration. Any lactic acid is converted into sugar and any cramp pains ease off and disappear.

Collect

- Set of weights
- String
- Pulley
- Timer

See how well your finger can recover when it has to exercise hard by lifting some weights.

1. Set up the experiment as shown below. You can decide how many grams to lift – as a rough guide try 200 grams to start with.

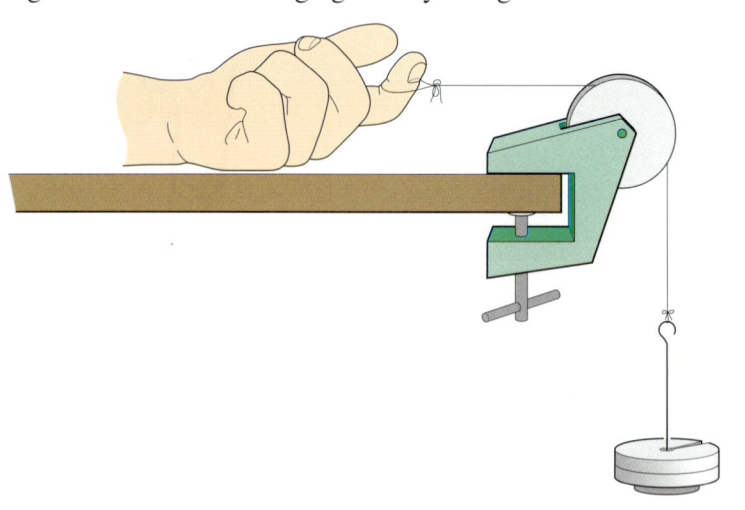

2. Start the clock. Count how many times you can lift the weights in one minute. Make a note of the result on scrap paper.
3. Rest for 15 seconds then make a second attempt. Note your result.
4. Have two more attempts.

1. Record the results of your experiment as a line graph.
   Hint: Put attempt number on the x axis and number of lifts on the y axis.
2. Give your graph a title.
3. Write a few sentences to **explain** the pattern of results. Use the ideas at the top of this page.

3.5 Extension

Fit for life

When you exercise your heart beat increases. If you are unfit it increases much more than if you are fit. It will also return to normal more slowly if you are unfit.

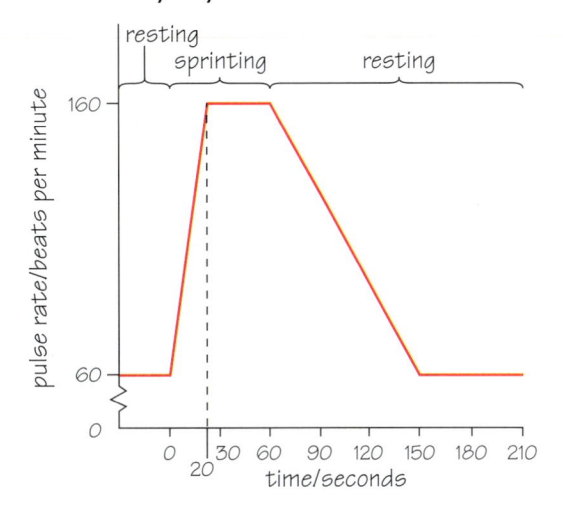

The fitter you are the better your heart and blood vessels circulate blood. You have less chance of getting heart disease. Training or regular exercise can help to make you fitter. By measuring your heart rate from your pulse you can be sure that any exercise is effective and safe.

Collect
- Stop clock

1 Pick your correct exercise range from the table.
  Calculate the heart rate you expect when exercising.
2 Find your pulse rate when you are at rest.

	Exercise range		
	Beginner	Intermediate	Fit
Heart rate when exercising	200 – your age	200 – (your age +20)	200 – (your age +40)

3 Run on the spot for two minutes. Stop and count your pulse for ten seconds. Calculate your pulse rate. Is it within your exercise range?
4 Find your pulse rate again after two minutes' rest. Is it back to normal?

Write a short report on your work. Include
- title
- a sentence explaining why pulse rates are used as indicators of level of fitness
- a table showing your pulse reading at rest, immediately after two minutes exercise and two minutes after stopping exercise
- your opinion of how fit you are.

3.6 Extension

CPR – Lifesaver technique

There has been a huge effort recently to teach as many people as possible how to resuscitate heart attack victims. Most heart attacks happen at home (about 70% in the UK) so it is important to know how to help a relative or friend who becomes ill in this way.

In about two hours you can learn the steps to keep the chain of survival going. The medical services then have a better chance of reviving the person when they arrive. The technique is summarised on page 139.

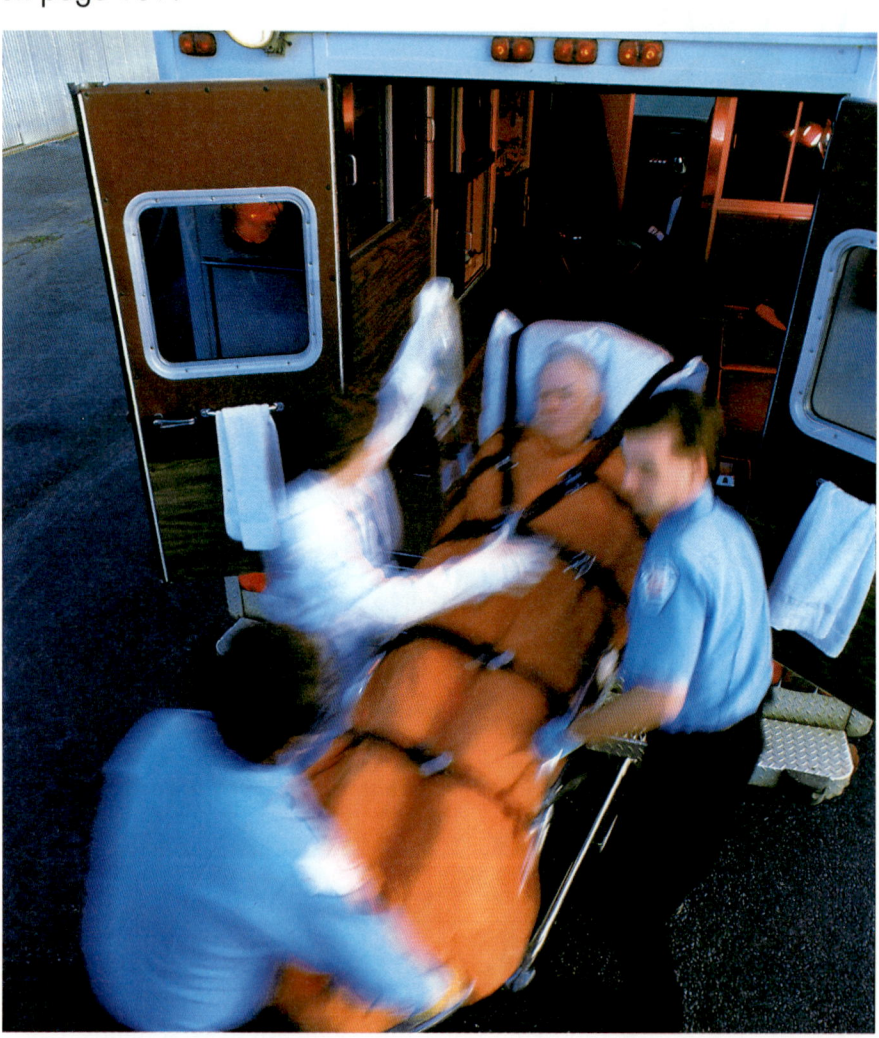

Collect

- Little Annie CPR model
- Antiseptic wipes
- Summary (when lesson has finished)

1 Learn the CPR technique from a qualified instructor.
2 Learn these techniques by practising on classmates
   a assessment of casualty
   b recovery position.
3 Learn these techniques by practising only on a dummy
   a kiss of life
   b cardiopulmonary resuscitation.

3.6 Extension

1 ✓ Check your own safety
2 ✓ Check the casualty's responsiveness
3 ✓ Shout for help

A Opening the Airway

make sure:
- the head is tilted back
- the chin is lifted, using two finger tips under the point of the chin
- the mouth is clear

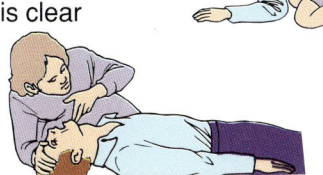

IF YOU SUSPECT A HEAD INJURY, HANDLE VERY CAREFULLY

B Look, listen and feel for Breathing

- *look* for chest movements
- *listen* at the mouth for breath sounds
- *feel* for air with your cheek—listen and feel for at least 5 seconds before deciding that breathing is absent

C Check the pulse for Circulation

- feel for a pulse in the neck
- ensure the casualty's head is tilted
- feel for the 'Adams Apple' in the middle of the neck about halfway between chin and upper part of the breastbone
- slide two fingers from the 'Adams Apple' towards you until they meet a strap like muscle
- feel for at least 5 seconds

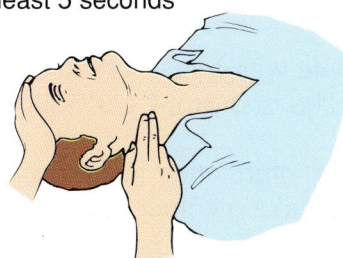

IF PULSE IS NOT PRESENT TELEPHONE 999 IMMEDIATELY

IF PULSE IS PRESENT BUT THEY ARE NOT BREATHING

Apply Ventilation

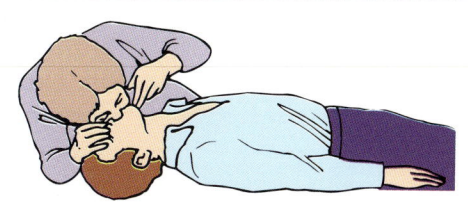

- keep the head tilted and the chin lifted
- pinch the soft part of the nose closed
- make sure you have a good seal on their mouth
- blow steadily into the mouth until you see the chest rise
- allow about 2 seconds for the full inflation
- take your mouth away and allow the chest to fall
- repeat this sequence to give about 10 inflations per minute
- telephone 999 for an ambulance
- return and reassess consciousness, breathing and pulse

IF PULSE IS NOT PRESENT

Apply Chest Compressions

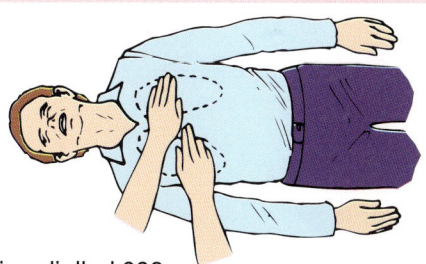

- having dialled 999
- ensure the casualty is on their back on a firm surface
- open the airway
- give 2 breaths of expired air ventilation
- identify the lower rib margins
- slide your fingers upwards to where the ribs join the sternum
- keeping two fingers on the bottom of the sternum place the heel of your other hand in the middle of the lower half of the sternum next to your index finger
- place the heel of your other hand on top and interlock the fingers of your two hands to ensure pressure is applied to the sternum only
- keep your arms straight, lean onto the casualty vertically
- release the pressure and repeat at a rate of approximately 80 compressions per minute
- give 2 full slow breaths after every 15 compressions
- continue until professional help arrives or pulse and breathing returns

139

3.7 Extension

Drug abuse

When chemical substances that are useful to us are misused, they can become dangerous. When drugs are taken or solvents like glue or gas are sniffed, chemicals are passed by the blood system to the brain. At first the person may feel good, but this feeling soon wears off. Drugs can make people lose control of their actions. Any damage caused by drugs is difficult to cure.

Some results of a survey of over 1000 fifteen-to-sixteen year olds are shown in the table below. The dangerous side effects of the drugs are also shown.

Drug	% Male abusers	% Female abusers	Effects
Cannabis	7.4	7.1	Similar to alcohol. Reactions slowed down, co-ordination poor.
Tranquillisers	5.4	5.1	Drowsiness, slow reactions. Addiction is possible.
Glues/solvents	5.4	4.0	Danger of addiction. Can cause heart damage, suffocation and death.
Other drugs	4.3	3.8	Many other drugs such as heroin, cocaine and crack are addictive. They can cause death.

The survey also found that people who tried these drugs were likely to be people who already smoked and drank alcohol.

1. Draw a bar chart to show the information in the first three columns of the table above. Make a colour key for your bar chart.
2. Write a letter to a friend to try and persuade them to avoid taking one of the substances from the table.

4.1 Extension

Force distorts

Think of what force can do to some of the things in your kitchen cupboard. With the force of your fingers you can

- make a dent in butter
- bend a piece of spaghetti
- snap a biscuit
- break off a piece of cheese
- stretch jelly.

Forces can change the shape of materials by bending, stretching and twisting them.

Collect

- Spaghetti
- Drawing pins
- Thread
- Ruler
- Graph paper
- Glue gun or sticky tape and heatproof board
- Newton spring balance
- Masses

1. Design a way of measuring how much you can bend a stick of spaghetti before it breaks. Try out a few designs. Choose the design that gives the most reliable result.
2. Use your invention to find out how the length of the spaghetti stick affects its strength. Predict what you expect to happen.
3. Remember to repeat each test several times and record the average on scrap paper.

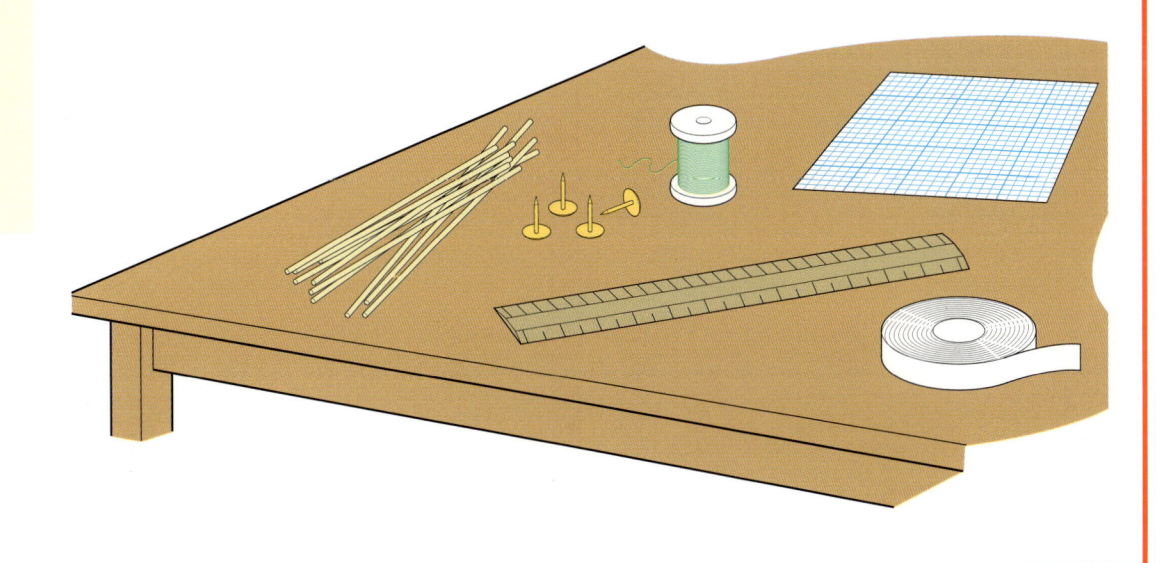

1. Make a drawing of your spaghetti strength tester. Label it to explain how it works.
2. Use your results to draw a line graph of length of spaghetti against strength.
3. Use the line graph to write a conclusion.

4.2 Extension

Ring the changes

Magnets are surrounded by a force field that exerts a force on other magnetic objects. You have to investigate the force field around two ring magnets.

Collect

- Wooden stand
- Two ring magnets
- Paper
- Cling film

The magnets have labels on them. The N stands for North pole, the S stands for South pole.

1. Slide one of the magnets down the rod. Note which side is facing upwards.
2. Investigate the effect the second magnet has on the first by sliding it down the rod. Note which side is facing downwards.
3. Repeat this but turn the second ring magnet the other way up.
4. Devise a way of measuring the strength of the magnetic field between the two magnets.

1. Write down two rules that describe how magnets interact.
2. Make a drawing of your experiment. Label it to explain how you measured the strength of the magnetic field.
3. If you have time investigate the effect on the force field of placing various materials between the magnets. Write a short report on your findings.

4.3 Extension

What a reaction!

It takes a lot of energy to blow up a balloon. Some of this is stored in the pushing force of the compressed air and the pushing force of the stretched rubber. If you let it go the balloon flies off in one direction as the air escapes in the other direction from the mouth of the balloon. It's a good example of equal and opposite forces acting.

You can see the same thing if you drop a ball on the floor. The ball exerts a force on the floor and the floor exerts an equal and opposite force on the ball. The ball bounces back up.

Collect

- Newton spring balance
- Balloon
- Sticky tape
- Straw
- Thread
- Metre stick
- Marker pen
- Help sheet (only if you need it)
- 2 retort stands

You can use the force of escaping air from a balloon to send it along a track. The drawing shows how you might do this.

Investigate the relationship between force and distance travelled in two stages.

1. Design a way of measuring the force exerted by the escaping air when the balloon is blown up a little, a medium amount and a lot. Think about how to measure

   - how much the balloon has been blown up
   - the force exerted by the escaping air.

2. Carry out experiments to show how the force exerted by the escaping air affects the distance the balloon can travel along the track.

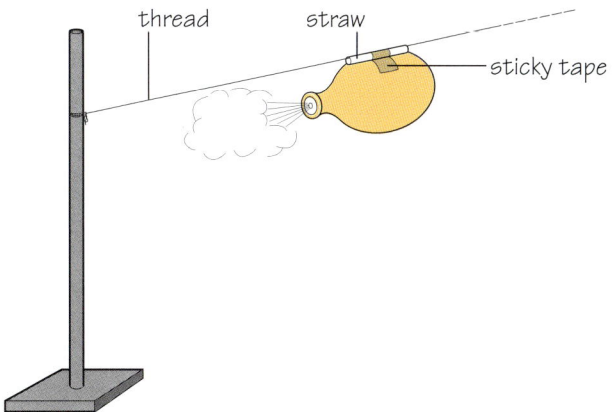

Write a full report to describe how you carried out this experiment. You must include a

- title
- description of the measurements you made, and how you made them (in words or labelled diagrams)
- description of the results (in words or tables)
- graph to show the relationship between force exerted and distance travelled
- conclusion.

4.4 Extension

Floating along

Cargo ships have a series of lines drawn on their hulls at water level. It shows the maximum depth to which the ship can safely be loaded. At this point the downward force of the cargo is balanced by the upthrust of the water. The lines are called the Plimsoll line after Samuel Plimsoll.

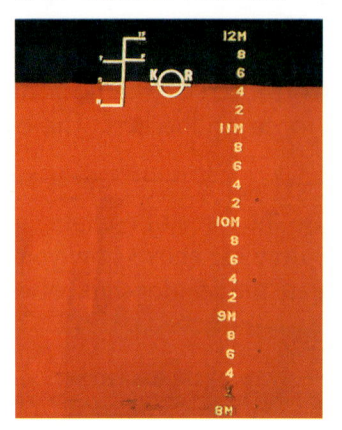

The Plimsoll line on a cargo ship

Samuel Plimsoll (1824–98)

Collect
- 4 test tubes
- 4 corks
- Sand
- Newton spring balance
- 4 solutions
- Marker pen

1. You have to produce a Plimsoll line for the 'HMS Test Tube'. You are given four different solutions

   A tap water
   B 2% salt solution (2 g of salt dissolved in 100 cm^3 of water)
   C 5% salt solution
   D 10% salt solution.

2. Use sand as a cargo for the ship 'HMS Test Tube'. You will need to solve the problem by trial and error and some logical thinking. The diagram should help.

3. Use the newton spring balance to measure the force exerted by the loaded test tube on the water.

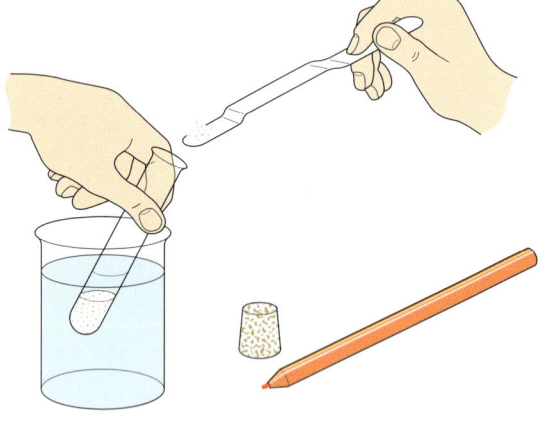

1. Write a short note to the Captain of the 'HMS Test Tube' giving advice on how to use the Plimsoll line when the vessel is being loaded with cargo. Tell the Captain where the ship can carry most cargo (2% salt solution: St Lawrence Seaway in Canada, 5% salt solution: Atlantic and Pacific Oceans, 10% salt solution: Dead Sea).

2. Make an accurate drawing of your Plimsoll line for floating test tubes.

4.5 Extension

Nothing for nothing

Levers are simple machines. They are often called force multipliers because they can convert a small applied force or **effort** on one side of a pivot into a larger force on the **load** on the other side of the pivot.

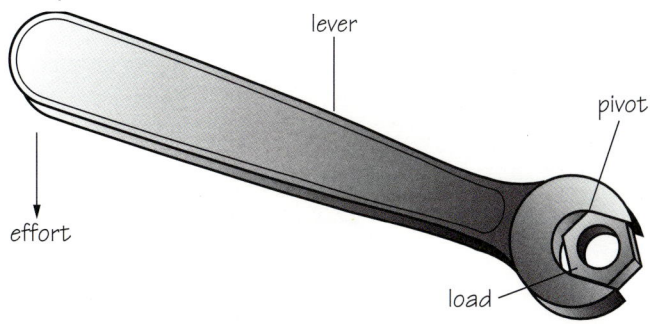

In a spanner a small effort at the end of the lever (the handle) produces a large force on the load (the nut).

Collect

- Newton spring balance
- See-saw apparatus
- Weights
- 2 pulley block-pulley
- Ruler
- Scrap paper

1. You have to investigate if a lever *or* a pulley (which is a moving circular lever) really gives you something for nothing by multiplying force.
2. Use a newton spring balance to measure the force required to lift three or four different weights.
3. Measure the distance travelled by the load and the distance travelled by the effort. 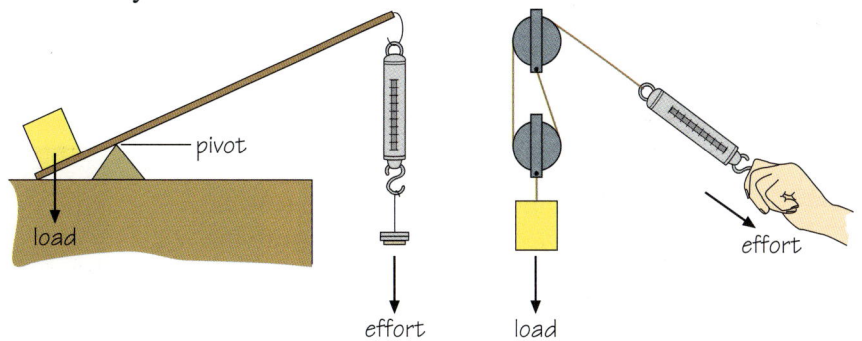
4. Keep a record of your results on scrap paper.

Effort (N)	Distance moved by effort	Load (N)	Distance moved by load

Produce a brief report on your experiments. Include a table of results. Do force multipliers give us something for nothing? Explain your answer.

4.6 Extension

Air resistance

Friction is a force that constantly opposes motion. This is quite obvious when a car tyre moves along the road, or when you have to push a heavy box along the floor. Friction forces also act against moving objects in the air and in water and this is often less obvious. The frictional force in air is called air resistance.

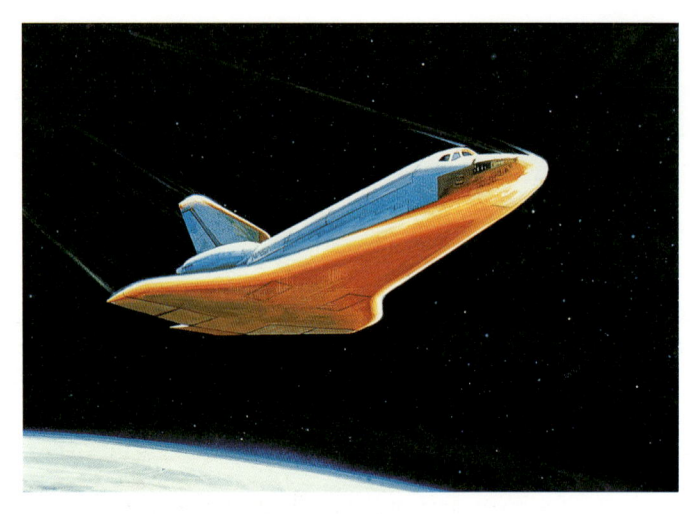

The space shuttle is covered in ceramic tiles to withstand the tremendous heat generated by friction on re-entry to Earth's atmosphere.

The streamlined body shape of sea mammals reduces friction and allows them to swim quickly.

In the natural world the seeds of some plants are adapted for wind dispersal. Their structure **increases** their air resistance, slowing them down as they fall. This means they have a better chance of being caught by a breeze and landing far away from the parent plant.

Collect

- Sheets of scrap paper
- Timer
- Metre stick

1. You have to design a seed that takes a long time to hit the ground. You also have to design a fair experiment to compare the seeds you design.
2. Use a single sheet of scrap paper for each design (make at least two). You can fold and tear or cut it into any shape you like. You may not throw any of the sheet away.

Draw your seed designs.
Note down the average time it takes for each to fall.
Explain why one of the designs takes longer to fall than the others.

146

4.7 Extension

Speed reading

We are fascinated by speed. Speed in the natural world and speed in the world of machines. Your task is to carry out some research into *one* of these areas.

Speedy animals　　　　　　　　　　　**Speedy machines**

Land

Water

Air

Collect
- Books
- Leaflets
- Video material
- Posters
- CD-ROMs

1. Choose speedy animals *or* speedy machines.
2. Choose three items from your list to find out about.

   Speedy animals
   - fastest land animal
   - fastest swimming fish
   - fastest flying bird
   - fastest flying insect
   - fastest human

   Speedy machines
   - fastest land vehicle
   - fastest water vehicle
   - fastest air vehicle
   - fastest underwater machine
   - fastest vehicle on rails

3. Use any available resource to find the information.

Record your research answers in a table.
Show the speed in metres/second.

4.8 Extension

Pressure puzzles

Air pressure is all around us. It depends on the moving gas particles of the air colliding with each other and with other objects. Differences in air pressure are the reason for many familiar events and effects.

Give an explanation for the events and effects shown below. You may want to do some research first. Use any available resources in the class or library to help. To give your explanations you could

- talk to your teacher
- write short answers
- record your ideas as a diagram or on audio tape.

Breathing
Breathing depends on changes in the volume of the chest cavity. (Look back at page 51.) What effect does this have on the pressure inside the lungs? Why is this important in breathing?

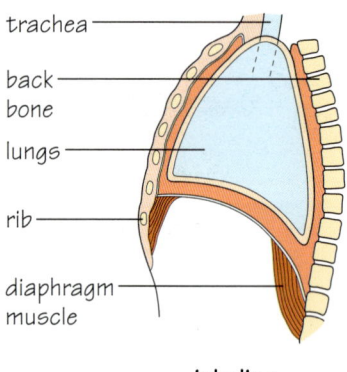

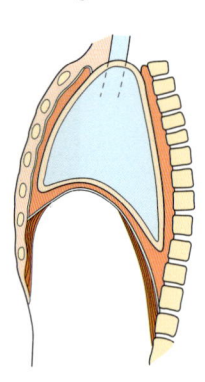

inhaling   exhaling

Wind
Wind depends on differences in air temperature between two places. What effect does temperature have on air pressure? What do the highs and lows on weather charts indicate?

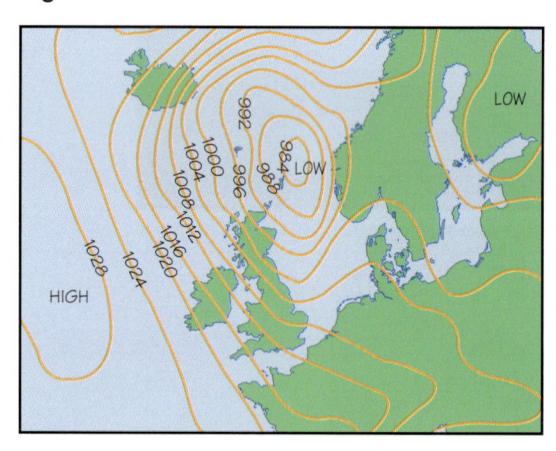

Jam jar
When jam is put into its jar it is hot. The lid is put on right away. What effect does the heat have on the air above the jam? Why is the lid hard to unscrew?

Hot-water bottle
In the morning a hot-water bottle contains cold water. Why does it often look like the diagram below? Why, when you open it can you hear a rush of air?

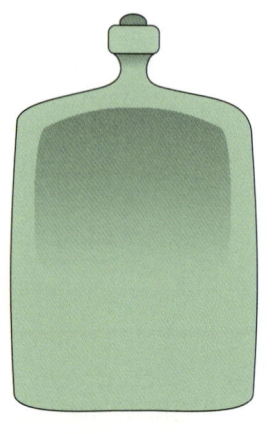

5.1 Extension

More active reactions

In a chemical reaction

- a new substance is formed and this can sometimes be observed
- an energy change occurs and this can sometimes be observed
- the change cannot be easily reversed.

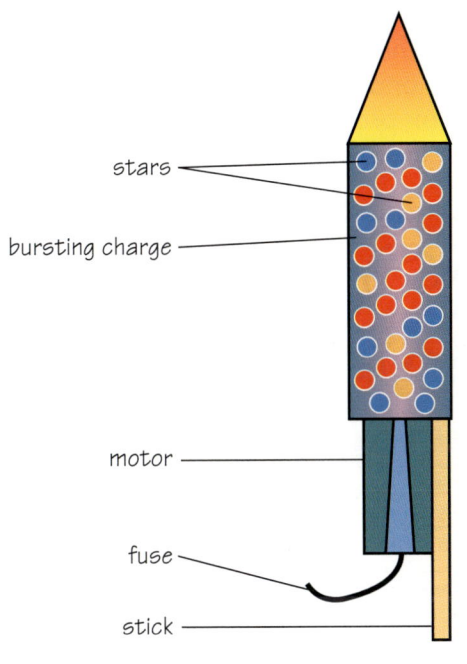

stars
bursting charge
motor
fuse
stick

Reactants

Give a little energy to start the reaction →

Products, energy change, not easily reversed

All the activities that follow involve a chemical reaction. For each activity

- write a suitable title
- list any evidence of a chemical reaction.

1 Watch your teacher demonstrate this . . .

2 and this . . .

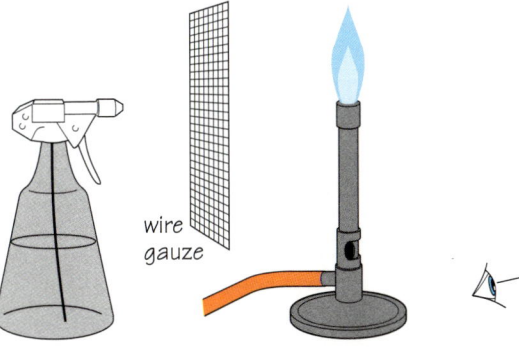

wire gauze

add liquid

3–8 Collect **one** of the activity boxes.
Follow the instructions and then return the box.
Write your report and then do another activity.

149

5.2 Extension

Rusting of iron: iron becomes iron oxide

Burning of petrol: petrol becomes carbon dioxide and hydrogen oxide (water)

Respiration of food: food becomes carbon dioxide and hydrogen oxide (water)

Tarnishing of silver: silver becomes silver oxide (tarnish)

Redox reactions

A reaction in which the reactant gains oxygen is called **oxidation**. Examples of oxidation are shown in the pictures.

When one substance gains oxygen, another must lose it. The loser in these cases is the air. A loss of oxygen is called **reduction**.

Oxidation and reduction are two halves of the same reaction story. They can only occur together and the whole process is called **redox**. A good example of a redox process is the smelting of copper. Smelting could have been discovered by accident like this.

The green copper ore is heated by the fire and forms black copper oxide. This mixes with the hot carbon ashes and a redox reaction occurs as described by the word equation

copper oxide + carbon → copper + carbon dioxide

The copper oxide has been **reduced**. The carbon has been **oxidised**.

Collect

- Green copper ore (malachite)
- Charcoal (carbon)
- Iron ore
- Any equipment you need
- Safety glasses

1. Design and carry out a laboratory experiment to find out if the reaction in the cartoon above is possible.
2. Find out if iron ore can be reduced by red-hot carbon.

Write a report about your investigations.

5.3 Extension

paint

grease

Investigating rust protection

Iron is a very useful material. Unfortunately it corrodes easily in air and water and forms rust. Rusting is a problem because the iron loses its strength as it turns into new compounds, mainly hydrated iron oxide. (Hydrated substances have water molecules combined with the compound.) There are different ways of protecting a metal from corrosion

- keep water and air away
- cover with a thin layer of another metal
- mix metals to form an alloy
- use electricity.

chrome electroplating

alloy

Investigate one (or more) of the questions on the cards below.

For each investigation, **collect** and follow the investigation card. The card lists the equipment that you need and gives some hints about which methods to try out.

In all the investigations use rust indicator to show up the corrosion of iron. Use salt water to make the rusting faster than it would otherwise be.

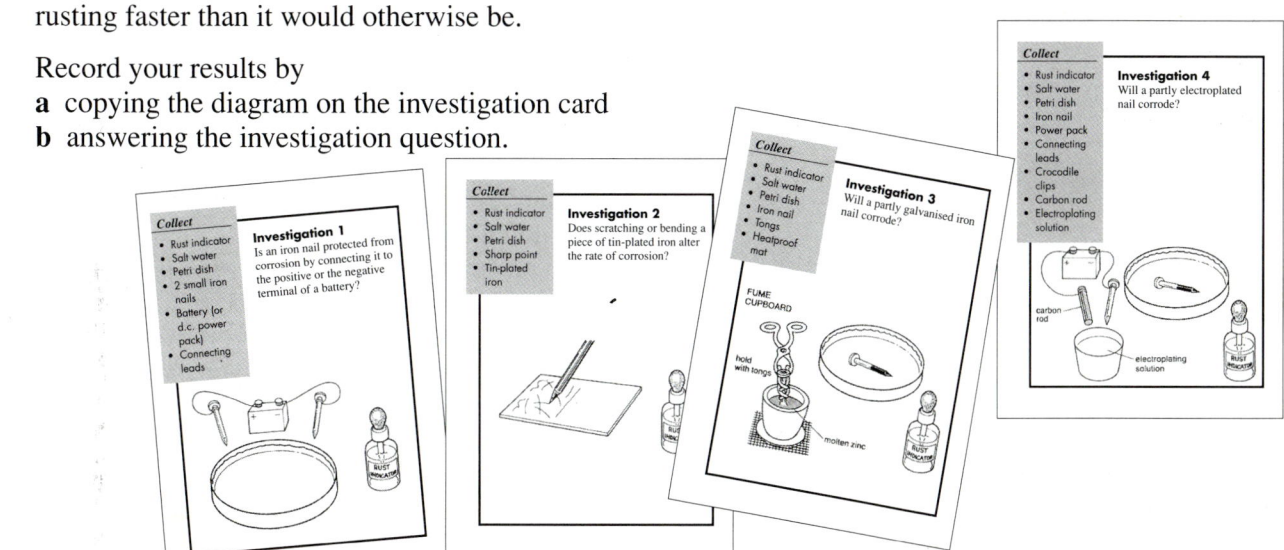

Record your results by
a copying the diagram on the investigation card
b answering the investigation question.

Investigation 1
Is an iron nail protected from corrosion by connecting it to the positive or the negative terminal of a battery?

Collect
- Rust indicator
- Salt water
- Petri dish
- 2 small iron nails
- Battery (or d.c. power pack)
- Connecting leads

Investigation 2
Does scratching or bending a piece of tin-plated iron alter the rate of corrosion?

Collect
- Rust indicator
- Salt water
- Petri dish
- Sharp point
- Tin-plated iron

Investigation 3
Will a partly galvanised iron nail corrode?

Collect
- Rust indicator
- Salt water
- Petri dish
- Iron nail
- Tongs
- Heatproof mat

Investigation 4
Will a partly electroplated nail corrode?

Collect
- Rust indicator
- Salt water
- Petri dish
- Iron nail
- Power pack
- Connecting leads
- Crocodile clips
- Carbon rod
- Electroplating solution

151

5.4 Extension

Activity plan

Some metals neutralise an acid to produce hydrogen gas.

Your task is to plan and do an experiment to find out the order of reactivity of the metals with vinegar (a weak acid).

Collect the following equipment and substances.

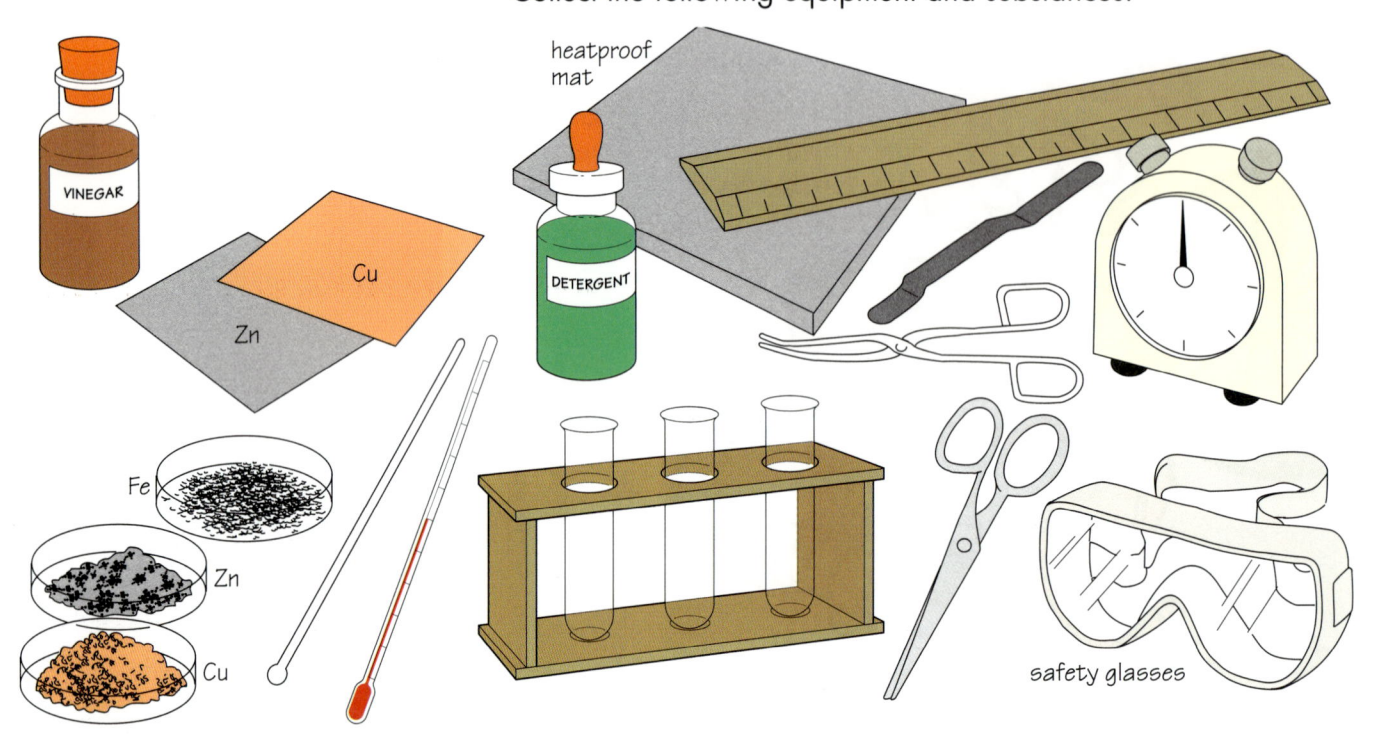

1. **Plan** your investigation.
   a. Look at the results of your experiment in Topic 5.2A and your answer to question 4.
   Write down your hypothesis about the order of reactivity of the metals with vinegar.
   b. Discuss the following with your partner(s) and **write down** your decision.
      i. Which *variable* will you change in your investigation?
      ii. What other variables will you have to *control* to make a comparison fair? List these.
         How are you going to control each one?
      iii. What can you observe and (if possible) *measure* about the reaction that will help you to decide how well each metal is reacting with the acid?
         It will be best to measure something if you can.
   c. Let your teacher read your plan.
2. Follow your plan. Record your results.
3. Write a comment on your results.
   Did they agree or disagree with your original hypothesis?

5.5 Extension

Sour water

The River Wiver flows past the town of Beesnees. There are three streams that join the river near the town. One of the streams is being polluted with acid – you have to find out which one. The local environmental health officer can then take action against the offenders.

Use the two diagrams below to help you plan and carry out your investigation.

Map

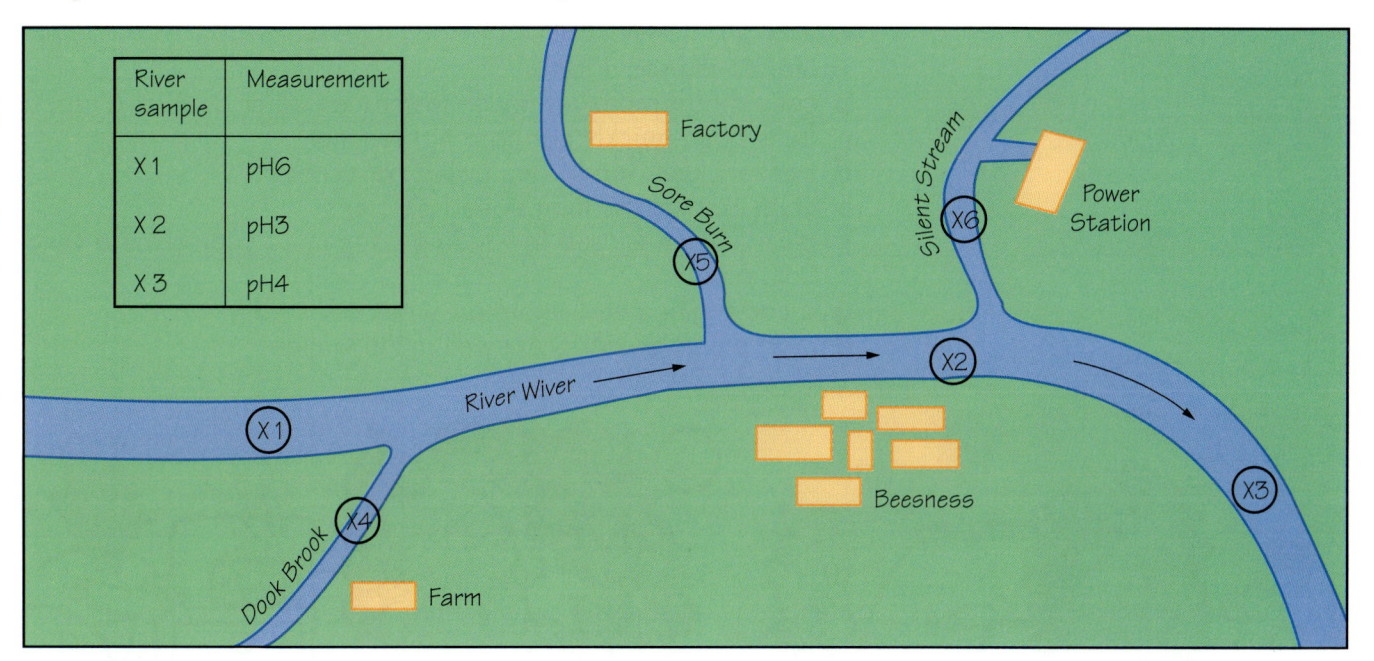

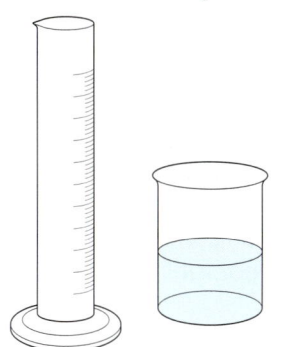

River sample	Measurement
X 1	pH6
X 2	pH3
X 3	pH4

Factory
Sore Burn
Silent Stream
Power Station
X5
X6
X2
River Wiver
X1
Beesness
X3
Dook Brook
X4
Farm

Titration technique

a Measured volume of water

b pH meter or add indicator

c How much alkali to neutralise?

d Compare results

Water sample	Amount

Write a full report about your investigation to the local environmental health officer. Make your method, results and conclusions very clear.

153

5.6 Extension

Speeding up reactions

Reactions can sometimes be speeded up by increasing the value of one or all of the following variables (see page 94)

- the temperature
- the amount of a reactant
- the number of pieces of a reactant (by decreasing their size).

1 Use these ideas to explain in a sentence why
   a powders that neutralise stomach acid work faster than tablets that do the same job
   b car exhaust pipes rust much faster than other parts of a car
   c fruits ripen quickly during a hot summer
   d freezers keep food from 'going off' quickly
   e chips cook faster than boiled potatoes
   f pure oxygen is used in welding equipment to produce a very hot flame
   g a car engine needs more air when it is cold
   h most plants do not grow well in the winter.

2 Write down three examples of reactions, one affected by the variable *temperature*, one by *amount of reactant* and one by *size of pieces of reactant*.

Collect
- Sodium hydrogen carbonate
- Acid crystals
- Anything else you need
- Safety glasses

If you have time, investigate whether the reaction that occurs in **cremola foam** is affected by the three variables mentioned above.

The reactants are an acid (*citric* or *tartaric*) and a neutraliser (*sodium hydrogencarbonate*). Report your findings.

6.1 Extension

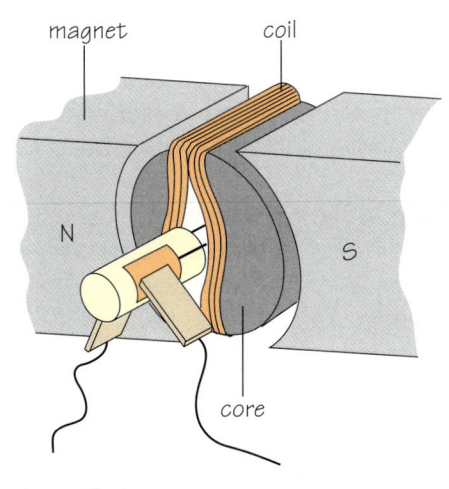

magnet *coil*

N S

core

A small electric motor

Electric motors

Many household machines contain an electric motor – vacuum cleaners, washing machines, tape recorders, electric clocks and toys. Electric motors also work underground trains and many mainline trains as well. They lift us up to the 22nd floor and open automatic doors for us.

Electric motors are quiet, efficient, easy to start or stop and can be very powerful. They all use electricity and magnetism to produce force and movement.

Small electric motors have two main parts – a **magnet** and a revolving **coil** of wire. The wire is usually wound on an iron **core** that can also rotate. When current is fed into the coil it magnetises the core, which is repelled by the magnet and forced to rotate.

Collect

- Electric motor
- Switch
- Power supply
- Variable resistor
- Construction kit

Build up a motor-driven machine stage by stage.

1. Connect a motor to a switch and a power supply, so that it can be turned on and off.

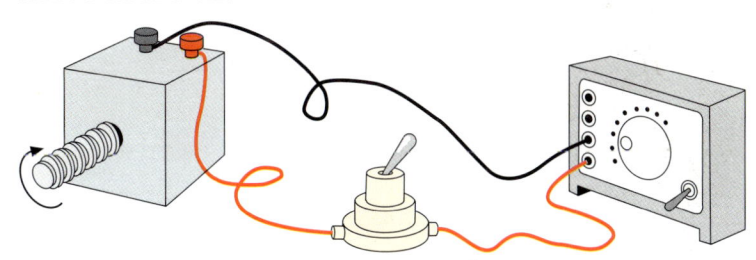

2. Make the motor do a job; for example, pulling up a model lift or driving a fan.
3. Build in a speed control.

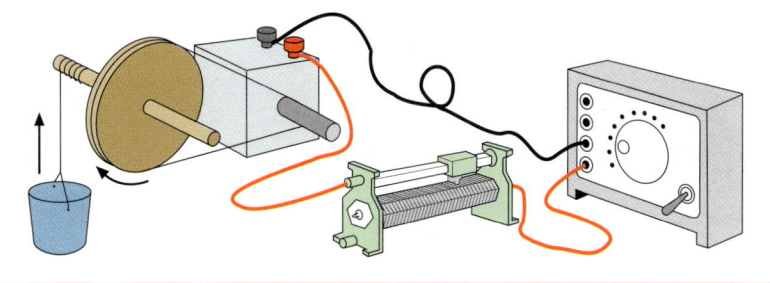

1. Make a drawing of the inside of a small electric motor. Find out the names of the main parts from a reference book. Label your picture to explain how the motor works.
2. Design (on paper) a motor-driven cat flap that only opens for *your* cat. Show how the motor opens the flap and how it is started and stopped by the cat.

155

6.2 Extension

Biotechnology with yeast

The process of brewing beer uses yeast microbes to ferment sugar into alcohol. This is traditionally done in a fermenting vessel with one batch of product being made at a time. The vessel must be cleaned before the next fermentation.

In some processes it is now possible to fix the microbes in one place and use them over and over again. For example, yeast can also be used to change raw cane sugar (sucrose) into glucose. The glucose can then be used to make sweets. This process will run continuously with the same microbes being used again and again.

Collect

- Tray of equipment
- Safety glasses

1. Clean all glassware and the bench with sterilising solution. Wash your hands.
2. Test the sucrose solution with Clinistix. (Use the index to find the method.) Check that there is no colour change.
3. Fix the yeast cells in small jelly beads by following these instructions.
   a. Stir 1 g yeast granules into 25 cm^3 water.
   b. Add this to 25 cm^3 sodium alginate solution. Stir all the time.
   c. Pour 200 cm^3 calcium chloride solution into a third beaker.
   d. Suck up some yeast/alginate mixture with a pipette.
   e. Drip this mixture from about 10 cm into the beaker of calcium chloride solution. Make lots of beads.

6.2 Extension

4 Now set up your production line.

jelly beads

sucrose solution

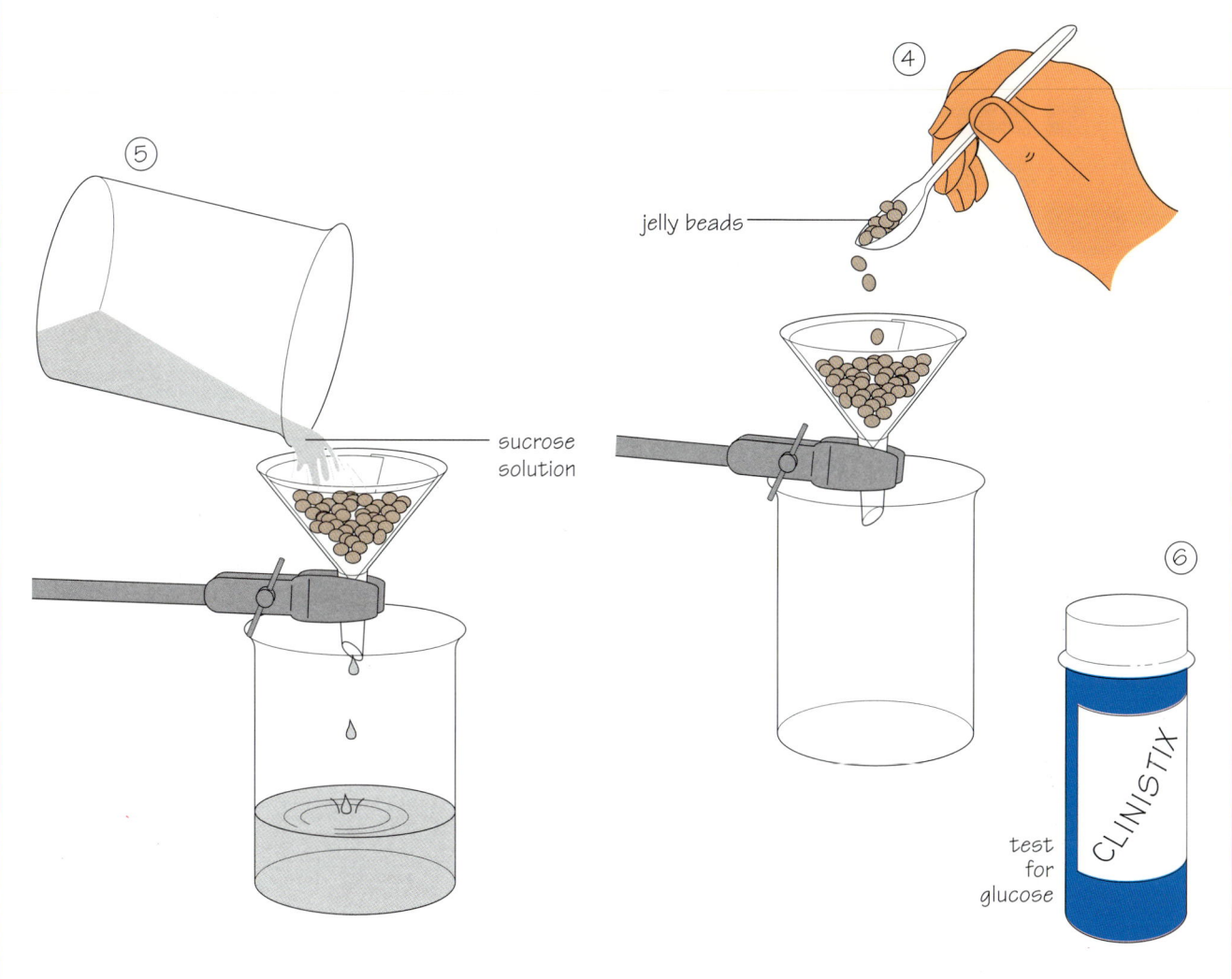

test for glucose — CLINISTIX

5 Pour the sucrose solution through the filter funnel twice.
6 Test a sample of the liquid you collect for glucose. If there is no change, pour the solution through the filter funnel once again and test it again.
7 If you have time, design a way of speeding up this reaction.

1 Explain the difference between a *batch* and a *continuous* process.
2 Imagine that you own a sweet factory! Why would yeast microbes be useful to you if sucrose was much cheaper than glucose?
3 Use the diagrams above to describe how your experimental production line worked.
4 What changes would you have to make to the experimental line if you were going to use it in a factory?

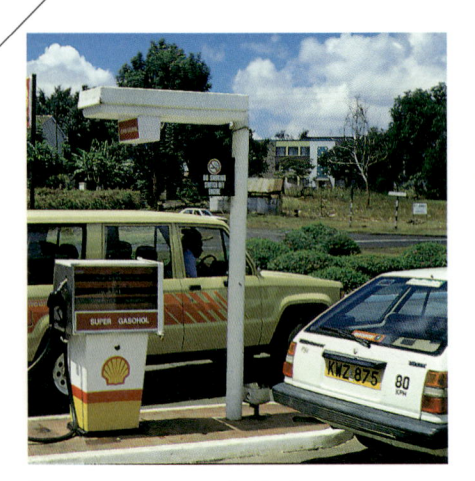

6.3 Extension

New fuels

Technology has produced different types of fuels. For example, alcohol and methane can be produced in large quantities by microbes. In Brazil petrol is very expensive. Cane sugar is plentiful and is changed into alcohol by yeast. Methane gas is used as a heating fuel. Certain bacteria convert farmyard manure and sewage into this valuable gas.

Cars can run on alcohol

Methane can be produced from sewage

Collect

- Distillation apparatus
- Bunsen burner
- Liquid from a yeast fermenter
- Safety glasses

1 The fermenters (from Topic 6.2B) use growing yeast to convert sugar into alcohol. Collect about 20 cm³ of the liquid from a fermenter.
2 Alcohol boils at around 78°C and water boils at 100°C. Use distillation to separate some alcohol from the liquid.
3 Ask your teacher to test the alcohol to see if it burns.

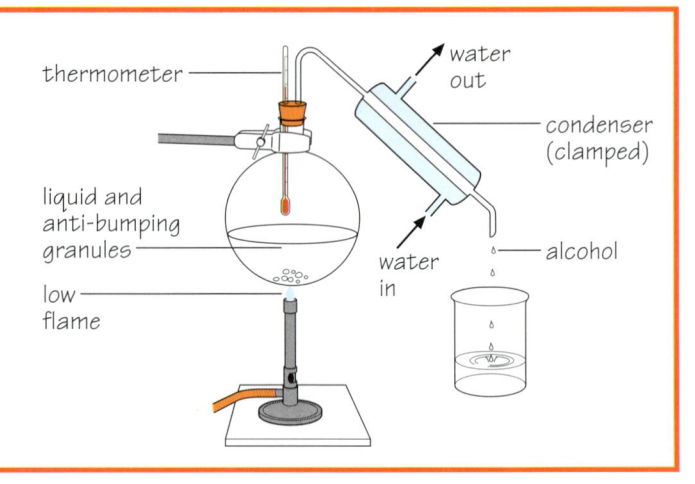

1 Write a report about this experiment. Include **only** the things that you think are important.
2 Making a summary of information is an important skill. In this unit *fuels* have been mentioned several times.
Use the index to find references to fuels. Read these pages and then complete the diagram.

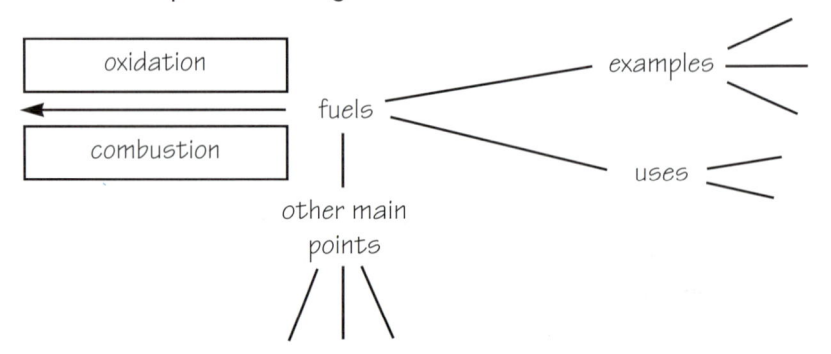

Index

A
acids 88
accounts, chemical 82, 84
adaptation 6–7, 15–16
advertising
   of alcohol 54
   of cigarettes 54
aerobic respiration 46, 136
air pressure 74, 146
air resistance 148
alcohol
   advertising of 54
   as a drug 53
   as a fuel 158
   making of 106
   unit of 53
alkalis 88
ammonia
   molecule 31
   properties 26, 128
anaerobic respiration 105, 136
animal
   counting of 8, 122
   kingdom 4
antibiotics 58
antibodies 57
arteries 48
artificial joints 78
atoms 24, 80, 127

B
bacteria 57, 104
   see also microbes
balancing 66–7
balanced diet 42, 47, 134
bases 90
beer 104, 156
bimetallic strips 20
   and fire alarms 36
biological washing powder 107
blood 57
   capilliaries 48, 50
brain 40
bread 104
breathing 50, 148
   see also respiration

Brown, Robert 27
Brownian motion 27
burning 83–4

C
calcium carbonate 92
cane sugar 156
carbohydrates 42
cells 40, 46, 50, 133
   blood 57, 133
chemical
   accounts 82, 84
   reactions 80, 81, 149
cigarettes 52, 54, 56
Clinistix 43, 157
compounds 24, 127
   coloured 125
   rust as a 86, 150
conservation 10
consumer reports 76
contact forces 62
contraction 132
Copernicus, Nicolaus 38
corrosion 83, 86
counting animals 8, 122

D
design features 77
diffusion 28, 129
digestive system 44–5
diet, balanced 42, 47, 134
diodes 115
distillation 158
drinking, see alcohol
drugs 58
drug abuse 146

E
electric motors 155
electromagnetism 102
electronics 114–15
electronic systems 115–16
electrons 114
elements 24
energy 34, 46–7, 108

environment 2, 14, 118, 121
   changes 8, 15
   conservation 10
   pollution 10, 153
enzymes
   and digestion 44–5
   fats and 135
   washing powders and 107
equations, word 93
expansion 132
   see also bimetallic strips
exercise 137
experiments 30
explanations 18–19, 24, 38, 124

F
fats 42
   digestion of 135
fermentation 105, 156
fermenters 106
fingerprinting 20
fire 110–11
fire alarms 36
fitness 137
flame colours 21
flammable materials 111
flotation 144
food
   digestion of 44–7
   preservation 95
   sources of 42–3
forces 60, 62–8, 141
forecasting, see predictions
friction 70–1, 146
fuels
   natural 108
   new 158
fungi 5, 57

G
Galilei, Galileo 38
gases 33, 34
gravity 62

INDEX

H
habitat 2–3, 6–8, 15–16, 121
health
  fitness and 137
  food and 42
heart 40, 48–9
heart attacks 138–9
heat
  particles and 35, 132
  pollution and 123
hip joints, see joints
human body 40
  defences 57–8
  digestion 44–5
  heart 48–9
  joints 78
  lungs 50–1
hypothesis 30, 38, 130

I
ideas 18–19, 38
immune system 57–8
indicators 88–9
infection 57
integrated circuits 115
invertebrates 4
iodine 43, 45
iron 151
  and magnets 100, 102
iron oxide 86, 97
  see also rusting

J
joints, artificial 78

K
key 119

L
lactic acid 136
levers 68, 145
light-dependent resistors 115
limestone, see calcium carbonate

lipase 135
liquid 33, 34
living things
  classification 4
  counting 8
  habitat 6
lungs 50, 52
  see also breathing

M
magnetic forces 100–3, 142
magnets and motors 155
map measurements 118
materials 96
  flammable 111
matter 22
methane 158
microbes
  brewing and 104, 156
  food 105
  fuel production and 158
  penicillin and 58
  respiration of 104, 105
milk 105, 135
minerals 42
molecules 24

N
natural fuels 108
nerve cells 133
Newton, Isaac 60
Newton's Law 64
neutralisation of acid 88, 90–1
non-contact forces 62–3

O
observations 18–20
organs 40
organisms 121
oxidation 82–3, 86–7, 95, 150
oxygen 86
  fuels and 110

P
paired statement key 119–20
pairs of forces 64–5
particles 24, 30
  and diffusion 28, 29, 129
  and energy 34–5
  heat and 35, 132
  hypothesis about 30
patterns 20, 125
penicillin 58
photocells 115
pH paper 89
pivot 68, 145
planets 130
plants 32
  and adaptation 16
  counting of 9
  kingdom 5
population 8, 122
pollution 10–11, 153
  thermal 123
predictions 18, 31, 32, 131
preservation
  of food 95
  of bodies 97–8
pressure 74, 148
protein 42, 47
pulse 48

Q
questioning 37, 126

R
reaction 31, 80–1
  chemical 149
  redox 150
  time 94–5, 154
reactivity 84, 152
redox reaction 150
reduction 150
resistors 115
respiration 46, 83, 105, 136, 150
  see also breathing
resuscitation technique 138–9
rust protection 151
rusting 86–7, 150, 151

INDEX

S
salt 90
sampling
   animals 8, 122
   plants 9
silicon chips 115
skin 57
smell 26
smoke 111
smoking, *see* cigarettes
solids 33, 34
   and heating 35, 132
species 119
speed 72
speed of reaction 94–5, 154
starch 45
stopping distance 72

T
thermal pollution 123
thermistors 115
tissues 40, 133
titanium 78
transistors 115

U
universal indicator 89

V
vaccine 58
vertebrates 4
viruses 57
vitamins 42, 134

W
washing powder 107
word equations 93

Y
yeast 104, 156
   see also fermentation
    and microbes
yoghurt 104–5